PUBLIC ZEN, PERSONAL ZEN

CRITICAL ISSUES IN WORLD AND INTERNATIONAL HISTORY
Series Editor: Morris Rossabi

PUBLIC ZEN, PERSONAL ZEN

A Buddhist Introduction

Peter D. Hershock

ROWMAN & LITTLEFIELD
Lanham • Boulder • New York • Toronto • Plymouth, UK

Published by Rowman & Littlefield
4501 Forbes Boulevard, Suite 200, Lanham, Maryland 20706
www.rowman.com

10 Thornbury Road, Plymouth PL6 7PP, United Kingdom

British Library Cataloguing in Publication Information Available

Library of Congress Cataloging-in-Publication Data
Hershock, Peter D.
Public Zen, personal Zen : a Buddhist introduction / Peter D. Hershock.
pages cm. — (Critical issues in world and international history)
Includes bibliographical references and index.
ISBN 978-1-4422-1612-9 (cloth : alk. paper) — ISBN 978-1-4422-1614-3 (electronic) 1. Zen Buddhism—History. I. Title.
BQ9262.3.H47 2014
294.3'927—dc23
2013040486

∞ ™ The paper used in this publication meets the minimum requirements of American National Standard for Information Sciences Permanence of Paper for Printed Library Materials, ANSI/NISO Z39.48-1992.

Printed in the United States of America

CONTENTS

ACKNOWLEDGMENTS

Some books fly into and through an author's life on wings of sudden and then surprisingly sustained inspiration—books that seem almost impossible not to write. This book had more reluctant beginnings and yet has proved to be unexpectedly rewarding. In 2006 I had the great pleasure to be able to invite Morris Rossabi to serve as a presenter for a faculty development program on the Silk Roads and China, hosted at the East-West Center in Honolulu under the auspices of a grant from the National Endowment for the Humanities (NEH). The lectures and discussions that Morris conducted were models of combined communicative ease and depth, marrying scholarly aplomb with urbane and yet utterly sincere friendliness in a way that was manifestly rare. When the opportunity arose to run a similar program in 2010, Morris was high on the list of presenters to bring back for a larger role in the program.

Out of that second occasion to have contributory shares in a vibrant community of inquiry (for which thanks are due to NEH) came a suggestion from Morris that I consider writing a book on Japanese Zen for his series on Critical Issues in World and International History. As someone trained in Asian and comparative philosophy, not history, I was both flattered and quick to offer reasons why that would not be a good idea, including the crucial fact that my study of Buddhism had focused largely on China, not Japan. Thankfully, Morris was not dissuaded and apparently gave a rather bright green light to Susan McEachern to approach me from the editorial offices of Rowman & Littlefield. The combination of Morris' personification of caring humanity and Susan's measured yet persistent invitations to give the offer serious consideration eventually dissolved enough of my reluctance that I actually began thinking about what kind of book on Zen I might be able to write, and how it might differ productively from the hundreds of titles already in print. To both Morris and Susan, then, go heartfelt thanks.

Thanks are also due to my many teachers, without whom I would not have been able to write this book. First to mention are the many scholars of Zen on whose work I have drawn and to whom readers are directed through endnotes and my suggestions for further reading. But included as well are such now "problematic" figures as D. T. Suzuki and Alan Watts, through whose writings I first encountered Zen as a teenager rationally dismayed by the arms race and the depredations of war in Vietnam and at home, and spiritually doubtful about the promises of either organized religion or individual (and often hedonistic) "self-discovery." Doors are sometimes opened by what hindsight might represent as unlikely hands.

Deeper thanks are due to my Buddhist teachers, Seung Sahn Dae Soen Sa Nim and Ji Kwang Dae Poep Sa Nim, through whom the personification of Zen became for me more than words on a page. Without Dae Poep Sa Nim's instructions to make my graduate school office into my "Bodhidharma cave," I most likely would have failed to finish my doctorate and continued looking *for* the Buddhist path rather than stepping (however lightly and awkwardly) onto it in practice. My indebtedness remains unfathomed.

Finally, thanks are due to my family. We are all sons or daughters, born through bonds of love and blood, a "red thread" stretching interminably behind us. And as vibrantly intimate as we can be with friends and colleagues, it ultimately is in our families that we are most profoundly and steadily refreshed in treading the infinite path of realizing appreciative and contributory virtuosity.

INTRODUCTION

Among Buddhist traditions of thought and practice, Zen has been one of the most successful in garnering and sustaining interest outside of the Buddhist homelands of Asia. Over just the last fifty years, thousands of books on Zen have been published in Western languages, hundreds of Internet websites have been launched on Zen history and practice, and the word "zen" has come to be part of the lexicon of global popular culture.

This relative popularity is somewhat ironic. For most of its fifteen-hundred-year history, Zen (Chinese: Chan; Korean: Sŏn) generally has portrayed itself as a return to Buddhist origins that requires extraordinary commitment and personal effort. Setting itself apart from (and often above) other Buddhist traditions, Zen has underscored its special status by claiming to replicate in each generation the enlightened mutual understanding that was realized when the Buddha held up a single flower and elicited a smiling response from his disciple Mahākāśyapa. Epitomizing this valorization of silently shared enlightenment, when the iconic ninth-century Chinese Zen master Linji Yixuan (J: Rinzai Gigen) was publicly invited to explain Zen, he responded that "as soon as I open my mouth, I will have made a mistake." Whereas other Buddhist traditions in China at the time identified themselves with particular texts or commentarial traditions, Zen came to identify itself as being "beyond words and letters"—a tradition centered on and sustained by "direct transmission, from heart-mind to heart-mind."

Given all this, why write yet another book about Zen? Part of the answer is that books are not written for traditions; they are written for readers. Zen might have identified itself as a tradition based on a special communication occurring "beyond words and letters," but this did not stop Zen teachers from writing, or from doing so extensively and with great erudition. In fact, the articulation of Zen has been so inseparable from written communication that imagining Zen without writing is like imagining a hand without bones. Another, related part of the answer is that whenever Zen teachings and practices have crossed cultural boundaries—as in being brought to the West—new kinds of writings developed, adapted to the needs and interests of new kinds of readers. Writing new books on Zen might well be said to be a crucial factor in the continued vibrancy and mobility of Zen.

One of the guiding assumptions in writing this book has been that if all things arise interdependently and are continually changing—two of Buddhism's founding insights—then Zen should be presented as having complex origins and as relentlessly dynamic. One implication of this is that the depth with which Zen is presented will be correlated with the breadth of consideration given to the contexts of its origins and development. That is, snapshots of Zen are not enough. Accordingly, a substantial portion of this book is historical—a presentation of Zen not as it *is*, but as it *has come to be*. A second guiding assumption has been that history and biography are intimately connected, and that the success of an introductory presentation of Zen will in some measure be related to how well it integrates both the "public" and "personal" dimensions of Zen.

In keeping with these assumptions, this book has been divided into three parts: Zen Origins, Public Zen, and Personal Zen.

Part I addresses the context for Zen's emergence in Japan in the late twelfth and early thirteenth centuries. It begins by offering a brief introduction to the origins of Buddhist teachings and practices in India and to the broad characteristics of its spread into China and the rest of East Asia. The second chapter tracks the importation of Buddhist teachings, practices, and rituals into Japan from Korea and China and how they factored into the crafting of a unified Japanese state and a common Japanese religious and cultural identity. Here, special consideration is given to the "localization" and elite mobilization of Buddhism in Japan from the sixth to the twelfth century, paying particular attention to the institutional and intellectual innovations involved in the founding of Japanese Tendai and Shingon Buddhism and their subsequent politicization. Against this broad historical and cultural backdrop, chapter 3 focuses on the conditions leading to the early development of Japanese Zen. After a centuries-long hiatus in official relations between Japan and China, reform-minded Tendai- and Shingon-trained monks traveled to China in the late twelfth and early thirteenth centuries seeking deeper understanding of their own traditions as well as ways to address the increasingly widespread and corrupt implication of Buddhist institutions in the power struggles among Japan's political and economic elites. What they discovered and brought home with them were the seeds of what would eventually evolve into the mature Rinzai and Sōtō Zen schools and reshape the religious landscape of Japan.

Part II explores the "public" dimensions of the consolidation and evolution of Japanese Zen. Chapters 4 and 5 address, respectively, the institutional development and cultural impacts of Rinzai and Sōtō Zen from the thirteenth to the mid-seventeenth century. These chapters show how the Rinzai and Sōtō traditions took inspiration from their Chinese "parent" traditions but became integrated into Japanese society by creatively responding to changing Japanese social, cultural, economic, and political realities. Chapter 6 considers the seventeenth-century arrival of the Ōbaku (Ch: Huangbo) line of Linji or Rinzai Zen from the Chinese mainland and the ways in which its rapid spread stimulated a new kind of critical self-consciousness within both the Rinzai and Sōtō communities. Finally, chapter 7 considers how Zen adapted first to the societal transformations brought about in the seventeenth and eighteenth centuries by the new military government established by the Tokugawa shoguns, and then to the even more dramatic changes that occurred as Japan was reopened to global contact after some two hundred years of self-imposed isolation and embarked on a self-conscious course of industrialization, modernization, and nation building.

Part III shifts attention from Zen's public faces to its personal expression—in Zen idiom, shifting focus from Zen's "skin" to its "flesh and bone." Chapter 8 explores the relationship among personal practice, communal discipline and ritual, and moral efficacy, as well as the promises and challenges of Zen partnership both within and beyond temple walls. Chapter 9 deepens engagement with the personal dimension of Zen by presenting and thinking through the life experiences of four Zen exemplars—two affiliated with Rinzai and two with Sōtō traditions—each of whom played crucial roles in shaping the emergence and maturation of Zen over its first six hundred years. The book concludes by considering the coming of Zen to the West, using the emergent tension between emphases on publicly documenting and personally demonstrating Zen as a springboard both for envisioning Zen's future prospects and for better understanding the Zen assertion that enlightenment is not something arrived at *through* practice, but rather as an ongoing achievement *of* practice.

It is somewhat unusual today to present Zen in a way that links complex origins with future prospects and that both acknowledges differences between Zen's public and personal dimensions and attempts to demonstrate their interdependence and interpenetration. The intent in doing so has been to express and respond to some significant features of contemporary writings about and interests in Zen.

In the history of Zen, the present moment is somewhat special. When Zen first developed in China in the seventh and eighth centuries and was subsequently carried to Korea and Japan, all of the new cultural environments in which Zen took root shared both the Chinese writing system and centuries-long histories of engagement with Buddhism. Because literacy was generally limited to elite members of society, the potential readership for writings about Zen was by modern standards both more limited and less varied than might otherwise be expected given the geographical and cultural scope of Zen's regional spread. In addition, since the core literary canon was based on Chinese classics, approaches to scholarship and history across East Asia were largely shared and relatively stable in terms of underlying intellectual assumptions.

None of these conditions has obtained during Zen's transmission beyond East Asia. In fact, the circumstances of Zen's arrival in the West were much more like those that obtained when Buddhism was first introduced in China. In both cases, the absence of a shared literary language led first to an emphasis on translation and interpretative works that attempted to accommodate or make a "place" for completely foreign teachings and practices within the frameworks of "local" knowledge systems. In China, the indigenous frames of reference were Confucian and Daoist, within each of which could be found relatively close parallels to such core Buddhist notions as the primacy of change and interdependence, and the moral centrality of relational quality rather than individual integrity. In marked contrast, the conditions of accommodation in the modern West were framed by religious and scientific assumptions about the nature of reality and the validation of knowledge claims that bore little resemblance to those which had shaped the articulation of Zen teachings and practices in premodern East Asia. In addition, the transmission of Zen to the West coincided with a period in which societal norms and structures were being actively challenged and reconstructed, and in which the moral and intellectual landscapes were being fundamentally transformed. These volatile circumstances dramatically shaped interests in and writings about Zen.

One result, particularly evident from our twenty-first-century vantage, has been the development of a deepening rift between what might be called objective/external and subjective/internal approaches to most effectively and accurately presenting Zen. Associated with the former approach has been a steadily growing and increasingly sophisticated array of translations, commentaries, and explanatory works written by academics committed to contemporary global standards of scholarship. Over especially the last forty years, in keeping with broad changes taking place in scholarly circles, this "objective" approach to presenting Zen has come to focus on using documentary and other kinds of empirical evidence to contextualize and critically assess traditional Zen histories and narratives. In contrast, those taking the "subjective/internal" approach to presenting Zen have generally continued to accept these traditional histories and narratives and have focused on producing interpretative and expository works written for readers less interested in textual and historical analysis than in Zen's immediate personal and spiritual relevance. These now very wide-ranging "Dharma works" go beyond describing or documenting Zen to advocate for it as a uniquely effective method of self-transformation— a liberating path of return to our "original nature."

Analogues to these approaches to writing about Zen can be found throughout Zen's past. Their sharp opposition, however, and the absence of any substantial middle ground between them seem to be a peculiarly modern artifact. As demonstrated, for example, in the writings of Guifeng Zongmi (780–841), one of the most prominent Zen writers in ninth-century China, these approaches were not generally seen as mutually exclusive. Zen writers adopted one approach or the other depending on circumstances and their intended readers. In contrast with the modern division of the world into public and private realms organized, respectively, in accord with collectively determined policy and individual conscience, the underlying assumption in premodern East Asia was that substantial continuity obtained from the grandest cosmic scale to the most personal, so that the fortunes, for example, of one's country and one's family were seen as naturally and intimately interconnected. Put another way, the underlying assumption was that the world is basically relational—a self-governing dynamic of horizonless interdependency.

As suggested by its title, this book is an attempt to move in the direction of closing the gap that has "come to be" between seemingly opposed "outsider" and "insider" approaches to presenting Zen, offering what aims to be a more "nondualist" approach to Zen. A book like this could not—and perhaps need not—have been written a generation or two ago. When it comes to Zen, the world beyond East Asia is no longer a blank slate. Global scholarship on Zen has undergone remarkable growth in the last fifty years and continues to do so. The fineness of resolution and the disciplinary spectrum of knowledge regarding the institutional, textual, and biographical aspects of Zen—as well as the contexts that have both shaped and been shaped by Zen—are without precedent. No less remarkable has been the sharing of experiences and insights among practitioners across cultural boundaries. Never before have so many people in so many different locales been able to participate in Zen practice and to actively compare, contrast, and creatively marry their realizations and authentications of Zen's personal and communal significance. Yet, as welcome as these developments are individually, their relative independence—and at times mutual disdain—has raised important questions about what it means to responsibly and accurately either present or represent Zen.

Presentations of Zen have always been partial in the sense of being incomplete. It is undeniable that for every historical detail and personal insight included in a presentation of Zen, many hundreds more have been left out. This difficulty has been greatly magnified by the staggeringly large volume of information and insights that might now be drawn upon in presenting Zen, but it is a difficulty that equivalently affects both "objective/outsider" and "subjective/insider" approaches to Zen. More problematic is the fact that presentations and representations of Zen can also be partial in the sense of being polemically biased. That is, they can foreground some teachings or traditions at the purposeful expense of others—a practice for which evidence exists in relation to even the earliest (tenth- and eleventh-century) attempts to present Zen traditions in an ostensibly comprehensive manner. Still, this kind of partiality has tended historically to be attributed either to the moral or other shortcomings of a particular exponent of Zen (often by those who disagree with his or her bias) or as a natural function of presenting Zen to different audiences for different purposes.

The questions being raised in light of the disparity of ostensibly "objective/outsider" and "subjective/insider" approaches to Zen, however, are not questions about partiality. Rather, they are questions about validity and utility that assume an absence of shared understanding and that forestall engaging differences between these approaches as openings for meaningful, mutual contribution. The modern convention of distinguishing between the public and personal dimensions of Zen—between the realm of Zen actions and institutions on one hand, and that of Zen motivations and experiences on the other—has opened potentials for greatly enhanced depth of understanding and engagement with Zen. But it seems to me that these potentials will be realized only when these approaches to understanding Zen are continuously attuned to shared purposes, just as depth perception results only when visual information from two sources is actively coordinated.

In writing this book, a coordinating principle has been to keep in mind that although Zen traditionally has identified itself as a transmission "beyond words and letters," it has also traced its own genealogy back to the intimate interpersonal encounter of the Buddha and a key disciple at a public gathering of more than ten thousand people. The origins of Zen were neither private nor arcane. Tracing a continuous line of transmission from the Buddha through medieval Japan to the present day may be a historical fiction. But it is a fiction that invites us to true our understanding of Zen by attending to the always dynamic interdependence of the public and the personal. That, ultimately, is the aspiration of this presentation of Zen.

Part I

Zen Origins

I

BUDDHA, DHARMA, AND SANGHA FROM INDIA TO CHINA

The origins and development of Zen are part of the larger story of Buddhism that now spans more than two and a half millennia. Granted the common association of Buddhism with seated meditation, it is perhaps surprising that this story has always been one about movement. In personal terms, it has been a story of experiential movement from the "here" of ongoing suffering (samsara) to the "other shore" of enlightening release (nirvana); conceptual movement along a "Middle Way" running oblique to prevailing and competing views about what exists, what matters, and why; and physical movement from the Himalayan foothills where Buddhism originated to Central, East, and Southeast Asia and beyond. At least a general understanding of this larger story is crucial to appreciating the history of Zen.

Consistent with its emphases on movement, the story of Buddhism has also been characterized by engagement with what James Clifford has termed the "predicament of culture"—a pervasive condition of "off-centeredness in a world of distinct meaning systems, a state of being in a culture while looking at culture" (Clifford, 1988:9). This condition has become more widespread and intense over the last two hundred years. But the need to respond reflexively to the interplay of distinct and often competing meaning systems has been a familiar reality for at least two thousand years in the multicultural trading hubs along the "silk routes" that linked Europe, the Middle East, and Asia; in the bustling ports that facilitated Indian Ocean trade; and especially in the great cosmopolitan cities of Eurasia like Chang'an and Baghdad.

Siddhartha Gautama—generally referred to as the Buddha or "enlightened one"—lived and taught in the culturally and linguistically diverse environs of what is now northern India and southern Nepal. There, and as his students began spreading his teachings southward and westward across the subcontinent, acknowledging and responding to the predicament of culture was perhaps inevitable. More than four hundred languages are spoken today in India. An equal number or more would have been spoken during the Buddha's lifetime (traditionally dated to 563–483 BCE), and early Buddhists clearly had to confront significant issues of translation and cross-cultural meaning making. In the *Araṇavibhanga Sutta* (*Majjhima Nikāya*, 139.12), for example, the Buddha instructs a group of monks to set aside attachment to his own words and phrasings, and to adopt and adapt local languages in spreading his teachings (Pali: Dhamma; Sanskrit: Dharma). He also cautions them against believing that any teaching could be wholly and exclusively correct. In a telling image, he described the Dharma as a raft: a purpose-built vehicle to be left behind after use, not a repository of absolute truths.

These linguistic issues of translation and interpretation were, however, only part of the picture. The intent of spreading the Dharma was not to share revelation, but rather to inspire: to enjoin, guide, and sustain practices that involved (among other things) an active deconstruction of both assumed and ascribed identities (*anattā*); critical appraisal of one's values, intentions, and actions (karma); and acknowledging the conventional and contingent nature of all social institutions. Buddhist teachings and practices can be seen, in other words, as having been aimed at actively inducing the "predicament" of being in a culture while looking at it—not to renounce the world entirely, but to realize the kind of freedom needed to revise its dynamics from within.

BUDDHIST BEGINNINGS

During the Buddha's lifetime and the centuries following, the Indian subcontinent was undergoing a dramatic rural-to-urban transition. Settlements had been developing around increasingly busy trade crossroads, a number of which eventually grew into major urban areas that became both manufacturing hubs and centers of regional political power. Into these new towns and cities streamed ever larger numbers of people willing to abandon the familiar, agriculturally focused life of the village to work in an expanding range of trading and manufacturing industries. While many of those who left their villages carried their natal religious and cultural traditions with them, moving to one of the new urban areas also enabled them to exercise significant upward or lateral social mobility. With heightened commercial activity came new prospects for wealth accumulation for a much broader portion of society, accompanied by heightened materialism and pleasure seeking. In these conditions of social and cultural dislocation, it was possible—and at some point perhaps imperative—to consider which identities and traditions to retain and which to abandon.

One apparent result of this was the emergence of new religious and philosophical teachings that openly challenged long-dominant Vedic traditions and the claims made by the brāhmanic elite that they alone could understand, transmit, and ritually manage sacred and cultural power. Many of these new religious and philosophical movements remained quite local and were organized around charismatic leaders practicing a purposeful withdrawal from society—rejecting both the strictures of Vedic religiosity and the moral vacuum of rampant materialism. In some cases, these movements seem to have been revitalizations of pre-Vedic religious beliefs and ascetic practices. Others, like Jainism and Buddhism, were no less critical of many prevalent societal norms and values, but in ways that allowed their progressive integration into society.

Like those who were migrating to and traveling among the emerging urban areas of the Indian subcontinent in search of improved life circumstances, the Buddha and the community of monks and nuns that grew around him were itinerant. But whereas traders and other seekers of opportunity left their ancestral homes without entirely departing from the sociocultural norms and traditions of their forebears, Buddhist monks and nuns self-consciously abandoned the "home life" as such. The early Buddhist community—the Sangha—was perhaps the world's first intentional community: a community consciously improvised by men and women from various walks of life who dedicated themselves to realizing freedom from conflict, trouble, and suffering through the Buddha's teachings and practices.

   The travels of the first generations of monks and nuns closely matched
the trade routes joining larger urban areas and the constellations of villages and towns surrounding them, and the early Buddhist community
was in significant contact with newly emerging urban elites. A survey of
the earliest recorded teachings of the Buddha shows, for example, that
while roughly seventy-five of the non-Buddhists featured in these narratives came from rural areas and the origins of two hundred are not specified, over twelve hundred came from urban areas, of whom nearly nine
hundred were *brāhmanas* or *ksatriyas* (the social, cultural, and political
elite), with the majority of the remainder being *vaiśyas* (merchants,
craftsmen, or landowners) (Bailey and Mabbett, 2003:88). Although there
persists—even in Buddhist contexts—an imaginary of the life of the early
Sangha as one of forest-dwelling renunciation, the historical reality was
much more complex. Concerns about the meaning-of and means-to a
skillful or virtuosic (*kusala*) intertwining of the personal and the public
were ongoing—concerns that, as we will see, would later factor powerfully in the development of Japanese Buddhism and the birth of Zen.

The Early Sangha

Some characteristics of the early Sangha can be usefully glimpsed by
considering the traditional division of early Buddhist literature (first oral
and then written) into "three baskets" (Pali: *Tipitika*; Sanskrit: *Tripitika*):
the *Suttas*, *Abhidharma*, and *Vinaya*. The first and foremost of these was
the *Suttas* (Sanskrit: *Sūtras*), a compilation of personally recalled "discourses" of the Buddha and his key disciples. These narratives depict the
Buddha in conversation, answering questions, offering guidance, and telling stories to various gatherings of people, often in the park-like environs
of an estate owned by an elite member of society. In the *Suttas*, we find
depicted an intensely communicative community—a community structured around rich exchanges of insights, puzzling through practical challenges, addressing issues of personality and class, and doing so with not
only intellectual rigor and sensitivity to difference, but also a disarming
combination of equanimity, compassion, and deftly enacted humor.

   The *Abhidharma* was compiled somewhat later and contains works
that articulate a comprehensive theoretical framework of key Buddhist
concepts and their philosophical implications. The *Abhidharma* not only
provides a record of the vibrancy of early Buddhist intellectual reflections

but reveals a community actively engaged in debates with non-Buddhists expressing skepticism about key Buddhist concepts and their logical implications. The *Abhidharma* is in this sense an interactive record of the early evolution of Buddhist thought.

The final basket, the *Vinaya*, or "discipline," contains works detailing the rules and norms that were developed to govern the conduct of monks (*bhikkhus*) and nuns (*bhikkhuni*), including the real-world cases that led to crafting each rule and norm as a means-to relational harmony both within the Sangha and in the relationships among monks, nuns, lay Buddhists, and society at large. The *Vinaya* reveals a community in the making—an ever-growing and increasingly well-defined "assembly" (*sangha*) of men and women responding to emerging challenges and changing circumstances as they traveled from city to town and village, and back again.

As members of the early Buddhist community ranged further and further from the Buddhist heartlands in the shadows of the Himalayas, traveling south and west along major trade routes, differences in the natural, social, economic, and political environment posed continual challenges. The result was the emergence of different lineages of decisions about what was proper conduct within the Sangha, and between Sangha members and the rest of society. According to tradition, the emergence of distinct "schools" of Buddhism came about through just such negotiations of the meaning of monastic discipline in response to changing circumstances, not through explicitly doctrinal disputes.

The day-to-day life of the early Sangha was one of remarkable and entirely voluntary simplicity. It included an "alms round" each morning in which monks and nuns walked silently through any nearby neighborhood or village, each carrying a single bowl into which offerings of food and other necessities could be placed by anyone moved to do so. All offerings were shared communally, and any perishable food would be consumed before noon, the final meal of the day. For the remainder of the day, the Sangha would engage in meditation, recitations, and discussions of teachings; rest; and participate in gatherings where the Buddha or other senior disciples would engage in teaching encounters with the local community and Sangha members. Importantly, other than during the monsoon season when travel was both physically challenging and hazardous—a period during which monks and nuns would reside in a fixed location—the protocol was for Sangha members to remain continuously "on the road." During much of the year, then, the Sangha was traveling in groups of varying sizes, staying only relatively briefly in one location, conveying the Dharma to local residents, and relying on them in turn to supply their own daily subsistence needs.

This is a crucial point. The men and women who had taken Buddhist ordination vows were neither beggars nor complete recluses. They were members of a voluntary association that offered something valuable to the communities they visited in exchange for food and other basic subsistence goods: the Dharma.

Core Teachings: The Dharma

The standard opening for all discourses attributed to the Buddha is, "Thus have I heard," followed by an identification of the place the discourse occurred and who was present. As they are recollected in the *Sutta Pitaka*, the Buddha's teachings did not provide revelations about the origins and nature of the cosmos. They did not offer a ritual technology by means of which one could propitiate the gods and instrumentally further one's own interests. Neither did they offer a regimen of progressive abstraction from the physical world that would result in ultimate bliss or union with a cosmic spirit. These kinds of teachings were available from other religious adepts and traditions, both old and new. Instead, what the Buddha and his students offered was a clearly and persuasively presented set of strategies for here-and-now authoring of one's own liberation from trouble, conflict, and suffering (*dukkha*).

Interdependence

The Buddha's pivotal insight was that all things arise and persist interdependently (*pattica-samuppada*). Nothing exists independently—not the self, the soul, or any of the Vedic gods; not mind; and not even matter. Although it seems to us otherwise, if we attend closely enough, it becomes evident that even what we refer to when we say "I," "my," or "me" is something that is only conditionally present and without any fixed or essential identity. Our bodily forms (*rūpa*), feelings (*vedanā*), perceptions (*saññā*), mental constructs (*sankhāra*), and sense consciousnesses (*viññāna*)—the five *khandha* or "aggregates" into which we can factor our presence as human beings—are all dependent on one another. Just as a stack formed of grain bundles stood on end and leaned against one another in a field at harvest time will fall down if any one of the bundles is removed, our presence depends on a relationship of mutual support among all five *khandhas*; remove any one of them, and "I" ceases to exist.

The same is true of experienced conflict, trouble, and suffering (*dukkha*). These experiences are not a matter of fate, accident, or either devilish or divine intervention. Conflict, trouble, and suffering occur only when certain patterns of mutual conditioning obtain. In other words, they are experiential evidence of interdependence gone awry—the result of relational dynamics being shaped by the interaction and distorting effects of our own ignorance (*avijja*), habit formations (*sankhāra*), and craving forms of desire (*tanhā*). In sum: conflict, trouble, and suffering are expressions of our karma.

Karma

The Buddhist concept of karma (Pali: *kamma*) differs from the earlier Vedic notion of a morally inflected and cosmically structured cause-and-effect relationship according to which bad actions inescapably bring bad results, regardless of why those actions were performed. In Buddhism, karma is understood as a verifiable function of intentional action. By paying close and sufficiently sustained attention, a very clear congruence becomes evident between the complexion of our values, intentions, and actions and the kinds of outcomes and opportunities we experience. Seeing this is not to see our "destiny." Although we can be bound by karma—especially if we are unaware of it—the karmic nature of our life stories is also what makes it possible to realize freedom from conflict, trouble, and suffering. Precisely because we are always in a position to change the patterns of values and intentions that have guided our actions thus far, our life stories are always open to revision. We are always in a position to generate new relational dynamics: new directions and qualities of interdependence.

Core Practices

Changing our karma, like changing a lifelong habit, is not easy. But as was attested by hundreds of the Buddha's students, it is possible. To do so, one need only realize Four Noble Truths: (1) *dukkha* exists, (2) *dukkha* arises when certain conditions occur, (3) *dukkha* ends when these conditions are dissolved, and (4) there is a way to actively dissolve these conditions. This final truth is the path of Buddhist practice, traditionally summarized as the Eightfold Path of realizing right or complete views, intentions, speech, actions, livelihood, effort, mindfulness, and medita-tion. Doing so, ignorance, habit formations, and craving forms of desire are dissolved through our embodied cultivation of wisdom (*paññā*), atten-tive mastery (*samādhi*), and moral virtuosity (*śīla*).

Wisdom

As a concrete means of embarking on this path, the Buddha recom-mended seeing all things as impermanent (*anicca*), as having no essence or fixed identity (*anattā*), and as troubled/troubling (*dukkha*). While there clearly are situations over which we have little, if any, personal control— situations we may be tempted to regard as intractable—seeing all things as impermanent is to see that change is already ongoing. The question is not *whether* our situation can be changed, but only in *what way*, with what impacts, and to whose benefit or harm? Seeing all things as without a fixed identity or essence is to realize that nothing is intrinsically good or bad, no one is inherently capable or incapable. Just as seeing the dynamic nature of our situation brings confidence that there are no "external" blockages to realizing liberating patterns of interdependence, seeing all things as *anattā* or empty (*śūnya*) of any fixed essence enables seeing that there are also no "internal" blockages to liberation. In this context, seeing all things as *dukkha*—that is, as characterized by trouble or stress—is not to indulge in horizonless pessimism, but rather to refrain from supposing that when things are good for me, or even for each of us as individuals, that they are good for all. As a function of relational distortion or degra-dation, *dukkha* is never simply mine or yours; it is in some degree always ours.

In the context of the pivotal Buddhist insight that all things arise interdependently, cultivating wisdom is thus a process, first, of realizing that relationality is more basic than "things" that "are related," and, sec-ond, that deepening wisdom is inseparable from expanding compassion. In other words, Buddhist wisdom is relational transformation.

Moral Virtuosity

Given this correlation of wisdom and compassion, it is not surprising that the cultivation of wisdom has been understood as both supporting and supported by *śīla*—a karma-transforming process of realizing harmonious conduct through the ongoing expression of moral clarity. The term *śīla* is most often translated as "morality" or "moral discipline," suggesting that it consists primarily in refraining from certain kinds of behaviors to live in accordance with preestablished rules or principles. This captures an important part of the conceptual scope of *śīla*. At a minimum, becoming a member of the Sangha means committing to refrain from taking lives, from taking what is not given, from sexual misconduct, from hurtful or harmful speech, and from using fermented drinks or other substances to the point of inducing heedlessness: the so-called Five Precepts. Those seeking ordination take on additional precepts aimed at ensuring that Sangha members conduct themselves, both publicly and privately, in ways that express Buddhist values and demonstrate a dignified willingness to forgo certain material comforts and pleasures in pursuit of more august ends. Over time, several hundred such rules for monastic training were codified.

All such rules, however, were explicitly understood as restraints one accepted, not in order to avoid sin or to become a morally upright individual, but rather as aids in the pursuit of freedom from *dukkha*—the realization of enlightenment. In fact, the umbrella term for all such rules or precepts was *patimokkha* (Sanskrit: *pratimoksha*), or "heading toward enlightenment." In keeping with this, *śīla* was often characterized as conduct directed toward harmony or coordination (*samadhana*), and was seen as one of the perfections or excellences (*pāramitā*) toward which all practitioners are striving, including generosity, patience, diligence, honesty, loving kindness, equanimity, and wisdom. In this sense, cultivating *śīla* can be understood as a means-to realizing the interdependent meanings-of harmony and relational virtuosity: putting wisdom into compassionate action.

Meditation

Anyone who is in a state of mental, emotional, or physical agitation, who is distracted and able to pay attention only fleetingly or by force of habit, or who is caught up in obsessive reflection and calculation, is in no position to heighten and sustain harmony and dissolve the conditions for conflict, trouble, and suffering. Doing so requires attentive mastery.

Buddhist discussions of meditation (Pali: *jhāna*; Sanskrit: *dhyāna*) eventually became remarkably detailed, but the most basic and often-discussed form of meditation in the *Suttas* is the relatively simple practice of mindfulness (*satipatthāna*) or direct and sustained attention to the moment-by-moment condition of body-mind-environment. Unlike meditative practices aimed at generating specific kinds of experiences, Buddhist mindfulness training consists in cultivating experiential immediacy—a letting go of physical, emotional, and cognitive intervention in whatever is occurring or "flowing together" in this situation, at this moment: the realization of what might be termed horizonless presence. The other broad categorizations of meditation practice—insight (Pali: *vipasannā*; Sanskrit: *vipaśyanā*) and calming (Pali: *samatha*; Sanskrit: *śamatha*)—can be understood as complementary extensions and intensifications of mindfulness practices: attention training practices focused, respectively, on exercising ever greater discernment regarding the contents of experience, and on exercising ever fuller and yet more fluid capacities for concentration.

As these brief descriptions suggest, the most basic forms of Buddhist meditation are not directed toward achieving a state of experiential abstraction—a departure or disengagement from the everyday world—but rather toward more complete immersion in it through realizing increasingly open and continuous awareness. Indeed, while the aim of cultivating wisdom, moral virtuosity, and attentive mastery was often described as nirvana (Pali: *nibbana*), a term that literally means "blown out" or "cooled down," it was also identified with the cessation of *āsrava* (Pali: *āsava*) or polluting "outflows" from the interplay of sensing consciousnesses and sensed environments. The function of meditation, especially in the early Buddhist tradition, was the expression of unhindered awareness—an approach to meditation that would come to be definitive for the traditions of Chinese Chan, Korean Sŏn, and Japanese Zen.

Giving

In addition to cultivating wisdom, moral virtuosity, and attentive mastery, giving (*dāna*) or the practice of increasingly open and skilled contribution was understood as a central Buddhist practice. This was true for all Buddhists, including monks and nuns. But it was recognized as especially important for those who continued living the household life. Giving could take the form of offering attention, time, or material support—sustaining an attitude of caring readiness, maintaining a pleasant and open demeanor, performing small acts of kindness, or making charitable donations.

But for lay Buddhists, it was understood that the most productive practice of giving was to make offerings to the Buddha, Dharma, and Sangha: the Three Jewels.

At a practical level, it is possible to see offerings to the Sangha as just a strategy for meeting basic subsistence needs of the monastic community, relieving monks and nuns of needs to secure food, clothing, medicine, and shelter, thus enabling them to wholeheartedly pursue enlightenment. But at another level, practicing generous giving of any sort was understood as having important karmic implications. Making offerings to those who are in need (the "field of compassion") or to the Three Jewels (the "field of reverence") was understood as a way of making merit (Pali: *puñña*; Sanskrit: *punya*)—a way of reconfiguring one's own prospects for the future as well as those of one's family and community.

Even during the Buddha's lifetime, there was a tendency for making merit to be described in terms that suggest a moral economy in which contributions to others are akin to making deposits in one's own "karma bank." For example, in the *Dakkhināvibhanga Sutta* (*Digha Nikāya*, 142), the Buddha is reported as declaring that while gifts to animals can be expected to repay a hundredfold, gifts to immoral ordinary people a thousandfold, and gifts to virtuous ordinary people a hundred-thousandfold, gifts to the "field of respect" will bring immeasurable returns. But as the prior-birth stories of the Buddha (especially the Vessantara Jataka) and the ideal of the bodhisattva or "enlightening being" make clear, the perfection of giving was understood as fostering a qualitative transformation that was tantamount to enlightenment.

In karmic terms, the perfection of giving involves both getting better at understanding what contributions are relevant and building the relational skills (*upāya*) needed to put that understanding effectively into action. It also entails, however, a continuous enrichment of our contributory capacities. This contrasts sharply with the karma of control and satisfying our individual wants and desires. To get better at getting what we want, we have to get better at wanting; but the better we get at wanting, the less we will ultimately want what we get. Far from being enriching, the karma of getting what we want is one of being continuously in want. In what might seem a paradox, it is the karma of giving which results in having ever more to give. As we will see, especially in East Asia, this understanding of the effects of generosity would powerfully influence expectations regarding the proper relationship among the Sangha, society, and the state—an ever-amplifying relationship of shared security and prosperity.

SANGHA, SOCIETY, AND STATE

Embarking upon and sustaining the karma-transforming cultivation of wisdom, moral virtuosity, attentive mastery, and generosity is not easy. Sustaining open and critical attention to our own values, intentions, and actions, and the impacts of their interplay on our own and others' experiences is impossible without extraordinary dedication and honesty. The values that inform our choices, the actions we undertake, and the patterns of outcome and opportunity that result from them define who we are, shaping the relational dynamics through which we are constituted as persons-in-community. Buddhist practice involves a deep and vigilant *critique of self*. And it is in the context of this critique that we must understand the repeated emphases in the *Suttas* and the *Vinaya* that coursing the Middle Way is best done in the intimate company of "good friends." Although it is possible to awake from ignorance, habits, and craving desires entirely on one's own, it is quite rare; enlightenment is much more readily realized through shared training and mutual reflection.

But, in fact, many of our most important values are not peculiar to us as individuals, and the critique of self is ultimately a *relational* critique that deepens through an expansion of the horizons of what we deem relevant. Far from being our personal inventions, the constellations of values that guide our decision making and conduct are significantly shaped by our cultures and collective histories. What we mean by being a good mother, daughter, son, or father is very much dependent on the time and place of our birth. Whether and how much we value independence, rationality, emotional intelligence, or relational harmony is not determined biologically but rather is shaped culturally and socially. And, insofar as cultural, social, economic, and political practices and institutions are both value laden and implicated in the occurrence of conflicts, trouble, and suffering, Buddhist practice at some level will also entail engaging in what might be called a *critique of culture*.

Neither of these critiques need take an antagonistic form. As the Buddha often insisted, declarations of opposition—especially those that take the form of personal attacks ("you are wrong," "I am bad") or presumptive exclusion ("this is true and all else is false," "only this way of life is truly exalted")—are a primary cause of conflict and enmity. [1] Instead, he recommended constructive critical engagement: exercising "wise attention" (*yoniso manasikāra*) to the roots or womb (*yoni*) of the present situation, bringing into focus the networks of causes informing it, and discerning how to skillfully foster and sustain a liberating turn in an already ongoing change process. Thus Buddhist "critiques" of self and culture have not typically involved direct contestations of personal, social, or political authority. Just as conveying the Dharma was not understood as a revelatory presentation of absolute truth, Buddhist engagements with prevailing cultural, social, and political norms were not aimed at revolution but rather at harmony-inducing and harmony-conserving revision.

This "conservative" approach to critique has been a cause of concern for some contemporary Buddhists—for example, late-twentieth-century Japanese exponents of "critical Buddhism" and Western advocates for a more progressive and activist "socially engaged Buddhism"—who see this apparent conservatism as evidence of either doctrinal drift or a failure to fully realize the Dharma. [2] Others are inclined apologetically to see this history of conservatism as evidence of Buddhist pragmatism or realism. For most of its history, the survival of the Sangha has depended on the favorable disposition of the state, and at various times across Asia, Buddhist institutions were subjected to purges of greater or lesser severity, violence, and duration. Threats of repression would clearly have encouraged institutional stances of accommodation toward the state, especially early in the process of integration into a new society.

Yet the story of Buddhism's spread across Eurasia seems to have been more complex than appeals to either of these classes of explanation might suggest. There is significant evidence in the earliest Buddhist literature of awareness that, as Buddhism became more fully integrated into society and incorporated into local cultural identities, its successes in this regard might ironically compromise its broader emancipatory effectiveness. The Buddha insisted that he was the most recent in a lineage of "enlightened ones" whose teachings had all long disappeared, and he openly addressed the rise of "counterfeit" teachings, on at least one occasion (recorded in the *Vinaya*) predicting that his own teachings would remain effective for only five hundred years. And, as Buddhism spread throughout the subcontinent and across Eurasia, it came to be widely believed that the age of the True Dharma would eventually give way, first to an age of the Counterfeit Dharma, and then to an age of the Degenerate Dharma.[3] All of this suggests that the predicament of bringing overlapping and interacting meaning systems into mutually productive accord was crucial to the development of Buddhist historical consciousness, and that over time it compelled considering whether claims about permanently resolving that predicament were not in fact evidence of the Dharma's imminent demise. More positively stated, ensuring the viability of the Dharma entailed ongoing improvisation or responsive virtuosity.

According to the Buddha, effectively conveying the Dharma to different kinds of audiences required "adopting their appearance and speech, whatever they might be," even before he had sat down with them or joined in their conversations; it was only after having first blended in that he "instructed, inspired, fired and delighted them with a discourse on the Dhamma" (*Mahāparinibbāna Sutta, Digha Nikāya*, 16.3.22). Moreover, when he was asked to describe those who are faring well on the path of Buddhist practice, the Buddha did not reference their individual psychological states or some set of experiential milestones that they had passed. Rather, he stated that they are distinguished by the fact that any situation in which they are present will be suffused with the relational qualities of compassion, loving kindness, equanimity, and joy in the good fortune of others—the so-called *brahma-vihāra* or "sublime abodes." Far from taking up residence in some utopia (literally, a "nonplace") utterly disconnected from the everyday world, those faring well on the Middle Way remain embedded in society as catalysts for a more harmonious and liberating reorientation of relational dynamics therein.

In keeping with this, the ideal societies described in the Buddha's discourses do not consist of small bands of contemplatives living in natural paradises. They are highly urbanized societies with large and varied populations engaged in many kinds of industry, teeming with artists and musicians, thriving in balance with their natural environs. Governed by rulers (Pali: *cakkavatti*; Sanskrit: *chakravartin*) who are dedicated to "turning the wheel" of the Dharma for the benefit of all, these societies are depicted as politically stable, economically vibrant, and as having long histories of peaceful and prosperous relations with all. This vision of the enlightened ruler and the flourishing state came to exert a powerful influence on South Asian imaginaries of good governance and just rule from at least the time of King Asoka (third century BCE) and would exert similar influence in imperial China, Korea, and Japan, and across Southeast Asia, even into the modern era. In this vision, often expressed in the form of allegorical tales (see, for example, the *Cakkavatti Sīhanāda Sutta*, *Digha Nikāya*, 26), good governance is explicitly consultative, and the successes of the universal ruler are understood as dependent on ongoing critical feedback and support given by loyal ministers and advisers, including religious or spiritual virtuosos whose contribution to the flourishing of state and society anticipate those that would come to be the historical norm for the Sangha across Asia: the provision of a protective moral compass for the pursuit of societal flourishing.

Indeed, the overwhelming evidence is that, prior to the modern era, the Buddhist "critique of culture" was predominantly a "countercultural" exercise of "soft power" carried out in a broad context of mutual support and accommodation. As is recounted in the *Suttas*, over the course of the Buddha's own teaching career, he was often in a position to offer guidance to political leaders of various kinds of polities, and not once did he recommend a regime change or a sweeping social or political revolution. Instead, his customary approach was to make use of some local governance practice (for example, performing animal sacrifices) as a metaphorical point of departure for exploring the meaning of wiser forms of leadership and governance (through, for instance, sacrificing one's own greed and narrow-mindedness). That is, his effort was directed toward helping leaders envision how to begin working out from within existing circumstances in new and more enlightening directions.

What we see in these canonical descriptions of the interplay of Sangha, society, and the state is a correlation of Buddhist intervention, political stability, state security, and socioeconomic flourishing that would become an explicit norm, playing an important role, for example, in the Sui dynasty reunification of China (589 CE), the seventh-century unifications of both the Korean Peninsula and the Japanese archipelago, and the expansion and acceleration of transcontinental trade.[4] This normative and constructive vision of the public role of the Sangha, however, had the liability of suggesting that when society came to be fraught with instability, dissension, poverty, and violence, it could be seen as an index of either the degree to which the Dharma was in decline or of the failure of Sangha members to fare well on the Middle Way—an index of Buddhist failures to make good on the promise of critically informed support. Indeed, this was an argument used at various points by Confucian and nativist critics of Buddhism, identifying disintegrating socioeconomic and political conditions with the Buddhist influences.

THE EMERGENCE OF BUDDHIST DIVERSITY

As we have seen, a major theme in Buddhist discussions about effectively conveying Buddhist teachings and practices is the need to adapt to local conditions. Since the purpose of these teachings and practices is to dissolve conditions that lead to *dukkha*—the lived experience of conflict, trouble, and suffering—and since these conditions include personally, culturally, and historically shaped patterns of values, intentions, actions, and institutions, there can be no "one-size-fits-all" Buddhism. In short, since the experience of *dukkha* differs from person to person, from time to time, and from culture to culture, so must the Buddhist response.

If the differences involved are relatively minor, this might not involve much more than a change of vocabulary or learning new kinds of body language. This was perhaps largely the case as Buddhism initially spread out of its North Indian homelands. Although there persisted very strong local and tribal cultural identities, increasing urbanization and the tendency for Vedic norms and institutions to serve as a kind of cultural constant would have been conducive to the prevalence of relatively soft or porous cultural boundaries. This was not the case as Buddhism moved north and west into Central Asia where Iranian, Turkic, and nomadic cultures predominated, and then across the Eurasian steppe and desert regions into East Asia. This marked the movement of Buddhism not only into entirely new cultural and natural environs, but also into ongoing interaction with entirely new worldviews.

Over this period, from roughly 300 BCE to 300 CE, Buddhist teachings and practices underwent considerable evolution. There emerged both new *means* for resolving suffering and significantly new *meanings* of Buddhist authority and liberation. By the third century BCE, marked differences had developed in the *Vinaya*, in the interpretation of key teachings and concepts and in the relative status accorded to *arahants* (those who had attained nirvana and were thus "worthy of reverence") and to bodhisattvas (those who voluntarily eschewed nirvana to work for the liberation of all sentient beings) as spiritual and authoritative ideals.

These differences were sufficient for some eighteen or twenty "schools" of Buddhism to be recognized under two major groupings.

One group of schools—the Sthaviravāda—broadly identified themselves as upholding the "way of the elders" (*sthavira*) and conserving the oldest teachings and institutional practices as they had been passed down through an authoritative lineage of *arahants*. Many of these schools remained active through the tenth and eleventh centuries. Texts associated with one of these schools, the Theravāda, were legendarily brought to Sri Lanka (Ceylon) by a mission from King Asoka in the third century BCE. In the fifth century, the Indian monk Buddhaghosa produced a commentary on the Theravāda texts and teachings preserved in Sri Lanka, which subsequently became definitive of the tradition. Sometimes known as "Southern Buddhism," the Theravāda was the only early Buddhist school to survive the Muslim conquest of South Asia.

The other major grouping of schools—the Mahāsanghika or "great assembly"—were broadly in agreement that *arahants* could be fallible in their transmission and interpretations of Buddhist texts, that the Dharma was open (not closed), that it was geared to the needs of specific audiences, and that Buddhism could be transmitted (perhaps most effectively) by other than textual means. It is within these more liberal schools that there began emerging teachings and practices which would later become definitive for Mahāyāna or Great Vehicle traditions that began consolidating sometime around the first century BCE. By roughly the fourth century CE, Mahāyāna traditions had become the dominant forms of Buddhism practiced in Central Asia and China, from which they were later transmitted into Korea, Japan, and Tibet. Although sometimes called "Northern Buddhism," Mahāyāna Buddhism in fact was prevalent (and at times dominant) across Southeast Asia from perhaps the sixth to tenth centuries, and remains the dominant form of Buddhism in Vietnam.

It should be stressed that even through the seventh and eighth centuries, when Chinese Buddhists made the first recorded journeys from China to India and back, monastic communities in India and Central Asia were not divided by school. Rather, the "followers" of many different schools could be found living together, causing Chinese monks like Yijing (635–713) to remark that it was hard to tell who belonged to the Mahāyāna and who to the Hīnayāna—a pejorative term meaning "Small Vehicle" that came into use at roughly the same time as "Mahāyāna" as a way of stressing that its adherents were concerned too narrowly for their own personal liberation (the *arahant* ideal) and not the liberation of all sentient beings (the bodhisattva ideal). In spite of their growing differences, all Buddhist traditions continued to accept the same basic teachings, practices, and rules for monastic conduct.

Nevertheless, differences among the major groupings of Buddhist traditions eventually became as dramatic as those between the land and climate of the Tibetan plateau and those of the Thai forest. Indeed, these major groupings can be seen as distinct "ecologies of enlightenment," each characterized by certain personal ideals, textual traditions, and ways of bringing into focus the means-to and meaning-of Buddhist enlightenment. By the time Zen began developing in Japan around the end of the twelfth century, the three such "ecologies" that are still flourishing today were already in existence: the Theravāda, Mahāyāna, and Vajrayāna.

Theravāda

The texts of the Theravāda or "speech of the elders" are written in the Pali language, which is reputed to be similar to the vernacular spoken by the Siddhartha Gautama, the historical Buddha. The personal ideal is to emulate the Siddhartha Gautama, leaving the home life to eventually become an *arahant*: one whose liberation, *nibbana*, takes the form of an irreversible "blowing out" or "cooling down" of craving desires and attachments to self. Liberation is understood as a release from samsara or being endlessly caught in the *dukkha*-laden cycle of being born, growing up, growing old, and dying. Although attaining liberation through insight (*vipasannā*) and calming/purifying (*samatha*) meditation is in theory possible for everyone, it may take an incalculable amount of time, and the practice of giving (and making merit) is crucial in bringing about the conditions for enlightenment. The authority of the historical Buddha is considered primary.

Although it largely disappeared from continental South Asia, the Theravāda tradition has been maintained in Sri Lanka since its original transmission there in the third century BCE, and it is from Sri Lanka that it was transmitted into Southeast Asia, where it has been the predominant form of Buddhism since approximately the twelfth century. The Theravāda line of female ordination was broken sometime around the eleventh century, and the Theravāda Sangha was thus male-only until very recently with the revival of female ordinations in the 1990s by way of East Asian lineages.

Mahāyāna

The primary texts (sutras and *sastras* or commentaries) of the Mahāyāna are in the Sanskrit language, an elite language of religious, cultural, and intellectual discourse that predated the development of Buddhism and that has been central to the Hindu and Jain traditions. Although Mahāyāna texts, teachings, and practices began developing as early as the second or third century BCE, Mahāyāna Buddhism begins to fully flower from perhaps the second century CE as Buddhism was being carried into Central Asia and across the "silk roads" to China. The personal ideal of the Mahayana is the bodhisattva who remains immersed in the cycle of birth and death (samsara) to work for the liberation of all sentient beings. Perhaps for this reason, Mahāyāna traditions have often been regarded as developing in response to the needs and aspirations of lay practitioners. Bodhisattvas are characterized by their achievement of unlimited responsive skills (*upāya*) through the strength of their vows. Mahāyāna traditions generally affirm the nonduality of nirvana and samsara, stressing that the world we are living in is itself a Buddha-realm. Considerable emphasis is given to the cultivation—by both monastics and laypeople—of six *pāramitās* or perfections: generosity, virtuous conduct, patience, energetic commitment, meditation, and discernment. While the historical Buddha is greatly revered, other "celestial" or "ahistorical" Buddhas are recognized and often accorded a central role in devotional practices.

Although Mahāyāna traditions first developed in India and Central Asia and were transmitted throughout all of Eurasia, they have remained dominant only in China, Korea, Japan, Tibet, and Vietnam.

Vajrayāna

The Vajrayāna traditions of Buddhism seem to have originated in northern India sometime from the sixth to the eighth centuries through an alloying of Mahāyāna Buddhist teachings and practices with tantric practices and teachings that challenged conventional distinctions between the pure and impure or the transcendental and the mundane. As is the case in the Mahāyāna, the primary canonical language of the Vajrayāna is Sanskrit. The term *vajra* refers both to a legendary weapon of the Vedic god Indra, the "thunderbolt," and to an indestructible "diamond-like" substance. And, like the Vedic Hindu traditions, Vajrayāna Buddhism strongly emphasizes the almost magical power of esoteric ritual and language, especially the use of mantra. Although recognizing the distinctive authority and ideals personified by the historical Buddha, *arhats* (Pali: *arahants*), and bodhisattvas, the Vajrayāna also idealizes the *mahasiddha* or spiritual adept whose attainment of enlightenment involves the acquisition of abilities to surpass the limits of "natural law." One of the most distinctive features of the Vajrayāna is the belief that particularly high-ranking adepts are empowered to choose the circumstances of their own rebirth.

Vajrayāna first flourished in what is now North India and Pakistan from the seventh to the eleventh centuries and, by the ninth century, had been carried to China, Japan (where it became highly influential through the Shingon teachings of Kūkai), Burma, and Indonesia (where it informed the building of the monumental stupa at Borobudur). While Vajrayāna was brought to Tibet relatively late—in the eleventh century—it has become so strongly associated with the Tibetan people that it is sometimes referred to as "Tibetan Buddhism." However, Vajrayāna is also the dominant form of Buddhism in Bhutan, Mongolia, and parts of Nepal and North India.

TRUING THE DHARMA

Although it is possible to classify Buddhist traditions into three major "ecologies," it must be stressed that remarkable differentiation has occurred—and continues occurring—within each of them. As a process that was keyed to transcontinental and transoceanic trade, and that was never centrally orchestrated, both the radiation of Buddhism across Asia and its ongoing differentiation have been nonlinear. Because of this, validation has been a continual Buddhist concern. The very first gathering of the entire Sangha took place during the monsoon retreat immediately following the death of the Buddha and was convened specifically for the purpose of verifying that discourses then being attributed to the Buddha could in fact be traced to actual conversations that had occurred at some point in his teaching career.

Even at this very early stage, validating the Dharma was complicated. Not only did the Buddha teach for forty years, interacting with thousands of people in groups of various sizes, almost certainly including relatively private conversations with small groups of students, but he also made no attempt to systematize his own teachings. Indeed, the Buddha gave no encouragement to those who tried to arrange his teachings into some grand and stable architecture, comparing his teachings to a mere handful of leaves fallen from the tree of his enlightenment and chosen simply for their convenience and immediate utility (*Samyutta Nikāya*, 56.31). With the advent of Mahāyāna teachings, the task of validation became vastly more complicated.

The emergence of the Mahāyāna coincided with the production of the first written (rather than oral) collections of the Buddha's discourses, and with the appearance of previously unknown and highly literary discourses that were often lushly imaginative and extensive, sometimes running to several hundred pages in length. Many of these new discourses reflexively portrayed themselves as realigning or truing the Dharma by conveying teachings of the Buddha that were more advanced than those which had been collected in the *Sutta Pitaka* and *Abhidharma*. Quite often, the core disciples of the Buddha—the *arahants* revered by the various schools of early Buddhism—were depicted as resting content with what they had heard at the feet of the Buddha, but without fully understanding or even remembering all of what they had been offered. In the *Vimalakīrti Sutra*, for example, one after another of the Buddha's key disciples are portrayed as reluctantly visiting the layman, Vimalakīrti, who had supposedly fallen ill, and to whom the Buddha had requested they bear greetings. Each of these disciples is drawn into debate by Vimalakīrti, who with both great intellectual skill and humor brings them to an awareness of their shortcomings in Buddhist understanding—especially regarding such core Mahāyāna teachings as emptiness (*śūnyatā*) and nonduality.

Ranking the Teachings

Importantly for the history of East Asian Buddhism, however, while these early Mahāyāna sūtras were clearly crafted to establish the validity and superiority of alternative—either new or not yet mainstream—ways of constellating and interpreting core Buddhist teachings and practices, they did *not* engage in a competitive, winner-take-all effort to disprove the

approaches of earlier schools. Rather than refuting their more conservative texts, teachings, and practices, the new Mahāyāna literature aimed at
relegating them to a lesser status.

This strategy of "argument by relegation" rather than "argument by
refutation" (Heisig et al., 2011:27) can be seen as deriving from the
Buddha's identification of all claims to absolute truth as causes of conflict and his caution that "anger, confusion, and dishonesty arise when
things are set in pairs as opposites" (*Kalahavivāda Sutta, Sutta Nipāta*,
4.11)—a caution that disposed early Buddhists to obliquely contrast the
true and real (*sacca*) with the confused or dull (*moha*) rather than with the
false and unreal (*asacca*). In East Asia, where the indigenous (Confucian
and Daoist) approaches to commentary focused on drawing out new and
apt implications of canonical texts rather than on zeroing in on a fixed
and essential meaning, Buddhist argument by relegation took the form of
positively recognizing and then ranking the truth value of all Buddhist
texts and treatises. The prevalence of this approach would play a powerful role in shaping the development not only of Buddhism in East Asia,
but of truly East Asian forms of Buddhism, especially the Chan, Sŏn, and
Zen traditions.

One of the results (and indeed drivers) of premodern transcontinental
trade between China and "the West" (Central Asia and India) was the
importation of large numbers of Buddhist texts destined for translation by
elite-sponsored international teams in China. By the fifth century, it was
evident to Chinese Buddhists that major differences of doctrine could be
found running through the unsystematic collections of texts flowing into
the country—texts that arrived without dates of composition or clear
provenance, representing the full range of early Buddhist and early
Mahāyāna traditions. Without any immediate reason to regard any given
text as anything other than an authentic record of the Buddha's teaching,
Chinese Buddhists looked for clues internal to these texts that would help
in their organization. What emerged over time were different systems for
interpreting the differences among and ranking the teachings, in which
the Mahāyāna concept of *upāya*—the unlimited responsive virtuosity of
the bodhisattva—came to play a crucial role.

Of the four major and enduring schools (*zong*, "ancestral lineages") of
Chinese Buddhism, three—the Tiantai (Heavenly Terrace), Huayan
(Flower Ornament), and Jingtu (Pure Land)—developed over the sixth to
eighth centuries, at least in part as a result of these efforts to rank Bud-

dhist texts according to the complexity, depth, and/or effectiveness of the teachings and practices offered in them. Each of these schools was organized around a specific text judged to be either the most profound and complete (Tiantai and Huayan), or as offering the most effective and certain means to liberation (Jingtu). All would prove to be profoundly influential in Japan. The fourth enduring school of Chinese Buddhism took a radically different approach. Instead of validating itself by reference to a particular text or group of texts, the Chan School insisted that Buddhist teachings cannot be fully or effectively transmitted through written texts, but only through the skillfully embodied interaction of teacher and student. What all four schools shared was a conviction that realizing enlightenment and conducting oneself as a bodhisattva was possible because each and every one of us has/is Buddha-nature (*fo xing*).

Buddha-Nature

The term "Buddha-nature" is a Chinese neologism that seems to have developed in the course of Chinese attempts to creatively synthesize a set of Buddhist concepts that, in India and Central Asia, were used by proponents of the Mahāyāna to explain the possibility of enlightenment, especially in light of the perhaps infinite accumulation of bad karma made over countless prior lives. They argued that although the seeds of negative experience created by certain kinds of karma are stored at a very basic level of consciousness –in the *ālaya-vijñāna,* or "storehouse consciousness"—so are seeds of enlightenment. Every sentient being is endowed with the "element" or "property" of enlightenment (*buddhadhatu*) in the form of a "womb/embryo" (*garbha*) of the Buddha, who was often referred to as the "thus come one" (*tathāgata*).

This *tathāgata-garbha* teaching was central to a group of Mahāyāna sūtras that were generally oriented toward offering a positive construction of liberation to counteract what some critics of the Mahāyāna took to be the "negative" association of enlightenment with the realization of emptiness. Over the fourth to seventh centuries, a number of these texts were translated into Chinese and became quite influential. But in the context of Chinese cultural emphases on relationality, an important shift occurred from seeing the *tathāgata-garbha* teaching as establishing the *possibility of enlightenment* to seeing it as confirmation of the *promise of enlightenment* for all.

On the basis of a strong interpretation of the teachings of interdependence and nonduality, it could be argued—as the seventh-century Chinese Buddhist thinker Fazang famously did—that interdependence ultimately entails interpenetration. Given this, it was a short step to concluding that if all things arise interdependently, they must ultimately also
share in the Buddha's enlightenment. And indeed, there were canonical
texts—like the *Vimalakīrti Sutra*—which straightforwardly proclaimed
that in a Buddha-realm, all things are doing the great work of enlightenment. All things have the Buddha-element (*buddhadhatu*). For the Chinese, this was most clearly summarized by the affirmation that all things
have or are Buddha-nature.

But in contrast with their Indian and Central Asian counterparts, the
Chinese were not inclined to understand this as a claim about some kind
of intrinsic essence. In the indigenous Confucian and Daoist traditions, all
things were understood as relationally constituted, and the nature (*xing*)
of a thing was thus understood not as a seedlike essence, but rather as a
distinctive pattern of dispositions or propensities. As the basic nature of
all sentient beings, Buddha-nature is nothing other than their *original and
responsive disposition for expressing the meaning of liberation.* It was
not only possible for everyone to become enlightened; it was in their very
nature to do so.

Even in China, however, claiming that all sentient beings have/are
Buddha-nature and are thus candidates for liberation was not uncontroversial. Some Chinese Buddhists found ample support in texts, such as
the *Lotus Sutra* and the Jataka tales, to support their convictions that all
sentient beings are capable of realizing full liberation as Buddhas and
bodhisattvas (even such infamous Buddhist "villains" as the Buddha's
murderously jealous cousin, Devadatta). Others were able to insist on
equally firm textual grounds that there are beings whose karmic debt is so
great that they are destined to endless bondage to the suffering-laden
cycle of life and death. In fact, the primary motivation for the sixteen-
year journey to India that was undertaken in the late seventh century by
the Chinese monk Xuanzang (the inspiration for the great medieval novel,
Xiyouji, or Journey to the West) was to find confirmation in the Buddha's
homeland that "Buddha-nature" was *not* a Buddhist concept.

Tellingly, while Xuanzang did return with the confirmation he had
sought and was greeted with imperial accolades, within three generations
his school of Buddhism had disappeared and Chinese Buddhists no long-

er entertained debates about the universality of our prospects of enlightenment.[5] Coinciding with this "canonizing" of the conviction that all
sentient beings have/are Buddha-nature, there was a dramatic waning of
interest in sending text-gathering missions to India. Perhaps under the
influence of texts (most prominently, the *Lotus Sutra*) that claimed the
Buddha's teachings would flourish only for a limited amount of time and
then go into decline, the assumption seems to have been that the Dharma
had already fallen into disrepair in the land of the Buddha's birth. Indian
Buddhism was relegated to a new and somewhat secondary status, while
China came to be viewed by Chinese as a true Buddhist heartland.

Questioning Authority

The emergence of the Tiantai, Huayan, and Pure Land schools of Chinese
Buddhism can be seen as a complex function of the Mahāyāna strategy of
argument by relegation being alloyed with the very early and very powerful Chinese association of writing with authority. As the Chinese cata-
logued, commented on, and interpreted Buddhist texts from "the West,"
they grew into Buddhist authorities in their own right. Although organized around key Mahāyāna texts from India and Central Asia, all of
these schools were distinctively Chinese. But at the same time, the specific constellation of concepts—especially *upāya*, karma, and Buddha-nature—by means of which Chinese Buddhists organized Buddhist texts
and established their own authority, they also resonated profoundly with
an equally early and powerful Chinese association of knowledge with
embodied realization. This ironically set the stage for Buddhist challenges to the ultimate authority of any text, and for questions about the
merit of predominantly intellectual and scholastic engagements with the
meaning of Buddhist teachings and practices.

Although the roots of these challenges can be traced back to the very
earliest strata of Buddhist texts in India, in the East Asian context a shift
occurs from doctrinal concerns (orthodoxy) to concerns regarding the
meaning of proper practice (orthopraxy) from around the middle of the
Tang dynasty in China. The Tang (617–907) is rightly regarded as one of
China's cultural high points, and as perhaps the most cosmopolitan of its
imperial dynasties. By the eighth century, the capital of Chang'an had a
multicultural and multireligious population of some two million people,
and the empire itself an official population of fifty-three million people

linked by highly sophisticated systems of transportation and trade. This reign of great prosperity and cultural flourishing underwent a cataclysmic shock, however, when a Chinese general of Turkic ancestry, An Lushan, attempted to overthrow the Tang. The rebellion began in 755 and was not fully suppressed until 764. Over this nine-year period, two out of every three people in China either died or went missing as a result of warfare, crop failures, infrastructure breakdowns, and epidemics. For the Chinese, this dire collapse into chaos was manifest evidence of the loss of the "celestial mandate" (*tianming*) of all those in authority—including the Confucian, Daoist, and Buddhist advisers to the court.

Two challenges to Buddhist orthodoxy and authority emerged in China just prior to and during this period of utterly tragic upheaval, each of which would eventually shape the course of Japanese Buddhism and the story of Zen. The first of these traces back to the arrival in China of Vajrayāna Buddhism. While Vajrayāna teachers did bring texts, these documents were considered important less for their verbal content than for their ritual efficacy. Emphasizing the necessity of orally transmitted instruction, the recitation of mantras and *dhāranīs* (short phrases imbued with spiritual force), and the performance of complex rituals, these early Vajrayāna teachers did not offer intellectual insights or philosophical systems comparable to the Tiantai or Huayan tradition, or devotional systems of the sort offered by Pure Land teachings; they offered the possibility of developing personally embodied *siddhi* or spiritual powers. In recognition of the central role played by the use of mantra—a Sanskrit term translated into Chinese as *zhenyan* or "true word"—the Chinese came to refer to Vajrayāna as the Zhenyan school of Buddhism.

By the middle of the eighth century, Zhenyan Buddhism was becoming increasingly widespread in the Chinese capital, in part because the efficacy of its rituals extended to the protection of the state—a very real need as the Chinese empire faced threats from Turkic peoples in the far west, from Tibetans to the west and south, from nomadic peoples to the north, and from Korea in the northeast. But perhaps most importantly, Zhenyan rituals also enabled practitioners to eliminate the obstructions of bad karma and appease "hungry ghosts" and other restless spirits whose deaths had been premature and harrowing—a "population" that could only have exploded in China during the traumatic years of the An Lushan rebellion and its aftermath. The Zhenyan emphasis on embodied understanding directly challenged the intellectual bias of the more text-focused schools of Buddhism. The Zhenyan tradition would eventually disappear in China, in part because the practices it emphasized were able to be absorbed by other Buddhist schools and emerging Daoist traditions. But it went on to flourish in Japan, informing the Tendai tradition—a Japanese adaptation of Chinese Tiantai—as well as the Shingon tradition founded in the early ninth century by the single most widely revered monk in Japanese Buddhist history, Kūkai (774–835), as a direct counter to the scholastically inclined Buddhist traditions that were then dominant in Japan.

Chan

The second challenge to the textual biases of the early Chinese Buddhist schools was the ancestor of Japanese Zen and Korean Sŏn: the Chan or "meditation" school. Unlike the other three enduring schools of Chinese Buddhism, the Chan tradition did not take any particular sutra as foundational. On the contrary, its proponents denied that any text could ever be an ultimate expression of the Buddha Dharma. As if drawing inspiration from and amplifying the Buddha's claim that those who are wise "do not hang on to anything, anywhere," and "do not enter into the mud of conceptual thinking" (*Sabhiya Sutta, Sutta Nipata*, 3.6), Chan teachers emphasized the realization of utter immediacy—the demonstration, in any circumstances whatsoever, of an unobstructed presence and responsive virtuosity. The iconoclastic eighth-century Chan master Mazu (J: Baso Doitsu) is recorded as having described this as an utterly flexible "harmony of body and mind that reaches out through all four limbs . . . benefiting what cannot be benefited and doing what can't be done" (*Ta Tsang Ching*, 45.408b). In short, practicing Buddhism is not about *getting* enlightened, it is about *demonstrating* enlightenment.

Consistent with this emphasis on the embodied demonstration of enlightenment—one's Buddha-nature—rather than tracing its authority to a particular text, by the late Tang, Chan exponents were tracing their genealogy back to the Buddha himself through a South Indian (or perhaps Iranian) monk named Bodhidharma (J: Daruma) who was said to have come to China in 527 as the twenty-eighth in an unbroken series of teacher-to-student transmissions. The relatively scant historical evidence we have suggests that Bodhidharma accepted a small circle of Chinese students and took a relatively mainstream Mahāyāna approach in his teaching and practice, stressing the realization of nonduality through sitting meditation (*dhyāna*).

A major turning point in the Chan narrative occurred in the eighth and ninth centuries as Huineng (J: Daikan Eno), legendarily represented as an illiterate son of a single mother whose only monastic experience was as a manual laborer, came to be accepted as the sixth Chan patriarch. For some time after this, Chan identified itself as a "rustic" tradition far removed from the sophisticated life of the imperial court and elite society—a tradition that, like the ancient classic, the Book of Songs, spoke with the voice of the Chinese people. Around the beginning of the Song dynasty (960–1279), Chan began explicitly proclaiming itself to be "a special transmission outside the teachings" that "does not establish words and letters" and instead "directly points to the human heart-mind" to enable "seeing (one's) nature and becoming Buddha."

With the crafting of Chan identity, Chinese Buddhists in effect announced their confidence in being able to shape and not merely interpret Buddhism—a confidence symbolized in the fact that Huineng's teachings were titled the *Platform Sutra*. Chan represented itself as a tradition of "homegrown Buddhas" who were not only capable of relegating all other Buddhist traditions to their proper places, but who were committed to actively "truing" the Dharma in spontaneous and virtuosic response to immediate situational needs and dynamics—a legacy of confidence and critical counterpoint that would profoundly inform the Japanese Zen traditions. For Chan, as for the Zen tradition which would carry on its legacy in Japan, the *personal realization* of enlightenment was considered virtually inseparable from the *public demonstration* of one's Buddha-nature.[6]

2

THE JAPANESE TRANSFORMATION OF BUDDHISM

Buddhism began taking root in Japan during the fifth and sixth centuries as immigrant communities from the Korean Peninsula established themselves as influential purveyors of new building techniques, new technologies (especially metalworking and writing), new institutional models, and new scopes and scales of imagination. Given the ruggedly mountainous geography of the Japanese islands, it had been natural for cultural, religious, and political authority to be structured traditionally around relatively small, local lineage groups or clans (*uji*). By the fifth century, as evidenced by the building of monumental burial tombs (*kofun*)—some as large as several hundred meters in length and up to thirty-five meters high—a degree of centralization had begun to occur around a set of lineage groups based on the Yamato plain. But political authority in Japan remained loosely structured and highly contested. From the continent, immigrant communities brought a vision of a hierarchic, functionally organized, and geographically vast imperial rule: an expansive imaginary of cultural, religious, and political authority in which Buddhism played both integrative and protective roles. This view of Buddhism had emerged with the reunification of China in the sixth century, and some understanding of this process is crucial for appreciating the interest of Japanese elites in this new foreign religion.

The collapse of the Chinese Han dynasty (221 BCE to 220 CE) had triggered a long period of relative political disunity emanating outward from northern China. Dozens of multiethnic and multicultural alliances attempted to assert imperial authority, but none was fully successful and the sustained intensity of their violent competition spurred the southward migration of as many as a million people. These refugees maintained a semblance of imperial rule in the Western and Eastern Jin dynasties (265–316 and 317–420, respectively), the capitals of which were each home to nearly one and a half million people and briefly vibrant centers of traditional Han culture. After the fall of the Jin, China was in political disarray for the better part of two centuries, divided among the so-called Sixteen Kingdoms.

This disarray did not entirely disrupt trade along the famed "silk roads." Indeed, by the fourth century the movement of goods and peoples was rapidly accelerating along the trade routes that skirted the Taklama-kan desert and merged at Chang'an (present-day Xian)—a city that grew to become the largest and most cosmopolitan in the premodern world, with a population of nearly two million people living within its walls and in its suburbs. The collapse of centralized political authority and the porous borders that prevailed from the Hindu Kush mountains in the west to the Korean Peninsula in the east were conducive to an extraordinary mixing of ethnic groups and cultures.

It was during this period that the famed Central Asian monk, Kumārajīva (344–409), produced benchmark Chinese translations of hun-dreds of Buddhist texts, working in Chang'an with an "international" team of some eight hundred people. Also during this period, the practice of carving monumental Buddhist statues from live rock—some as tall as 180 feet—spread across Eurasia from Gandhara (present-day Afghani-stan) to northwestern China. So strong was Buddhism's appeal that from the late fourth to early sixth centuries, for example, the previously no-madic rulers of the Northern Wei dynasty commissioned the carving of more than fifty thousand Buddhist statues at a single site (the Yungang grottos near present-day Datong). In this remarkably cosmopolitan era, Buddhist thought, practices, and rituals provided a shared frame of refer-ence across the continent—a conceptual and practical framework for achieving both political unification and economic growth. During the period that immigrants from the Silla and Paekche kingdoms on the Kore-an Peninsula were creating alliances and intermarrying with powerful families in central Japan, they could with considerable justification claim that all civilized lands from the far western regions to the Korean Penin-sula were Buddhist.

If for no reason other than as a means to political consolidation, then, it was perfectly natural for elite Japanese families to welcome the arrival of Buddhism in the archipelago. Buddhism was, however, clearly an imported religion. Tradition has it that when a Buddhist statue was presented to the Yamato court as a gift from the Paekche kingdom in 552, it triggered considerable debate about whether officially embracing this foreign religion would offend the indigenous Japanese *kami* (spirit forces) from which Japanese lineage groups ultimately drew their own authority and upon which they relied for help in bringing about and sustaining prosperity. This resistance to officially embracing Buddhism dissolved over the latter half of the sixth century as the immigrant-descended, pro-Buddhist Soga family engineered a series of victories in royal succession struggles that eventually resulted in the ascent of Empress Suiko to the throne in 593 and the appointment of her nephew, Prince Shōtoku (572–622), as regent the following year.

It was at the height of these succession struggles in Japan that China was finally reunited in 589 by Yang Jian (541–604), founder of the Sui dynasty (581–618). Born in a Buddhist monastery and raised for a time by a nun, Yang Jian took the name Wendi (Emperor Wen) and began instituting policies aimed at reinvigorating China's material economy (symbolized by the construction of the iconic Grand Canal), and at constructing a new, Buddhist economy of imagination. In a move that would set a precedent for rulers throughout East Asia in the centuries to come, Wendi mandated the creation of a protective network of 111 sites housing Buddhist relics across the empire, sponsored temple complexes at each of the five sacred mountains in China, encouraged spiritual pilgrimages to these sites, and established continuous recitations of Buddhist sutras at the imperial court.

Seen first through immigrant eyes and then through official emissaries sent to the Sui court in 600, it was evident to many in Japan that China's reunification, the harmonization of its diverse peoples, and the rapid growth of its economy occurred in conjunction with the dramatic ascent of Buddhism. Throughout the known world, Buddhism was evidently both a unifying force and a civilizing one. According to traditional Japanese historical accounts (for example, in the eighth-century *Nihon shoki* and *Kojiki*), it was precisely this vision that inspired Prince Shōtoku to compose the founding document of the unified Japanese state in 604—the so-called Seventeen-Article Constitution.[1] Urging a collaborative approach to governing in accordance with the rhythms of nature that made complementary use of Confucian values to structure public actions and Buddhist teachings to shape inner motivations, Shōtoku's Constitution articulated a basic template for the conception of Japanese identity that would be essentially unchallenged for nearly a thousand years.[2]

Much as in Sui dynasty China, the consolidation of imperial-style rule in Japan was interwoven with efforts to root Buddhism in the Japanese landscape. By 624, there were forty-six Buddhist temples in Japan that supported nearly fifteen hundred monks and nuns. By the middle of the eighth century, hundreds of temples had been built, and the larger individual monastic complexes often comprised dozens of buildings and had populations of several hundred monastics. In contrast with China, however, the political and cultural drivers for these compounding efforts to spread and deepen the presence of Buddhism in Japan would eventually result in a substantial blurring of boundaries between the state and the Sangha. By the end of the Heian period (794–1185), the extent of this blurring and the corruption resulting from it would become crucial factors in the emergence of Zen as a critical Buddhist "counterculture."

WRITING AND AUTHORITY: THE GROWTH OF BUDDHISM IN JAPAN

As epitomized by Shōtoku's Constitution, the Japanese model of imperial rule was an adaptive blending of native and imported conceptions of order. A key dimension of the model of imperial statecraft imported from the continent was the profound association of writing with authority—an association that had been explicitly scripted into Chinese legends of the origins of their own culture and that had factored importantly in their initial respect for and growing appreciation of Buddhism. This association was critical in the esteem accorded in Japan to the immigrant communities that first brought Buddhist practices and institutions, as well as Chinese/Confucian models of statecraft, to the archipelago. The skills in reading and writing Chinese that these immigrants possessed positioned them to serve as gatekeepers both to continental sources of political authority and to the literary sources of cultural refinement (*wen*) that in China were understood as complementing and ultimately completing the work initiated by the exercise of martial prowess (*wu*). Given this, it is no surprise that the spread of Buddhism in Japan was carefully and centrally orchestrated by elite families and the imperial court; that the *kami* from which leaders of individual clans (*uji*) drew their authority were gradually accorded important but subordinate places in an overarching Buddhist cosmology; or that the unifying sense of Japanese identity that emerged during the late Yamato, Nara (710–784), and Heian (794–1185) periods was a distinctive alloy of indigenous inspirations and imported aspirations.

Perhaps the single most important effect of the historical context of Buddhism's arrival in Japan was the development of an almost symbiotic relationship among Buddhist and state institutions as sites for the accumulation and hereditary transmission of wealth and power. Due in part to the centrality of written texts for Buddhist thought, ritual practices, and institutional dynamics, it was natural that practically all of the first generations of Japanese monks and nuns were from elite families. In fact, the first Buddhist temples built in Japan were not public institutions. They were family or clan temples intended to further the fortunes of those related by blood, marriage, and hierarchically ordered patterns of mutual loyalty.

Through the Nara and Heian periods, although Buddhism spread beyond the boundaries of elite society, strong and abiding connections with leading families continued to characterize important Buddhist centers. Indeed, the line between the imperial court and the monastic cloister became sufficiently blurred that a term was coined for emperors and empresses who formally abdicated the throne only to exert ongoing influence from within the monastery as an ordained monk or nun. The Emperor Shōmu (701–756), who was one of the first of Japan's imperial rulers to go into such working retirement as a "cloistered emperor" (*Daijō Hōō*), was responsible for mandating the construction of a "temple for the protection of the country" (*kokubunji*) in every province and for nearly bankrupting the government in the course of lavishly outfitting the headquarters of this network—the famed Tōdaiji or Great Eastern Temple—the main Buddha Hall of which remains the largest wooden building in the world.

A second major effect of the historical circumstances of the transmission of Buddhism to Japan and its spread through the archipelago was the early predominance of Chinese schools that were in heated intellectual debate with one another, jockeying for the status of offering the most sophisticated and complete articulation of the Buddha Dharma. These disputes were brought to Japan—along with the texts and styles of argument supporting them—by both native Chinese exponents and those members of Japanese elite society who had been chosen to take part in official imperial missions to the Sui and Tang courts. In the eighth century, there were seven such missions, each involving between five- and six-hundred "men of promise." Perhaps expectedly, when transplanted to Japanese soil, Chinese intellectual disputes were grafted onto a complexly shifting array of inter-familial animosities and alliances, with ever-expanding political, social, and economic stakes.

It was substantially in response to the intellectualism of the so-called Six Schools of Nara Buddhism—the Ritsu, Kusha, Jōjitsu, Sanron, Hossō, and Kegon schools—and the ways in which disputes among them were inflamed by and drafted into serving elite power struggles that the first schools of distinctively Japanese Buddhism began developing around the beginning of the ninth century. These new schools—Tendai and Shingon—remained wedded to the ideal of a mutually supportive relationship between the Sangha and the state. But their founders explicitly advocated a basic reconfiguration of that relationship. Buddhism had been welcomed to Japan in connection with an imaginary of social, political, and spiritual integration, and all of its core teachings were emphatically oriented toward dissolving the conditions for conflict and suffering. Yet the spread of Buddhism in the Nara period had become synonymous with competitions—both intellectual and material—that mirrored those taking place among Japanese elites. Very much in the spirit of Shōtoku's constitutional vision, Tendai and Shingon Buddhism emerged as inclusive and unifying responses to this factionalism.

RITUAL AND AUTHORITY: THE EMERGENCE OF JAPANESE BUDDHISM

In the final decades of the Nara period, the capital was awash in political intrigues and scandals in which Buddhist institutions were crucially implicated. While the imperial Taika Reform (645) and Taiho Code (702) had resulted in more centralized control over land distribution, taxation, and religious institutions, these reforms had not had the desired effect of neutralizing power struggles among aristocratic families. The new imperial policies of mandating temple and monastery construction in every province, granting land to government officials and noble families for their private use, exercising bureaucratic control over Buddhist ordination rituals, and awarding tax-exempt status to Buddhist institutions had the combined effect of opening a loophole through which elite families could amass both wealth and political power. By donating land and labor to Buddhist temples and monasteries, and by ensuring that family members were ordained and appointed to leadership positions within them, aristocratic families were able to build productive capacity and influence without being taxed or subject to direct imperial oversight.

A dramatic confrontation with the corrupting impacts of this instrumental merging of religious, economic, and political fortunes occurred in the mid-760s. After having left the throne in 758 to become a Buddhist nun, the Empress Kōken responded from within the cloister in 764 to crush an attempted imperial coup plotted by one of Nara's elite families. Reinstating herself as Empress Shōtoku, she appointed as her prime minister a Buddhist priest and healer, Dōkyō, with whom she had developed a complex (and perhaps sexually intimate) personal relationship. In doing so, she effectively created a personal bridge between the secular Council of State Affairs and the religious Council of Kami Affairs. Not long afterward, in a move that shocked the Nara establishment, the empress made this bridge explicit by granting Dōkyō the honorary status of a "Dharma king," and in 769 he was sufficiently emboldened to orchestrate the promulgation of an oracle that suggested he should be made emperor. Although he was foiled by those loyal to the concept of an imperial bloodline and died in exile, Dōkyō's bald ambition to erase the boundary between religious and political power laid open to widespread and incisive condemnation the competitive and elite-empowering collusion of Buddhist and state institutions.

The virulent competitiveness and corruption associated with this collusion of secular and sacred authorities likely informed the decision of Emperor Kammu to abandon Nara in 784, relocating the capital first to Nagaoka and then to Heian (modern-day Kyōto). Among his edicts regarding the new capital was a ban on Buddhist temples within the city proper: the legal imposition of geographical separation between political and religious elites. Emperor Kammu was not, however, averse to Buddhist institutions as such. Among those who traveled to China as part of the imperial mission to the Tang court in 804 were two monks—Saichō

(767–822) and Kūkai (774–835)—who founded on their returns, respectively, the distinctively Japanese schools of Tendai and Shingon Buddhism, both with the emperor's enthusiastic support.

The life paths that led Saichō and Kūkai to officially supported passage to China were very different. Saichō had been raised in a Buddhist family, entered monastic training at age twelve, and developed a lifelong interest in combining doctrinal studies, meditation, and esoteric ritual. His motivation in going to China was to bring back Tiantai texts that argued for a definitive ranking of Buddhist teachings and, by extension, promised an end to competition among the doctrinally based schools of Nara Buddhism. Kūkai was sent to study at the government university in Nara in preparation for a bureaucratic career, but he became disenchanted with the heavily Confucian curriculum and dropped out to undertake an intensive, independent study of Buddhism, including long periods of solitary meditation in the mountains near Kyōto. After encountering a text central to the Zhenyan tradition—the *Mahāvairocana Sūtra*—he became convinced of the need to go beyond an intellectual grasp of Buddhist knowledge to its embodied activation by studying in person with a master of esoteric Buddhism in China.

What Saichō and Kūkai shared prior to their travels to China were two convictions: the highly politicized and scholastically inclined schools of Nara Buddhism were incomplete vehicles for realizing either the personal or the collective benefits of Buddhist practice, and Buddhism would not flourish and truly benefit Japanese society without restoring strict monastic discipline. As it happened, their efforts would not succeed in permanently eradicating the troubled relationship among the imperial state, elite society, and the Sangha. Indeed, the persistence and intensification of political and religious conflicts and corruption at the end of the Heian period were important factors in the appeal of the Zen, Nichiren, and Pure Land schools of Buddhism that developed in the early Kamakura period (1185–1333). Nevertheless, the schools founded by Saichō and Kūkai did succeed in marking out a field of interrelated concepts, symbols, practices, problems, and sensitivities that came to define the terms of religious and cultural development in Japan for more than half a millennium. Crucial to both was the importance of esoteric (*mikkyō*) forms of Buddhist teaching and practice, and an insistence that enlightenment was not something to be realized only in an incalculably distant future or by only a select few.

Tendai

After his early introduction to Buddhist meditation and doctrinal studies, and at about the same time that the imperial capital at Nara was being dismantled, Saichō decided to go into retreat on the wooded flanks of Mount Hiei near Kyōto. He remained there, meditating and studying Buddhist texts for nearly a decade. During this period, Saichō was most strongly attracted to Kegon (Chinese Huayan) works that undermined Buddhist sectarianism by offering a One Vehicle (*Ekayāna*) teaching that relegated all other Buddhist teachings to the status of "skillful means" used by the Buddha to address the needs and limitations of those he encountered over the course of his teaching career. The core Kegon text, the *Avatamsaka*, or *Flower Ornament Sutra*, was claimed to be the very first teaching of the Buddha—an undiluted expression of the Buddha's enlightened insight, to the explanation of which many of the best minds of China had devoted their lives. It was in such a commentarial work that Saichō encountered references to Chinese Tiantai and the writings of its primary philosophical architect, Zhiyi (538–597).

In Zhiyi, Saichō discovered an exemplary model for combining meditation and doctrinal study in a way that few of Saichō's contemporaries were able even to consider. Not only did Zhiyi write the seminal Chinese Buddhist treatise on meditation, but he had also devised a masterful and comprehensive system for ranking all Buddhist texts and teachings built around the self-referential claim made in the *Lotus Sutra* (*Saddharmapundarīka Sūtra*), the core text of the Tiantai tradition, that it was the final and most complete expression of the Buddha's teachings: a disclosure of the ultimate meaning of being Buddha or an "enlightened one," based on a lifetime devoted to effective teaching. This was precisely what Saichō had been seeking.

A parable-filled Mahāyāna text that portrays itself as offering the Buddha's most profound and complete teaching, the *Lotus Sutra* sets itself apart from both the lesser (Hīnayāna) and greater (Mahāyāna) turnings of the wheel of the Buddhist Dharma, claiming that all other teachings of the Buddha were expressions of his *upāya* or responsive virtuosity, but not his peerless insight and true nature. Only the *Lotus Sutra* transmits the ultimate truth of the Buddha, and in a way marvelously accessible to all. Moreover, as Zhiyi emphasized, the *Lotus Sutra* effectively denies the existence of grounds for distinguishing among those who are caught in samsara and those who have successfully crossed over from samsara to nirvana by means of one of the so-called Three Vehicles—those who have achieved awakening through hearing a Buddha's teachings (*śrāvakabuddhas*), those who are self-enlightened but unable to teach or guide others (*pratyekabuddhas*), and those rare few (like Siddhartha Gautama) who are fully self-enlightened and both capable of and committed to teaching and guiding others (*samyaksambuddhas*). Instead, the *Lotus Sutra* presents an all-encompassing One Vehicle (*Ekayāna*) teaching: not only is the Buddha always compassionately omnipresent, but the world in which we find ourselves is a continuous expression of innumerable meanings and infinite potentials for enlightening conduct; not only are all beings already on the Buddhist path, but they are already acting as bodhisattvas, demonstrating unlimited skillful means or responsive virtuosity, even when they do not think that they are doing so.

As Zhiyi interpreted it, and as Saichō would come to affirm, the *Lotus Sutra* offers a way beyond the apparent opposition of existence and emptiness; the opposition of what arises provisionally as a function of causes and conditions, and what obtains unconditionally; and the opposition of what can be specified and expressed, and what is ambiguous and inexpressible. While other Buddhist teachings remain caught in contrasting *conventional* truths about the world as mundanely experienced and *ultimate* truths about reality in the absence of all conceptualization, the *Lotus Sutra* presents an integrative Threefold Truth: a vision of the mutual penetration and convertibility of provisional existence, emptiness, and the middle path of manifesting unlimited and universally liberating responsive virtuosity. Put somewhat differently, enlightenment manifests *as* existence, *as* emptiness, and *as* the middle path of reconciling existence with emptiness. Each thing and every being, precisely as they are right now, are already expressing the Buddha Dharma.

For Saichō, the One Vehicle and Threefold Truth approach of Tiantai made it possible to relegate the six schools of Nara Buddhism to a lesser status without refuting any of their specific teachings—a nonconfrontational and yet openly hierarchic approach to altering the dynamics of Buddhist (and, by extension, social and political) interaction in Japan. Indeed, while he was in China, it became clear to Saichō that the kind of sectarian divisions that prevailed in Japan—divisions based in part on patronage practices that effectively fostered the physical segregation of monks and nuns from different traditions—were not the norm in China.

There, those devoted to all the major Buddhist schools lived together in the same monastic complexes without the competitive rancor that seemed so prevalent in Japan.

The inclusiveness of Chinese Buddhist institutions enabled Saichō to complement his study of Tiantai with the study of other Buddhist traditions. And, in fact, the Tendai tradition that he developed after returning to Japan in 806 was not simply a local iteration of Tiantai; it was a distinctively Japanese alloy of Chinese Tiantai and elements drawn from the Chan, Zhenyan, and Vinaya schools—an alloy that Saichō believed was suited to clearing a path beyond both sectarian struggles and the moral lassitude that had come to characterize monastic life in Nara. His vision made a sufficiently positive impression on Emperor Kammu that Saichō was granted the right to ordain two monks annually to launch his new Tendai School.

Saichō's decision to fuse Chinese Tiantai and esoteric (*mikkyō*) Zhenyan teachings and ritual practices would prove to be a decisive factor in Tendai's ascent into preeminence over the Heian period—a fusion of openly transmitted, conceptually focused, and textually articulated streams of Buddhist practice and insight with one that was secretly transmitted, corporeally focused, and ritually articulated. Having received basic initiation into esoteric Buddhism in China, Saichō continued studies on his own in Japan, making use of texts he had brought back with him, convinced that the teachings of the *Lotus Sutra* as interpreted in Tiantai were in essence identical to those transmitted by Zhenyan—a fact reflected in the curriculum of the Tendai school where these two sets of teachings were understood as parallel courses.

With the return of Kūkai to the capital in Kyōto by imperial order in 809, Saichō and his students intensified their study of esoteric Buddhism under his tutelage, even as Saichō himself became increasingly involved in establishing the superior credentials of his own Tendai School and dealing with the disputatious struggles that were ironically emerging within it. Eventually, Saichō and Kūkai broke off relations. This was at least in part because Saichō was convinced of the ultimate equivalence of the teachings presented in the *Lotus Sutra* and those transmitted through the esoteric texts and rituals of the Zhenyan tradition, while Kūkai maintained the superiority of the path of esoteric practice and insisted on the necessity of secret, oral transmissions from masters to disciples. But it may also have been a result of their taking rather different approaches to realizing the conditions under which their distinctively new formulations of Buddhist thought and practice could take firm root and flourish.

Kūkai seems to have adopted an accommodating stance toward the Nara Buddhist establishment, even as he cultivated increasingly close relations with the imperial court, focusing his attention on presenting Shingon as serving an intermediary function: explaining why and how the exoteric structures of thought, speech, and action that were made manifest in existing Buddhist practices were in fact effective, especially in securing and promoting the vitality of the state. That is, Kūkai presented Shingon as revealing the esoteric warp on which the various schools of Nara Buddhism had been weaving their own traditions—an esoteric infrastructure without which their texts, chants, and rituals would have been incapable of functioning as intended.[3] Saichō adopted a more explicitly advocatory stance. Wedded to Zhiyi's ranking of Buddhist teachings, he found that his attempts to articulate a hierarchic and yet fully inclusive approach to organizing Buddhist thought and practice drew the considerable ire of the Nara establishment. And in fact he became embroiled in what could be regarded as one of the single most important intellectual debates in Japanese history.

Over roughly a four-year period, Saichō engaged in a series of increasingly incisive exchanges with Tokuitsu, a monk in the powerful Hossō School, at the center of which was the concept of Buddha-nature (J: bussho). Following the famous Chinese monk Xuanzang, the principal exponent of the Chinese Faxiang tradition to which the Hossō School traced its roots, Tokuitsu insisted that there are sentient beings whose karmic burdens are so great that they are not candidates for enlightenment; no matter how hard or long they try, they will never become a Buddha. For Saichō, this marked a basic misunderstanding of the nature of Buddhist practice—seeing it as a necessary but not sufficient means to enlightenment—and implied a fundamental rejection of the overarching thrust of the Lotus Sutra: that all beings are destined for the realization of unsurpassed enlightenment. Making use of the One Vehicle and Threefold Truth teachings of Tiantai, he argued that all sentient beings have/are Buddha-nature and that this was not something to accept on faith, but rather to realize in practice.

In the later Tendai tradition, this argument was taken to its logical conclusion by the proponents of so-called original enlightenment (hongaku) who maintained that even "the grasses, trees, mountains, and rivers all

attain Buddhahood," insisting that to realize the Threefold Truth of emptiness, conventional existence, and the middle way was to realize the
ultimate identity or mutual convertibility of all things. Precisely as it is,
the world of daily experience is a Buddha-land; just as we are, each and
every one of us is Buddha.[4] From the late Heian to the modern era, this
profound affirmation of the mundane world as intrinsically enlightened
and enlightening was a nearly ubiquitous trope in literature, art, and thea-
ter.[5]

At Enryakuji, the temple Saichō founded on the slopes of Mount Hiei
just outside of Kyōto, monks committed to remaining in residence for
twelve years, undergoing a training regimen centered on strict adherence
to the *vinaya* (monastic code), rigorous meditation, and extensive doctrinal and ritual studies. During Saichō's lifetime, Enryakuji remained rela
tively modest in both size and influence. At his death, there were perhaps
a few dozen monks in residence. But Enryakuji grew steadily through the
efforts of his successors. By the end of the Heian period, the Tendai
complex at Mount Hiei included some three thousand buildings housing
some thirty thousand resident monks.

It was not, however, a unified community. From the time of Saichō's
death in 822, there were nearly continuous controversies about who
would serve as head abbot of Enryakuji and as at least the titular leader of
the Tendai community as a whole. In addition, over the ninth and tenth
centuries, the growth of Buddhist institutions and the fortunes of aristocratic elites became increasingly and often problematically entangled as a
result of the dramatic expansion of *shōen*, or privately run agricultural
estates that were granted to those who cleared forests for agricultural use
or who played important roles in administering and protecting the state's
interests, including members of the court, local elites, and Buddhist institutions. Because *shōen* were able to operate tax free and with considerable legal autonomy, they were often conflict-ridden nexuses of use
rights, obligations, and aspirations for wealth and influence. They were
also a major factor in the gradual erosion of imperial power and the
increasing militarization of the countryside that eventually escalated into
outright war among competing power blocs—a process that culminated
in the establishment of the Kamakura shogunate in 1184 by the victorious
Minamoto clan.

As ritual specialists capable of promoting and protecting the interests
of elite sponsors, Tendai monks were deeply embroiled in this complex

process of political and religious factionalism. In fact, to protect their own land and holdings, many monastic complexes found it necessary to develop their own security forces: groups of monks (*sōhei*), often from aristocratic families, who possessed both arms and the training to use them.[6] By the end of the tenth century, internal conflicts on Mount Hiei were intense and violent enough for the head abbot, Ryōgen (912–985), to issue a twenty-six-article proclamation intended to restore order and moral integrity to a Tendai community that was in tatters from fighting among divisively aligned bands of "vicious monks" (*akuso*). The changes he instituted did succeed in restoring a measure of dignity to the community on Mount Hiei, ushering in what would come to be regarded as the "golden age" of Tendai history. But this came at the cost of a split between two loosely coordinated factions within the Tendai School: the so-called Mountain and River, or Sammon and Jimon, groups. And, in ways broadly emblematic of Japanese society at the time, violence over succession issues, land claims, and political alliances would plague Tendai (and other Buddhist schools in Japan) through at least the sixteenth century.

Although the Tendai School did not live up to Saichō's unifying vision, it did succeed in becoming institutionally central to the imperial court and, through its rigorous educational programs, came to serve as a breeding ground for both Buddhist and secular leaders through the end of the Heian period. Indeed, all of the founding figures of the new Buddhist traditions that emerged in the Kamakura period—Eisai (Rinzai Zen), Dōgen (Sōtō Zen), Hōnen (Pure Land or Jōdo-shū), Shinran (True Pure Land or Jōdo-shinshū), and Nichiren (Nichiren Buddhism)—were originally trained as Tendai monks on Mount Hiei.

Shingon

Unlike Saichō, Kūkai did not return from China to immediate imperial welcome. It was not until 809, three years after his return, that he was summoned to the capital. This was occasioned by him submitting to the imperial court a document that detailed the texts, artifacts, and ritual techniques he had brought back from China, and that also explained why this marked the advent of a new era in Japan—an era built around the promulgation of the most advanced Buddhist technology for harmonizing the state, assuring the conditions for societal flourishing, and realizing enlightenment "in this very body" (*sokushin-jōbutsu*). Within a year,

Kūkai had become close enough with the newly enthroned Emperor Saga to exchange calligraphy and poetry and write official letters for him, and sufficiently respected by the Nara Buddhist establishment to be appointed administrative head of the Great Eastern Temple, Tōdaiji. Just two years later, with imperial approval, he conducted a public esoteric Buddhist initiation ceremony for leading court officials, members of the aristocracy, and important Buddhist leaders, including Saichō and a number of his disciples. Within three years of returning to the capital, Kūkai was acknowledged as the preeminent master of esoteric Buddhism and as an increasingly prominent contributor to Japan's political and cultural dynamics.

Kūkai's mercurial rise in both imperial and Buddhist circles is dramatic evidence of both his intellectual gifts and the inspirational force of his personal presence. And his subsequent achievements in philosophy, linguistics, poetry, calligraphy, architecture, civil engineering, and public administration over the next twenty years were impressive enough for him to attain permanent legendary stature in Japan's cultural landscape. But Kūkai's ascent was also a testament to the skillfulness of his initial depiction of Shingon as a framework for explaining and extending the efficacy of rituals already a part of the practices of Nara Buddhism, and the fortuitousness of his identification of the experienced world *as* the thoughts, words, and deeds of the Buddha Dainichi (Sanskrit: Mahāvairocana), or "Great Sun Buddha." Not only did this identification resonate powerfully with both the mythic descent of the royal line from the Sun Goddess (Amaterasu), but it also enabled seeing Shintō *kami* veneration as fully consistent with the ultimate truths of Buddhism, thus dissolving the grounds of competitive tension between indigenous Japanese religion and the imported, continental traditions of Buddhism.

The skill with which Kūkai articulated spaces of mutual accommodation did not, however, deter him from asserting the preeminence of esoteric Buddhism or from insisting on proper recognition of his status as the only Japanese to have received full transmission from the Chinese lineage holder of the Zhenyan tradition, Huiguo. By 815, Kūkai's hierarchic distinction between exoteric and esoteric Buddhism and his understanding of his role as lineage holder had sharpened considerably enough to precipitate an end to formal interactions with Saichō and his still-nascent Tendai School. For Kūkai, although there were esoteric elements embedded within the texts and practices that were definitive of Nara Buddhist traditions, and although Saichō was intent on incorporating explicit esoteric elements into Tendai, neither the Nara schools nor Tendai could offer a direct revelation of the ultimate truth of Buddhist realization. Making use of a long-standing distinction in Chinese efforts to rank Buddhist teachings and practices, Kūkai argued that only Shingon offered a "sudden" and complete path to enlightenment: a path to enlightenment in this life, with this body. The paths offered by all other forms of Buddhism in Japan were "gradual" and partial—results of the historical Buddha's *upāya* in responding to audiences of different capacities and commitments. Through a line of secret and direct transmission from master to disciple, only Shingon afforded access to the uncompromised teaching of the Dharmakāya Buddha.

By claiming that Shingon directly expressed the teaching of the Dharmakāya, Kūkai was effectively asserting that Shingon was not a "shortcut" to enlightenment or even, properly speaking, a "path" at all. Shingon opened prospects for *immediate* enlightenment. The concept of the Dharmakāya can be traced to the early Buddhist distinction between the collection or body (*kāya*) of the Buddha's teachings (*dharma*), and his body as a material form (*rupakāya*). In Mahāyāna Buddhism, this distinction was further developed to include three exemplary embodiments of enlightened and enlightening presence—the Dharmakāya, Sambhogakāya, and Nirmānakāya. The Nirmānakāya, or "apparent body," was generally identified with the historical Buddha: the exemplary presence of enlightening intent in human form. The Sambhogakāya, or "reward/response body," was understood as the personally embodied presence of unimpeded compassion and responsiveness and was often identified with cosmic bodhisattvas abiding in other-than-human realms. The Dharmakāya, or "reality-body," was conceived as the ever-abiding, formless presence of enlightened realization: the unborn, unlimited, and unqualified manifestation of awakening in and of itself.

For most Mahāyāna Buddhist thinkers, the Dharmakāya was understood as being beyond the reach of images, ideas, and words. According, for example, to one of the most important Buddhist commentaries in East Asia, the *Dacheng Qixin Lun*, or Raising Confidence in Mahāyāna,[7] Mahāyāna ultimately consists in the realization of "one-mind." This can be accomplished through either the "seed/category gate" of Suchness (Ch: *zhenru*; Skt: *tathatā*), or that of samsara—that is, either through the nondualistic presence of all things as they are in and of themselves, or through their phenomenal "arising and perishing." Manifest *as* Suchness, while one-mind is empty or free of all identifying marks and beyond the reach of all concepts, it also has the nature of expressing all meritorious qualities and virtues. Manifest *as* the phenomenal world of arising-and-perishing, one-mind is the "treasury consciousness," hidden in the midst of all things with the function of harmonizing the nonarising and nonperishing with the arising and perishing. This consciousness is the site of expressing the meaning of both enlightenment and nonenlightenment, revealing the truth that the *dharmadhātu*, or "realm of reality," is precisely the equivalent of Suchness and the Dharmakāya. It is because of this that we can distinguish "original enlightenment" and "incipient enlightenment," literally the "root" of enlightenment and its sprouting in practice.

Kūkai accepted the broad strokes of this account: Buddhist practice ultimately is realizing oneness with the Dharmakāya. But he rejected the idea that the Dharmakāya is a transcendent, abstract principle of enlightenment. If the Dharmakaya and the Suchness of all things are equivalent (literally, of "level rank"), enlightenment is realizing that the world of our daily experience *is* the Dharmakāya. And, since the *Mahāvairocana Sutra* identifies the Dharmakāya with Vairocana Buddha, this is to realize the ultimately personal nature of the cosmos. For Kūkai, the Dharmakāya is the "body of the six great elements" (earth, water, fire, wind, space, and consciousness)—the basic constituents of the material world, all sentient beings, and all enlightened ones. And, as such, the six great elements are mutually nonobstructing and in uninterrupted harmony or yoga (literally, "mutual correspondence"). The cosmos, in its entirety, is nothing other than the perpetual meditative practice of Dainichi.

In accordance with this vision, Kūkai structured Shingon practice around the "three mysteries" of realizing harmony (mutual correspondence) with the functioning of the Dharmakāya's body, speech, and mind through ritually performing *mudrās* (gestural sequences), reciting mantras (spiritually charged words and phrases), and imagining or physically creating mandalas (symbolic representations of the ultimate relational structures of the cosmos). For Kūkai, ritual was not a *means* to some separate, experiential end; ritual was enacting the *meaning* of the Dharmakāya's teachings. This was possible, he argued, because language itself is a function of differentiation, and the experiential differences occurring in the six consciousnesses (visual, auditory, tactile, gustatory, olfactory, and cognitive) are thus ultimately nothing other than letters—

the spontaneously and continuously realized language of the Dharmakāya's preaching. Original enlightenment, nonenlightenment, and incipient enlightenment are simply different *expressions* of Dainichi. In Kūkai's beautifully poetic words, "Soaring mountains are brushes; vast oceans, ink; heaven and earth, the box preserving the sutra. Yet contained in every stroke of its letters is everything in the cosmos. From cover to cover, all the pages of the sutra are brimming with the objects of the six senses, in all their manifestations."[8]

Kūkai's absolute affirmation of the world of everyday experience and his insistence on the essential equivalence of everything in it established a powerful bridge between the spiritual and the sensory that had a deep and lasting influence on Japanese art and aesthetics. His poetry, calligraphy, and painting were not only received with acclaim during his lifetime as works of literary and artistic genius, but they came to be seen as standards of exemplary practice and continue to be regarded as such today. But even more importantly perhaps, they also established very powerful precedents for insisting that "realizing enlightenment in this very body" was not an exclusive right of those of noble birth or elite connections. Since enlightenment is simply "to know one's own mind as it really is," it is a universal possibility. In keeping with this conviction, he founded a private school of arts and sciences that combined religious and secular curricula and was open to any good student, regardless of class. With free tuition, room, and board, it was a revolutionary instantiation of Kūkai's esoteric and yet egalitarian vision.

Like Saichō, Kūkai did not simply import Chinese esoteric Buddhism to Japan. He said of poetry and calligraphy that one should penetrate and fully absorb the great works of the past but not imitate them, and this certainly applied both to his philosophical and religious appropriation of Chinese Zhenyan. Like Tendai, Shingon was the progeny of a cultural marriage. But whereas Saichō promoted Tendai as a superior *institutional* alternative to the Nara-based schools of Buddhism in Japan, Kūkai was more interested in infusing existing religious and political institutions with esoteric Buddhist content, ultimately bringing about, not their replacement, but rather their transformative revision from within. While one of Saichō's central ambitions was to break the Nara schools' monopoly on monastic ordination and to be granted imperial permission to found a separate and distinctly Tendai ordination lineage, Kūkai's manifest ambition was to meld meditative seclusion with public participation by transmitting ritual practices that enabled both "realizing enlightenment in this very body" (*sokushin-jōbutsu*) and "pacifying and defending the nation" (*chingokokka*). If Kūkai was interested in supplanting anything, it was not existing Buddhist institutions, but rather the effective hegemony of Confucian and Chinese legalist discourse in structuring the interplay of the religious, cultural, social, and political spheres—the so-called *ritsuryō* state.

In this, Kūkai was unquestionably a success. Through his efforts, the religious orthodoxy of the state came to be deeply suffused by Shingon practices, and a decisive shift was realized from writing to ritual as the basis of religious authority and social flourishing. True, the temple complex that he designed on Mount Kōya as the Shingon headquarters was not completed during his lifetime. And while Shingon grew in stature over the course of the Heian period and has remained influential to the present day, it never enjoyed either the institutional eminence or influence achieved by Tendai. But in large part due to his combination of public service and personal realization, and to the force of his philosophical, linguistic, and literary works, Buddhism did come to be firmly established as the dominant episteme of Heian society. For the next five hundred years, both the basic frameworks for intellectual, moral, and aesthetic discourse and the underlying "common sense" of Japanese society would be unmistakably and unapologetically Buddhist.

BUDDHISM AS A PREVAILING COMMON SENSE

The narrative presented thus far of Buddhism entering and taking root in Japan has focused on how Buddhist imaginaries and institutions from the continent shaped the processes of Japanese state formation and cultural identity construction, and on how erudite visionaries like Saichō and Kūkai came to articulate new and distinctly Japanese Buddhist traditions. As such, it has been an undeniably partial narrative—one almost exclusively concerned with events taking place at elite levels of society. In part, this is a function of the peculiar dynamics of the initial transmission of Buddhism into Japan. But it is also in part due to the literate (and thus necessarily elite) nature of the available historical sources. The beliefs and practices of those living beyond the borders of literate society simply were not deemed "historic" at the time. Even in the available sources, however, there is considerable indirect evidence that, from the pre-Nara period onward, Buddhism was having mounting effects on the lives of the general population.

Among the first waves of monks who traveled from Japan to China in the early part of the seventh century was the founder of the Japanese Hossō School, Dōshō (629–700). While often remembered primarily for his founding of the Hossō School and introducing Chan meditation techniques to the growing Nara Buddhist community, Dōshō also spent part of his life as an itinerant monk, living among and teaching the common people. During a period when Buddhist monks and institutions were being ever more aggressively implicated in the religious and political ambitions and power struggles of the capital, Dōshō put into action a countervailing set of ambitions aimed at enabling the growth of Buddhism to benefit the people as a whole, not only the competing architects of the emerging Japanese state.

He was not alone in these ambitions. There were many who devoted themselves to leading a demonstrably Buddhist life, but who elected to forgo ordination, devoting themselves instead to lay Buddhist practice and teaching. In addition to these *ubasoku* or lay seekers and teachers, there were also relatively large numbers of "meditation masters" (*zenji*)—some officially ordained and formally trained, and some self-ordained—who underwent ascetic training in the mountains. Many of these "mountain ascetics" developed what was known as "natural wisdom" (*jinen-chi*)—including shamanistic powers of forecasting and healing—and enjoyed close relationships with the villagers who supported them.

The earliest documented mass Buddhist movement in Japan occurred in the first half of the mid-eighth century, led by a charismatic, Hossō-trained monk by the name of Gyōki (668–749), who later came to be associated with the cult of Prince Shōtoku and hence with the creation of Japanese identity. Other than the fact that he was a kinsman of Dōshō, we know next to nothing about Gyōki's life until the years just prior to a smallpox epidemic that devastated Japan from 735 to 737, resulting in the deaths of roughly a third of the Japanese population. Defying imperial edicts that prohibited teaching Buddhism to commoners, Gyōki left the Nara Buddhist establishment to embark on a mendicant career. Traveling around the Japanese countryside and begging for his own sustenance, Gyōki dedicated himself to organizing lay Buddhist communities centered on performing meritorious deeds that included building bridges and waterways, conducting spirit (*kami*) propitiation ceremonies at crossroads in the emerging state-supported highway system, and providing charitable relief to those in need of basic subsistence goods and medical attention. Although his activities were initially sanctioned and subjected to scathing criticism, Gyōki managed to gather a devoted and almost cultic following of thousands of laypeople—a populist movement that was apparently large and powerful enough to ward off direct suppression. By the end of his life, however, Gyōki's activities were granted positive imperial recognition, and he eventually came to be one of the most widely known Buddhist figures in Japanese history.

By the end of the eighth century, the numbers of unofficial "monks" or *shidosō* were increasing rapidly enough to be of considerable state concern and the target of repeated imperial edicts aimed at restricting their activities and pressuring their return to sanctioned societal roles. Some of these "monks" were evidently motivated primarily by gaining access to insiders' leverage in the ongoing aristocratic power struggles being conducted through Buddhist institutions. But many of these informally or self-ordained monks simply were interested in leading largely secular lives outside of the imperial- and elite-supported system of temples and monasteries, devoting themselves to meditation; to conveying basic Buddhist teachings, often in dramatically delivered narrative form; to performing healings and divinations; and to encouraging regular and sincere merit-making conduct.

The picture that emerges, then, is that by the beginning of the ninth century, in spite of official prohibitions on spreading Buddhism outside of the regulatory purview of the state, a crucial threshold had been crossed: Buddhism was no longer strictly a religion of the elite. The popular appeal and spread of merit-making activities, for example, could not have occurred in a religious or conceptual vacuum, but only in the context of a newly emerging set of common convictions about the world and its dynamics—a new vision of the cosmos and of our human place and prospects within it. Like elite sponsorships of ritual adepts and Buddhist institutions, popular investments in merit-making activities were expected to result in improved relational prospects—a positive inflection of one's personal and family fortunes. In both cases, the plausibility of these expectations depended on the assumed validity of a Buddhist cosmology in which movement from one birth realm to another is as natural as moving from one set of mundane living conditions to another, and in which the scopes of one's own possibilities are an intimate result of one's own karma. Over the course of the Heian period, Buddhist teachings of karma, impermanence, interdependence and nondualism, and the representation of enlightenment as "knowing one's own mind as it really is" came to suffuse all levels of Japanese society as a prevailing cultural common sense. By the time classic works like Lady Murasaki's *Tale of Genji* and Sei Shōnagon's *Pillow Book* were being composed at the end of the tenth and early eleventh centuries, poetry, art, literature, and drama were all laced with Buddhist themes and concepts, not due to any self-conscious efforts, but simply because these themes and concepts were part of the experiential fabric of people's daily lives.

Mappō: The Decline of the Dharma

During the Heian and Kamakura periods, the notion that the readiness to understand and practice the Buddha's teachings was relative to changing historical contexts was woven thoroughly into the Japanese worldview. Based on a few remarks the Buddha was recorded as having made about how long his own teachings would be effective, there had developed a theory of historical progression from the age of Right Dharma during and just after the Buddha's lifetime, through a period of the Counterfeit Dharma, into an era of the End of the Dharma or *mappō*—an era of collapsing readiness for personal practice, natural disasters, and widespread social, moral, and physical degeneration. Different lengths of time were assigned to these three "ages" of the Dharma. But beginning in the early ninth century and intensifying markedly in the tenth century as Kyōto suffered a string of natural disasters, a general consensus emerged in Japan that *mappō* was imminent if not already under way.

One Buddhist response, from Tendai monks like Kūya (903–972) and Genshin (942–1017), was to admit the degenerate nature of Japanese society and spiritual capacities and to adapt to these conditions by offering alternative methods of Buddhist practice. Taking the path of the itinerant religious adept (*hijiri*), Kūya developed a considerable following by engaging in charitable works and dancing in public as he led common people in the practice of *nembutsu*, continuously thinking about or reciting the name of the Buddha. The aim of this practice was not to achieve liberation here and now "in this very body." Living in *mappō* made this next to impossible. Rather, the aim was to achieve rebirth in the Western

Paradise through the saving power of Amida (Buddha Amitābha, the Buddha of Infinite Life). From there, enlightenment was guaranteed to be only a single lifetime away. Genshin accepted the validity of Kūya's approach but chose to spur devotion to Amida by writing a descriptively powerful account of the six birth realms, including various kinds of "hells" in which one could come to be embodied. Arguing that those living in *mappō* can only be assured a way around migrating downward through the birth realms by opening to Amida's grace, Genshin advocated the combined practice of a contemplative form of *nembutsu* and visualizations of Amida.

In the context of the open warfare that led to the end of the Heian period and the political dominance of the Kamakura shogunate or military government, this turn toward the saving grace of Amida came to full fruition with Hōnen's (1133–1212) founding of an independent tradition of Jōdo-shū or Pure Land Buddhism. After having lost his own father to a political assassin, Hōnen ordained as a Tendai monk but found no liberation in the practices and political intrigues conducted on Mount Hiei. Convinced that neither the ritual complexities of Tendai and Shingon nor the scholastic debates of the Nara Buddhist schools were effective in such a degenerate age, he advocated the exclusive use of *nembutsu* as a means to salvation, insisting that only a single, simple practice was necessary— one that required no initiations and no reading of ancient or arcane texts. In sharp contrast with the heroic aspirations of visionaries like Saichō and Kūkai, Hōnen argued that it was no longer possible to realize liberation through one's own power (*jiriki*); liberation was possible only through the other-power (*tariki*) of Amida's grace.

In addition to the power struggles that were driving Japan toward open civil war between factions aligned with the Minamoto and Taira clans, the capital seemed trapped in an unbreakable catastrophic cycle that left very few people unconvinced that *mappō* had not already arrived. In 1177, a fire devastated a third of Kyōto, leaving tens of thousands dead or homeless. As the capital was rebuilding, a whirlwind struck in 1180 that destroyed hundreds of homes. From 1181 to 1182, famine and epidemic disease were so severe that over forty thousand people died in a single month, with many of their bodies simply left in the streets or thrown into the river. Finally, dozens of earthquakes struck the capital, culminating in the great quake of 1185, the most powerful in contemporary memory. Describing this string of calamities in his essay, "An Account of My

Hut," Kamo no Chōmei (1153–1216) asked how anyone could fail to appreciate the unpredictably fleeting and fragile nature of life and the futility of seeking permanent eminence or wealth. Seeing this, what could be wiser than to retreat from intrigue and struggle as he had, taking up the simple life of a Buddhist recluse content with little and seeking nothing?

In reality, reclusion was more an ideal than a real possibility. By the final quarter of the twelfth century, there were few places of immunity from violent struggles over authority—a fact as evidently true in the Buddhist temple complexes outside the capital at Mount Hiei and Mount Kōya as in the environs of the court. One of the ironies of the success of both Tendai and Shingon is that their founders' shared emphases on nonduality and the efficacy of esoteric rituals in bringing about both spiritual and material rewards had proved conducive to dissolving boundaries between the secular and the sacred, but also to continued sectarianism and institutionally sustained corruption. Tendai broke into such virulently competing factions in the late tenth century that the temples of both factions were burned to the ground. And for the next two hundred years, beset by patronage and succession conflicts, Tendai temples underwent increasing militarization and were not infrequently sites of armed violence. As a result of similar tensions, Shingon underwent a schism in the mid-twelfth century that was rancorous enough to involve the destruction of temple buildings and physical intimidation.

It should be stressed that the strife cutting through Buddhist institutions during this period was not something exceptional. In striking contrast with the idealized inclination toward gentility and aesthetic refinement that prevailed in the imperial court and the upper reaches of the aristocracy, violent confrontation and warfare were increasingly viewed as legitimate forms of "conflict resolution." Although the Heian period began with a strong and active central government, the steady decrease of tax revenues that were a result of strategic land grants to provincial elites and Buddhist institutions led to a dramatic atrophy of central government power. Outside the capital, those with wealth and property had no recourse but to build private security forces, creating a growing "market" for those skilled in the military and martial arts. By the middle of the twelfth century, the emperor reigned but did not rule, and the real "law of the land" was not imperial but rather a function of hierarchically structured loyalties based on a volatile mixture of blood relations and blood spilled.

Under such circumstances, when even the great Buddhist institutions of learning and ritual mastery were failing to provide the moral compass needed to chart a public course toward peace and prosperity, it was perhaps inevitable that Buddhist "countercultures" would emerge. The distinctive Buddhist traditions that were founded at the beginning of the Kamakura period—Jōdo-shū (Pure Land), Jōdo-shinshū (True Pure Land), Nichiren, and Zen—all shared a contrarian perspective regarding the complex scholastic and ritual pursuits of the Nara and Heian Buddhist institutions. Rather than the authority of writing or of ritual, each of these new forms of so-called Kamakura Buddhism stressed the authority of sincere commitment to a single practice through which anyone, with nothing more than their own body and mind, could secure their own liberation from conflict, trouble, and suffering.

3

FROM CHINESE CHAN TO JAPANESE ZEN

Zen is not just transplanted Chinese Chan. Much as Tendai and Shingon are more than merely Japanese versions of Chinese Tiantai and Zhenyan, the Zen traditions that began emerging in the late twelfth and early thirteenth centuries are not merely reproductions or imitations of Chan on Japanese soil. As implied by the word for "schools" of Buddhism in Japan, *shū* (a word that literally means a clan or lineage group descended from a common ancestor), the birth of Zen in the early Kamakura period is perhaps best understood as the result of an "arranged" cultural marriage. And so, while it is possible to discern in Zen features inherited from Chinese Chan, they are incorporated and expressed in new and characteristically Japanese ways.

The birth of Zen is often depicted as a rejection of the corruption that was consuming Buddhist institutions in and around Nara and Kyōto, and as a response to the spiritual needs of a population torn by the violent transition from imperial to military rule. According to such a telling of Zen's early history, Zen's success—like that of the Pure Land and Nichiren traditions that developed during the same period—was a function of the directness of its teachings, the simplicity of its practice, and the charismatic commitment and sincerity of its founders. In Zen's case, its core teaching can be neatly summarized by the oft-repeated phrase, "Seeing one's own nature, becoming a Buddha"; its core practice identified as the utterly simple meditative practice of "just sitting"; and the founders of its two main branches (Rinzai and Sōtō) identified, respectively, as Myōan Eisai (1141–1215) and Dōgen Kigen (1200–1253). Inspired by what they had encountered in the Chan monasteries they had visited in China, Eisai and Dōgen each broke away from the Tendai School in which they had received their early Buddhist training and established communities committed to the uncompromising pursuit of enlightenment in this very life.

This story has its merits. But, it does not do justice to the complexity of Zen's origins or their relevance today. Teachings and practices associated with Chinese Chan were known in Japan from early in the Nara period. As previously noted, Dōshō—the founder of the Hossō School—apparently introduced Chan meditation practices to Japan in the late seventh century. The Chinese monk Daoxuan (702–760) brought northern Chan teachings to Japan along with those of the Huayan and Vinaya schools. And the monk Yikong (n.d.) spent several years in Japan, during which he is said to have introduced Chan teachings to the Emperor Saga (r. 809–823) and Empress Danrin. But there does not seem to have been any inclination to develop an independent Chan tradition in Japan prior to the late Heian period.

In part, the Japanese lack of focused interest in Chan may have been related to the fact that textual precedents for many of the core teachings of early Chan could be found in the literature that the Tendai and Shingon traditions were drawing upon. In other words, early Chan was not doctrinally distinctive. An additional factor may have been that the Chinese did not translate the Sanskrit term for meditation (*dhyāna*), but instead transliterated it using a character now pronounced "chan" in China and "zen" in Japan. While the term would eventually become strongly associated with Chan as the "meditation" school, all Chinese Buddhist schools incorporated *chan* as part of their practice regimen. Thus, in Japan, anyone who developed particular skill in meditation (*dhyāna*) was known as a *zenji*—a "meditation master"—and *zen* was simply assumed to be an integral part of Buddhist practice, along with observing Buddhist precepts, studying Buddhist texts, and performing Buddhist rituals.

But a more important factor in the late interest of Japanese in Chan was the fact that Chan only gradually coalesced in China as an independent tradition and did not become a prominent tradition for several centuries. Although references to Chan as a distinct (and distinctively Chinese) approach to Buddhist thought and practice were becoming common by roughly the mid-eighth century, there were no monasteries devoted solely to Chan prior to the tenth century. Those who identified with the still-emerging Chan "school" or "gate" did not live in separate communities, but rather alongside those who identified with other Buddhist traditions. Moreover, although a characteristic body of Chan teachings was already developing in the late seventh and early eighth centuries, the writings of Chan masters remained full of rhetorical approaches and concepts found in sutras and commentaries central to the already established Tiantai, Huayan, and Zhenyan schools. Chan did not yet have a unique "voice." For Japanese monks traveling to China—primarily to the capital, Chang'an, and the monastic complexes on the sacred slopes of Mount Tiantai and Mount Wutai, and primarily in search of new textual and ritual resources—Chan would not have stood out as either a unique or particularly important Buddhist tradition.

FROM PERIPHERY TO CENTER: THE CHANGING STATUS OF CHAN

According to traditional accounts, the late Tang was a period of rapid and transformative growth for Chan. During this period there consolidated a distinctive, "countercultural" Chan identity centered on making a revolutionary break from the textual and formal biases that had come to characterize the major schools of Buddhism in China—an identity based on returning to the purportedly "primordial" Buddhist practice of embodying (ti) the function (yong) of enlightenment by publicly and spontaneously demonstrating one's own Buddha-nature. By the middle of the ninth century, sensitized to the recursive danger of imposing a means-end structure on the relationship between Buddhist practice and Buddhist enlightenment, a significant number of Chan communities had adopted a critical and iconoclastic stance toward the gradualism of a Buddhist establishment that insisted on disciplined study and practice as a necessary precursor to expressing one's own, originally enlightened and enlightening nature. This stance was graphically epitomized by Linji's (d. 866) denunciation of Buddhist scriptures as "hitching posts for donkeys" and his fierce insistence that true practitioners must be ready even to "kill 'Buddha'" en route to becoming "true persons of no rank," responding to each situation as needed to improvise an enlightening turn in its dynamics. [1]

Although contemporary Buddhist scholarship suggests that these traditional accounts might best be seen as imaginative reconstructions of an idealized past, rather than as accurate historical records, it is clear that

Chinese Buddhism was undergoing especially profound changes over the period from roughly the An Lushan Rebellion in 755 to the imperial purge of Buddhist institutions that occurred from 842 to 845. In contrast with the esoteric rituals and highly philosophical readings of Buddhist texts that prevailed in the great metropolitan temples—and that were of greatest interest to Japanese like Saichō and Kūkai who were intent on fostering stable and productive state–Sangha relations—Chan valorized abandoning ritual invocations and abstract affirmations of the nonduality of all things to realize directly the nonduality of our own human heart-mind (*xin*) and Buddha. Granted confidence in that nonduality, what need is there to pore studiously over arcane texts, to conduct elaborate rituals, or to engage in efforts either to "cultivate" our Buddha-nature or "purify" ourselves of the emotional and sensual riches of daily life? As Mazu (709–788) succinctly put it, Buddhism is simply realizing that our "ordinary, everyday mind is Buddha" (*Ta Tsang Ching*, 45.406a).

Although many Chan masters in the ninth century and thereafter continued to refer to important sutras and commentaries in their talks and writings, those associated with the more "countercultural" streams of Chan typically did so to authenticate the *radical* nature of Chan as a tradition "rooted/originating" (*ben*) in the Buddha's direct, mind-to-mind transmission of the meaning of enlightenment. The dominant forms of Chan coalescing in the ninth and tenth centuries had little use for disputes about orthodoxy or for composing carefully crafted treatises in literary Chinese. Adopting, instead, a highly vernacular and avowedly improvisational approach to written and oral communication, by the end of the tenth century a distinctive Chan "voice" was being powerfully articulated in retellings of lively and at times quite earthy conversations between Chan masters and their students. Often depicted as occurring in the midst of day-to-day activities, these dialogical encounters were remembered, rehearsed, and gathered into collections of "public cases" (Ch: *gongan*; J: *kōan*) that were then reworked to become a body of strikingly vibrant and naturalistic literature that valorized relational genius and responsive virtuosity.

Because it was being developed primarily in rural monasteries and smaller cities in relatively outlying provinces, this new voice of Chan would not have been one that Saichō, Kūkai, or other Japanese pilgrims would have encountered during their time in China; and if they had, it would not have been a voice to which they would have been inclined to listen. Although Mazu became the most successful Chan master of his day, attracting more than eight hundred students to his temple in Hong-zhou, his iconoclastic approach to Buddhism was naturally viewed with considerable skepticism by many members of the Buddhist elite who criticized it as espousing an amoral doctrine of neither cultivating the good nor cutting off the bad, celebrating the potential for acting freely, experiencing emotions, and undergoing passions and desires as demon-strations of Buddha-nature.[2] That, critics argued, was liable to result in justifications of heedlessness and a failure to discriminate even between the slovenly and the sublime. This was certainly the view of Saichō's disciple and successor, Ennin (794–864), when he traveled in China from 838 to 847. In the diary that he kept of his sojourn in China, Ennin several times mentions meeting Chan monks, but his only comment is a succinct and damning dismissal of them as exhibiting "extremely unruly heart-minds" (Reischauer, 1955:210).

Japan did not send an official mission to China after 838 and formally cut off relations with the Tang court in 894. This turn away from official interest in China was not without cause. Ennin was still in China when Emperor Wuzong ordered what was to be the most virulent purge of Buddhist institutions in Chinese history. Beginning in 842, climaxing with a total proscription of Buddhism in 845, and ending only with Wu-zong's death in 846 (as a cumulative result, ironically, of ingesting Daoist "immortality" pills), this purge resulted in the dismantling of some 4,500 temples and 50,000 shrines, the forced laicization of more than 250,000 monks and nuns, and the destruction of virtually every major Buddhist library in China. The proscription of Buddhist institutions was rescinded by Wuzong's successor, but China was beset by political and economic instabilities that culminated in widespread depredations during the Huang Chao Rebellion (874–884) and the eventual fall of the Tang dynasty. Only a small handful of monks are known to have traveled from Japan to China from the mid-ninth century until the mid-twelfth century. In the intervening three hundred years, the status of Chan changed dramatically.

Although the 845 purge had been indiscriminate in its destructiveness, its impacts were disproportionately devastating for the more scholastic and text-dependent Chinese Buddhist traditions. The disbanding of mo-nastic communities, the razing of temple complexes, and the burning of libraries dealt a near mortal blow to the Huayan, Tiantai, and Zhenyan traditions. The least severely affected were communities associated with so-called Southern Chan: communities that prided themselves on exemplifying a "special transmission outside the teachings" that was "not founded on words and letters." Many of these Chan communities were located in rural and mountainous settings and evinced an iconic ethos of self-sufficiency that Mazu's successor, Baizhang (720–814), neatly summarized as "a day without working is a day without eating."

Chan continued growing in both size and prestige through the Five Dynasties period, and by the beginning of the Song dynasty (960–1276), not only were entire monastic complexes devoted solely to Chan practice, but Chan had also become the dominant form of elite monastic Buddhism. One factor in Chan's rising fortunes was the Song policy of sharply differentiating between private and public Buddhist monasteries and temples. Private monasteries and temples were defined as those in which the selection of abbots was undertaken internally—a "familial" or "hereditary" line of succession in which an outgoing abbot was replaced by the most senior of the monks he had ordained. Support for institutions of this type was entirely private and almost invariably local. In contrast, the identification of successors in "public" (literally, "ten directions") monasteries and temples was a competitive process in which a wide range of candidates were reviewed by a group of leading abbots from nearby public monasteries, who then nominated the most accomplished and charismatic candidate possible for approval by the local prefectural government. Headed by the most gifted monks of their generation, these public monasteries were accorded high prestige and patronage by both the imperial court and influential members of the literati.

By the end of the eleventh century, the majority of public monasteries were designated specifically as Chan monasteries. While public monasteries devoted to Tiantai and Huayan traditions did exist, these were given the special designation of public "teaching" monasteries, underscoring their distinct and implicitly subordinate status. The reasons for this intimate connection between Chan and the institution of public monasteries are not entirely clear. However, among the likely contributing factors were the damage done to the textually defined schools of Chinese Buddhism, mounting reservations about Buddhist reliance on complex metaphysics and ritual technologies, and the adoption of a distinctive Chan monastic code—said to have originated with Baizhang's community—that not only accorded with the wishes of the Song state to exercise oversight regarding the selection of spiritually adept abbots for public monasteries, but also emphasized long periods of daily sitting meditation, twice-a-day public Dharma talks and debates, and opportunities for private interviews with abbots. This monastic code in effect created spaces for laypeople, especially literati, to participate in the intellectual and spiritual life of Chan monasteries and to develop personal relationships with abbots who were by design both personally inspiring and culturally conversant. The Chan code also stipulated that Chan monasteries would not be centered architecturally or relationally on a Buddha Hall, but rather on a Dharma Hall, in effect transferring spatial preeminence from the historical Buddha (or one of the cosmic Buddhas of the Mahayana) to the Chan master. The authority structure of the Chan monastery, in other words, was one in which the proximate allegiance of both monastic and lay practitioners was not to a "foreign ancestor," but rather to a "homegrown Buddha."

Another factor in the growing favor that Chan was accorded in the early Song was the broad social, cultural, and political resonance of a tension within Chan circles between those convinced that sudden enlightenment was a function of sudden practice in which literary learning was irrelevant, and those convinced that sudden enlightenment could only occur as the culmination of sustained "gradual" practice in which literary learning played a necessary and important role. Among the implications of the traditional Chinese conception of political authority as "celestially mandated" (*tianming*) are that dynastic transitions are never accidental, and that the founding of a new dynasty necessarily entails establishing a new heading on the basis of crucial—and fundamentally moral –lessons learned. In the still turbulent first decades of the Song dynasty, there had developed a general consensus among the intellectual and aesthetic elite that a primary cause of the fall of the Tang was excessive cosmopolitanism and a drift away from core Chinese cultural values. Some literati followed precedents set by Confucian critics of Buddhism in the Tang and faulted the religious and economic authority that had been vested in Buddhism as an essentially foreign tradition. Others blamed the irrational and otherworldly nature of both Buddhism and Daoism. But most literati, in keeping with a metaphor that would be made famous by the Song emperor Xaiozong (1127–1194), took Confucianism, Daoism, and Buddhism to be like the three legs of a *ding*—a ceremonial bronze vessel associated with the origins of Chinese culture in the Shang dynasty. Chan's deepening focus on the teachings of "homegrown" Chinese buddhas and its iconoclastic proclamations about established forms of "imported" Buddhism went a long way in making this metaphor of unity a plausible one. Most importantly, perhaps, it also happened that, among those debating what heading to take in securing the celestial mandate for Song rule, there was a tension between those advocating "studying the Dao" (*daoxue*) and those stressing "literary learning" (*wenxue*)—a tension that corresponded closely to that occurring in Chan between so-called sudden or gradual approaches to Buddhist practice.

Literati in the first camp insisted that the Dao—the Way, or path and method, of the natural and emergent self-ordering of the cosmos—can only be realized directly and intuitively as the spontaneous revelation of one's own true nature or heart-mind. This realization might be occasioned or inspired, perhaps, by reflecting on a small handful of classical texts exemplifying the distinctive spirit of Chinese culture. But according with the Dao is not a matter of studying the ancient sages; it is a matter of becoming a sage oneself. Those in the second camp insisted that access to the Dao is possible only through cumulative familiarity with the full spectrum of cultural media—poetry, calligraphy, painting, music, and literary commentaries on the great classics—combined with the cultivation of one's own creative genius. Realizing the Dao is something that is accomplished interactively, through an essentially social process of furthering an ongoing and aesthetically informed conversation.

This parallelism of debates within Chan regarding the means-to and meaning-of enlightenment and those among the literati regarding the means-to and meaning-of an era-defining Song ethos and culture was, it would seem, both a consequence and cause of the majority of public monasteries being identified with Chan lineages. Although all public monasteries were the property of the Buddhist Sangha as a whole, each public monastery depended on material sponsorship of the imperial court and literati. The Chan code's normative emphasis on public teachings and debate, as well as on private interviews held in the abbot's quarters, fostered multifaceted interactions between secular and sacred elites in which friendship, sponsorship negotiations, intellectual debate, and spiritual mentoring were readily interfused. Like their secular counterparts, abbots of Chan monasteries were almost invariably capable of making fluent use of the Confucian, Daoist, literary, and artistic canons, and their quarters often became liminal spaces for blending the secular and sacred spheres through shared meals, joint reflection, and appreciative exchanges of calligraphy, poetry, and paintings.

Although many of the institutional features of Chan would not be inherited by Zen, the association of Chan with cultural refinement and leadership would be an important part of Zen in Japan. There, however, rather than taking the form of relatively even exchanges among secular and Buddhist elites, this relationship would play out as one in which Zen monks and monasteries offered opportunities for the emerging samurai or warrior class to acquire highly desirable cultural credentials from those fluent in the latest developments in China.

FROM CHAN TO NASCENT ZEN

When significant numbers of Japanese began traveling again to China in the mid-twelfth century, most of the great public monasteries in China were officially designated as Chan monasteries, and many of these had several thousand monks and nuns in residence. Regularly visited by high officials, poets, painters, and calligraphers, Chan monasteries were renowned as places of spiritual power and cultural vitality, and for being capable of bringing the more material benefits of peace and prosperity to their area. Five "families" or "houses" of Chan, encompassing seven distinct transmission lineages, were officially recognized by the Song government as part of a state-supported network referred to as the "five mountains and ten temples" (*wushan-shicha*) that would later become the model for the medieval Japanese *gozan* ("five mountains") system. Each of these Chan "families," and the temples belonging to them, were understood as being under the guidance of a unique "living Buddha" who had received the "true Dharma eye treasury" (*zhengfan yanzang*) through participating in an unbroken series of person-to-person transmissions that originated with the Buddha's mind-to-mind conferral of enlightenment recognition to his disciple Mahākāśyapa. Compilations of Chan masters' "recorded sayings" and "encounter dialogues" were not only being widely circulated due to the spread of print technology; they were popular even among literati committed to developing resolutely Confucian approaches to self-cultivation. The preeminent form of Buddhism in China was no longer Tiantai, Huayan, or Zhenyan; it was Chan.

In the early twelfth century, the public face of Chan was dominated by two of the five main transmission lineages: the Linji line, which would be carried forward in Japan as Rinzai Zen through the founding efforts of Eisai (1141–1215), and the Caodong line, which would be carried forward as Sōtō Zen through the founding efforts of Dōgen (1200–1253). These two lineages were in broad agreement about embodying the true function of Chan: seeing one's own nature and becoming a Buddha. But Linji and Caodong Chan differed markedly in how they conceived of meditation as the nondualistic means-to and meaning-of realizing enlightenment.

For Linji Chan, the realization of nonduality—the *actualization* of our original enlightenment or Buddha-nature—was not something developed incrementally or intellectually; it was a sudden and transformative breakthrough that required total body-mind investment. To bring this about, the leading master of Linji Chan, Dahui Zonggao (1089–1163), advocated the innovative practice of *kanhua* (J: *kanna*)—literally, "observing key phrases" from the *gongan* (J: *kōan*) or public cases that recounted enlightening exchanges between Chan masters and their disciples. According to Dahui, although sitting meditation (Ch: *zuochan*; J: *zazen*) is fine, the concentration of energy needed for an awakening breakthrough is most effectively generated by total interrogative immersion in *kanhua*—an unrelenting investigation, even in the midst of one's mundane activities, of the meaning of inhabiting the relationally dynamic space of demonstrating and transmitting enlightenment.

For the proponents of the Caodong Chan tradition, realizing our Buddha-nature was not a function of some explosive breakthrough; it was a function of embodying and sustaining the attentive transparency needed for one's original, enlightened Buddha-nature to manifest. By remaining resolutely and quiescently present, the turbulent play of our sensations, thoughts, and feelings eventually settles, allowing our originally enlightened mind to naturally shine forth. In keeping with this methodological minimalism, although Caodong Chan also used *gongan* (*kōan*) as important source texts for Chan teaching, it advocated the primary practice of unencumbered mindfulness or "just sitting" (J: *shikantaza*)—the demonstration of a luminous awareness in which (perceiving) self and (perceived) other have both been dissolved. The Caodong master Hongzhi Zhengjue (1091–1157) described this approach to Chan practice as one of "silent illumination" (Ch: *mozhao*; J: *mokushō*)—a practice that reveals the world's myriad things as already speaking the Dharma through their mutual correspondence, radiantly dissolving the need for any striving.

For the Japanese monks traveling in twelfth-century China, the emphasis placed on embodying an enlightened and enlightening presence by both Linji and Caodong Chan would have recalled Tendai and Shingon idealizations of realizing enlightenment in/through this very body. But the daily regimen and authority structure of Chan monasteries would also have suggested a profound difference. In the Tendai institutions that dominated the late Heian and early Kamakura monastic landscape, monks in the *zenshū*, or "meditation group," who were responsible for performing daily ritual offerings, chants, and meditation were seen as lower-class subordinates of textual and ritual specialists (*gakusō*). In Chinese Chan monasteries, the most respected and revered monks were renowned first and foremost as practitioners (*gyonin*). And, whereas the great Japanese monastic complexes were embroiled in various kinds of economic and political struggles and maintained regiments of armed monks who were powerful and numerous enough to force even the founder of the Kamakura shogunate, Minamoto Yorimoto (1147–1199), to bow to pressures from the Tendai headquarters on matters of taxation and rent payments, Chinese Chan monasteries were focal points of apparently harmonious sociopolitical relationships and Song cultural life. In short, the first generation of monks traveling to Song China in the mid- to late twelfth century would have witnessed both the viability of an inverted authority structure in which issues of orthodoxy (right doctrine) were subordinate to those of orthopraxy (right practice) and concrete examples of how to go from merely talking about original enlightenment (*hongaku*) to directly manifesting it.

The inspirational impact of visiting thriving Chan communities clearly played a key role in shaping the lives and teachings of Eisai and Dōgen, traditionally regarded as the founders of Zen in Japan. Each of them returned from China energized and committed to orchestrating a renewal of Japanese monastic life through promoting strict adherence to the Chan monastic code and its idealization of monastic self-reliance, social harmony, daily meditation practice, and regular interpersonal teaching. Yet the first efforts to establish a fully independent Zen school in Japan were not initiated by someone who had traveled personally to China, but rather by Dainichi Nōnin (n.d.), a charismatic Tendai-trained monk whose only encounter with Chinese Chan was through reading and conversations with those returning from China, and who apparently viewed monastic precepts and regimented practice as neither necessary nor sufficient for living an enlightening life.

We know relatively little about Nōnin and the Darumashū or Bodhidharma School that he sought to establish as an independent Buddhist tradition. In the course of doctrinal studies included in his Tendai training, Nōnin seems to have encountered some early Tang dynasty Chan texts that emphasized the possibility of a "special transmission outside the teachings" based on the fact that "mind is originally enlightened." Inspired by these texts, Nōnin began practicing meditation on his own and eventually attained an awakening that was sufficiently powerful and transformative for him to attract a large number of both ordained and lay students, and to establish his own, independent temple. Through doing so, he also attracted the critical attention of the Tendai establishment.

In apparent response to questions about the legitimacy of his awakening and teachings, Nōnin sent two of his students to China in 1189. They carried with them a poem and gifts to present to Fuzhao Deguang (1121–1203), a Dharma heir of Dahui, along with a request to authenticate Nōnin's enlightenment. They returned later that year with a laudatory letter and sacred relics as evidence of Nōnin's enlightenment and his receipt of a "special transmission" in the Linji-Dahui line of Chan. This at least nominally linked Nōnin to Dahui's *kanhua* Chan. But Nōnin's teachings more strongly resembled antinomian expressions of Chan like those that Mazu had rejected as conducive to self-serving interpretations of "original enlightenment" and the teaching that "ordinary mind is Buddha."

This certainly was Eisai's opinion, who returned from his second trip to China in 1191 to vehemently contest the confirmation of Nōnin's enlightenment and claims to transmission in the Linji Chan lineage. Having been granted transmission in the Huanglong branch of the Linji line, Eisai wanted to infuse Japanese Buddhism with Chan meditative and institutional approaches, blending Chan with Tendai rather than seeking to establish an entirely separate tradition. Arguing that the irregularity of the "transmission" claimed by Nōnin was compounded by the irregularities manifest in his construction of Zen practice, Eisai characterized Nōnin's teachings as rooted in a "false emptiness" that legitimized sensory and emotional indulgence—a path of eating when hungry, sleeping when tired, and generally ignoring both monastic discipline and the rigors of daily meditation practice. Caught by the easy allure of such a path, Eisai claimed, one would have no reason either to externally avoid wrongdoing or to internally aspire to benefit others. A generation later, an almost identical and no less scathing set of criticisms would be leveled at the Darumashū by Dōgen after several prominent members of the group had joined his budding Sōtō community.[3]

Yet the Darumashū articulation of nonduality and its apparent disdain for rigidly compartmentalizing the sacred and the secular clearly resonated with a wide range of people, contributing significantly to the Darumashū's success in attracting both lay adherents and monks dissatisfied with the formalism and factionalism of the Buddhist establishment. In addition to teaching that our minds are originally enlightened and that awakening can be accomplished without either textual or personal intermediaries, Nōnin also insisted that a result of Zen awakening was that "whatever is searched for is obtained." Realizing that "mind is Buddha" is realizing that our mind is originally a "wish-fulfilling gem"—a common Mahāyāna metaphor for the dissolution of barriers between the world as mundanely experienced and the world experienced as a wondrously enriching Buddha-realm. For Nōnin, Chan meditation and awakening did not require either cutting off afflictions and emotions or the "blowing out" (nibbana/nirvana) of passions and desires. His nondualistic view of enlightenment would have recalled for his Japanese interlocutors the passage in the Vimalakīrti Sutra where the concept of meditation held by Śāriputra, the most skilled among the Buddha's disciples in preaching the Dharma, is critically discounted by the layman Vimalakīrti in a brilliant demonstration of the viability of enlightenment—even for laypeople—in this very body.

Thus, although Nōnin's critics charged him with offering license to abandon institutionally regulated moral self-cultivation, his teachings were consistent with mainstream Mahāyāna and Chan, as well as with many of the values that had informed the development of earlier Japanese Buddhist traditions. The independence that Nōnin sought for the Darumashū can, in other words, be understood as a "countercultural" response to existing Buddhist institutions rather than as one of exclusive opposition to them. And, in fact, much the same can be said for Eisai's and Dōgen's adaptive use of Chan practices and ideals in their efforts to reshape Japanese Buddhist realities. The Darumashū, Rinzai, and Sōtō expressions of Chan can be seen, in other words, as competing attempts—at a time of dramatic political and social transformation in Japan—to establish a productive religious counterpoint to the esoteric, textual, and ritual tenor of especially the Tendai tradition out of which each had emerged.

This presence of competitive tension within Zen might be attributed to personal aspirations for influence and authority among those at the vanguard of marrying Chan ideals and Japanese realities. It is true, after all, that even as simple a matter as having the land on which to build a new temple required either a cooperative arrangement with existing monastic institutions or collaboration with secular elites of a sort that would have made the attractions of power and influence continuously and palpably present. But it is also true that Chan itself originated in context-rich reflexive considerations of the meaning of Buddhist practice and enlightenment. In other words, Chan identity itself involves calling into question the meaning of being Buddhist and of practicing Chan as a radical commitment to realizing nonduality, not by erasing differences, but by their productive harmonization. In this sense, tensions among the initial articulations of Japanese Zen can be seen as a legitimate legacy of its Chan heritage.

As in China, lineage concerns were central to the tensions both among and within the formulations of Zen put forward by Nōnin, Eisai, and Dōgen. Part of the "radicalism" built into Chan and Zen identities is a concern for intergenerational dynamics—the tracing or creation of an unbroken line of transmission that roots the present generation in the relational interplay of the Buddha and his disciples. Indeed a major axis of tension between Eisai and Nōnin centered precisely on such genealogical concerns about lineage-holding legitimacy. For Nōnin, inclusion in the genealogy of Chan masters was a matter of personal realization; institutionally granted recognition was, for him, incidental. For Eisai, who sought to nurture Chan roots within the framework of Tendai traditions, the public dimensions of being accorded a place in the spiritual genealogy of Chan were crucial. And given the complex nature of the early transmission of Buddhism to Japan and the close relationship between Buddhist institutions and the state, it is perhaps unsurprising that issues of institutional structure and monastic discipline were central to both Eisai's and Dōgen's critiques of the Darumashū, and that these issues would come to be an enduring axis of tensions within Zen. Put somewhat differently, tensions between what we might call public Zen and personal Zen were, from the very beginning, a part of Zen identity.

Part II

Public Zen

Zen has often been "represented as emerging suddenly and definitively in the context of Japan's turbulent transition from aristocratic to military rule—a shift of power from the imperial court to samurai-led "tent governments" (*bakufu*). Traditional narratives of Zen's emergence have been predominantly structured around the activities and attributes of exemplary "founders" and the unique lineages through which their teachings and styles of practice have been transmitted. A common image is of Zen's founding luminaries rejecting the corrupt interplay of imperial and monastic institutions, going into meditative seclusion, and then returning to articulate new foundations for the expression of spiritual authenticity. In more historical accounts, Zen has often has been depicted—like the Pure Land and Nichiren traditions that also emerged in the early part of the Kamakura period—as part of a groundswell of religious innovation in response to the crises and widespread suffering of the late twelfth and early thirteenth centuries. Like these other forms of so-called Kamakura Buddhism, Zen rejected state-supporting public rituals to offer a "single practice" approach to gaining individual salvation.

The best evidence, however, is that Zen's emergence was neither sudden nor definitive, that the idealization of meditative prowess and reclusion were not peculiar to Zen, and that the emergence of Zen as an independent Buddhist tradition in Japan was inseparable from both support from and support for new political elites. While Zen, Pure Land, and

Nichiren did spread dramatically in the early Kamakura period, the six schools of Nara Buddhism, Tendai, and Shingon also remained quite powerful. In short, Zen neither refuted nor replaced previously existing forms of Japanese Buddhism. Instead, it developed gradually and complexly as a kind of Buddhist counterculture—a critically informed and alternative approach to Buddhist spirituality that nevertheless retained many of the core values and ideals of Japanese religiosity and culture.

Perhaps the most strongly and significantly shared norm among Zen, other forms of Japanese Buddhism, and Japanese culture more broadly was the valorization of embodied realization. In the phrasing championed by both Saichō and Kūkai, enlightenment is not something to be realized in some distant future or heavenly realm, but here and now "in this very body." For Zen, as for other Japanese Buddhist traditions, the concept of embodied realization includes that of enlightenment realized in our very own personal bodies. But our individual bodies exist only interdependently with all other things, including the land, water, plants, animals, air, and sunlight on which we depend for our basic sustenance and shelter, as well as our family members and communities. Realizing enlightenment "in this very body" thus also connoted the possibility of enlightenment in (and perhaps of) the "body politic." The full story of Zen's emergence is thus a story of intimately interrelated Zen exemplars and Zen institutions: a story of the interdependence and interpenetration of the personal and the public.

The four chapters that comprise this section will forward accounts of one part of this story. The first three chapters provide a historical overview of the three major schools of Zen: Rinzai, Sōtō, and Ōbaku. The fourth chapter addresses the encounter of Zen and global modernity. Although Zen exemplars played crucial roles in establishing the monastic communities and spiritual ideals through which these schools came to affect Japanese lives and to be affected by them in turn, the emphasis here will be institutional rather than interpersonal—an emphasis on Japanese Zen's "skin" and "flesh" rather than its "bones" and "marrow."

As noted in the introduction, this narrative division of the more public and institutional aspects of Zen and those that are more personal and experiential is ultimately just a useful artifice. In much the same way that the living human body is a function of the systemic interrelationship of skin, flesh, bones, and marrow, living Zen is a function of the interfusion of the public and the personal. A related artifice is the treatment of Rinzai, Sōtō, and Ōbaku as independent entities, with separate origins and paths of development. In Japanese, these three traditions are referred to as distinct *shū*—a term that can be translated as "school" but that has primary connotations of the "ancestral" or "kindred" and points toward emotionally charged intergenerational and interpersonal connections. And so, Rinzai, Sōtō, and Ōbaku are perhaps best seen as different branches growing out of (or in the case of Ōbaku, grafted onto) the trunk of Zen's "family tree"—traditions informed and sustained through intimately shared roots.

In fact, although Rinzai, Sōtō, and Ōbaku Zen will be variously referred to as distinct "schools" or "traditions" for the sake of convenience, these are perhaps somewhat misleading terms. Rinzai and Sōtō Zen did not exhibit the kind of ideological or practical boundaries usually associated with these terms for centuries after first beginning to take root in Japan. Instead, the shapes eventually taken by Zen's various "branches" and the "fruit" growing on them evidence the different patterns of relationships that coalesced around the lineages of Chinese Chan being transmitted to Japan. The monks who played key roles in this process—especially through the end of the thirteenth century—did not generally regard their adaptations of Song dynasty Chan institutional frameworks, practices, and teachings as constituting autonomous entities or "sects." To push the arboreal metaphor a bit further, the emergence of Rinzai and Sōtō did not represent the appearance of mangoes and papayas on the same tree, but rather different kinds of mangoes. And so, while something like sectarianism did develop in the early modern era, care must be taken not to read this back into the premodern origins of Zen.

4

RINZAI ZEN

The Rinzai Zen tradition traces its origins in Japan to Eisai's founding efforts. During his first trip to China in 1168, Eisai focused on furthering his Tendai studies. During this trip, although he encountered Chan practitioners, his personal interests remained focused on recent developments in Chinese Tiantai. It was during his second, longer trip to China from 1187 to 1191 that he was positively impressed by Chan teachings and institutions and came to appreciate how powerful a role they might play in transforming Japanese Buddhism.[1]

Unlike Nōnin, who sought to establish a fully independent Chan lineage in Japan, Eisai sought to merge Chan meditation and teachings with Tendai esoteric practices and scholasticism. Even so, his efforts met with considerable resistance from within the Tendai community and the imperial court, many members of which had come to associate Chan with Nōnin's iconoclastic and potentially anarchistic inclinations. To distinguish his own efforts, Eisai publicly denied that Nōnin was a legitimate lineage holder within the Linji Chan tradition and followed the Tendai lead of claiming that Nōnin's Darumashū was potentially a threat to the harmony of state and Sangha relations. He argued that, in contrast, the legitimate tradition of Linji Chan was perfectly suited to advancing the interests of the Japanese state and society, offering a distinctive new approach for realizing increased security and flourishing for all. In spite of this accommodative approach, however, it was not until Eisai moved to the new capital of Kamakura that he was able to establish a temple dedicated to adapting and practicing Zen in Japan.

As a blend of Chinese Chan, Tendai esotericism, and a renewal of commitments to strict monastic discipline, Eisai's formulation of Zen has often been termed syncretic—the result of a merely partial embrace of Chan. More charitably, Eisai's efforts can be understood as aimed pragmatically at opening a lasting conduit for Chan practices and institutions to flow into Japan in ways suited to transforming Japanese Buddhism from within. What can be said with some historical certainty is that for the first half century of its development, Rinzai was relatively inclusive and did not live up to the later identification of Zen with the "single practice" approaches to Buddhism that became popular later in the Kamakura period. Although one of Eisai's third-generation disciples, Daikatsu Ryōshin, did try to "purify" Zen of Tendai esotericism and scholasticism, through the middle of the thirteenth century those who carried on Eisai's Rinzai lineage remained eclectic in approach, and their elite sponsors seem to have been more interested in the mundane benefits accruing from Zen ritual practices than in rigorously pursuing sitting meditation.

For many early Zen sponsors, a good deal of Zen's appeal also lay in the fact that—in keeping with the Chan model in Song China—Zen marked a move in the direction of political and military neutrality. In contrast with the heavily armed Tendai monastic complexes of the late twelfth century and their extensive landholdings, the new Zen communities initially played neither on connections with the imperial court nor on deeply entrenched relationships with the Kyōto aristocracy. Rinzai teachers and temples distinguished themselves by offering access, not to the old Japanese elites and power structures in Nara and Kyōto, but to the latest religious and cultural developments on the continent. For the shoguns and samurai who were Japan's new political leaders, Zen opened a highly desirable avenue for acquiring more than just military legitimacy.

Nevertheless, through the first half of the thirteenth century, Rinzai Zen institutions remained few, their memberships small and volatile, and their influence relatively minor. A crucial turning point occurred with the return from China of the Rinzai monk Enni Ben'en (or Shōichi Kokushi, 1202–1280). Initially trained in the Tendai tradition before studying under several of Eisai's followers, Enni had been intrigued by Rinzai teachings and practice but had felt compelled to gain more complete and authentic instruction in China. Sponsored by a wealthy Chinese merchant in the Hakata region of Japan, Enni spent seven years in China studying under the Linji Chan master Wuzhun Shifan (1177–1249) and eventually received transmission as one of Wuzhun's Dharma heirs. On his return to Japan in 1241, with further support from the Chinese merchant who had funded his China sojourn, Enni built a number of temples in Hakata and came to the attention of Kujō Michiie (1193–1252), one of the most powerful figures in Kyōto court society.

A devout Buddhist, not only did Michiie himself serve as either regent or senior adviser to two Japanese emperors, but his sons also rose to considerable power, with one serving as imperial regent, another rising to become the fourth Kamakura shogun, and still others serving as abbots at influential Buddhist monasteries in both Nara and Kyōto. This was an extraordinarily powerful family, and Enni's growing connections with it greatly amplified Rinzai's prestige and institutional viability. In 1235, Michiie commissioned the construction in Kyōto of what he intended to be the largest, most architecturally advanced and religiously comprehensive monastic complex in Japan. This temple complex, Tōfukuji, took nearly ten years to build, and when it was completed Michiie invited Enni to serve as its founding abbot.

As a disciple of the leading Chan master in Song China, and with training not only in the esoteric Buddhism of the Tendai and Shingon traditions but also Indian metaphysics and epistemology, Enni was an ideal choice as the abbot of what Michiie hoped would become Japan's greatest and most influential temple. But while Enni was perhaps even more comprehensive in his studies than Eisai, he was adamant that the core practice at Tōfukuji would be daily *zazen*, or sitting meditation. For him, although it contained buildings devoted to the study of both Shingon and Tendai, Tōfukuji was essentially a Zen monastic complex.

Although Enni traveled to Kamakura on a number of occasions, his connections there remained relatively modest. In and around the military government headquarters in Kamakura, Rinzai Zen did not attract patronage anywhere near as influential as that provided by Michiie, and it was not until Hōjō Tokiyori (1227–1263), the samurai regent to the Kamakura shogun, met an immigrant Chinese Chan monk by the name of Lanqi Daolong (1213–1278) that Rinzai began to be vigorously sponsored and to flourish in the new center of political power. Both a skilled warrior and an astute statesman, Tokiyori nevertheless had a strong interest in Buddhism and had studied Tendai and Shingon esotericism, as well as the syncretic approaches to Rinzai taught by Eisai and Enni. Meeting Lanqi seems to have cemented his commitment to focusing his personal practice on Zen, in particular a "pure" Zen modeled on the monastic regimen that prevailed in Song China.

Lanqi apparently traveled to Japan on his own initiative in 1246, arriving first in Hakata and then spending some time in Kyōto before traveling to Kamakura where he stayed with Daikatsu Ryōshin, Eisai's third-generation Dharma heir. With his excellent credentials in the Linji Chan lineage and a personal introduction from Ryōshin, Lanqi quickly developed a deep and lasting relationship with Tokiyori. Under Lanqi's guidance, Tokiyori embarked on a serious and lifelong course of regular *zazen*, *kōan* study, and personal interviews or debates (*mondo*). As a show of respect for his teacher, Tokiyori commissioned the building of Kenchōji—the first fully "independent," Song-style Zen temple in Japan—and invited Lanqi to serve as founding abbot on its completion in 1253. Uninterested in scholarly pursuits, Lanqi deemphasized textual study and instituted a policy of strict adherence to monastic behavioral codes (*vinaya*), sitting meditation (*zazen*) four times a day, and engaging in regular *kōan* study.

In keeping with the mutually supporting pattern of Sangha–state relations upheld in Song China, Lanqi also explicitly framed Zen's social role as one of complementing and safeguarding secular norms. This appealed to Tokiyori and others in Kamakura, in part because of the sharp contrast of this Zen ideal and the political and economic realities in Kyōto and Nara, where Tendai and (to a lesser extent) other Buddhist institutions were active and often disruptive agents in struggles for power and authority. But a perhaps more important reason for Zen's appeal was the shocking success of the Mongol alliance in overrunning much of Eurasia, including northern China, and the resulting recognition that a vibrant sense of imperial or national unity might well prove to be a necessity for survival in the years to come.

Building on the military exploits of his father, Chinggis Khan, Ogōdei Khan crushed the Jin rulers of northern China in 1234 and within two years had effectively encircled Song China, including the brutal capture of much of the agriculturally rich territory of what is now Sichuan Province, where Chinese casualties exceeded a million people in the area around Chengdu alone. By 1242, Mongol armies had reached as far west as present-day Poland and controlled virtually all of what are now eastern Europe, Russia, Central Asia, Turkey, the Middle East, Tibet, Mongolia, Korea, and both North and Southwest China. Although the Mongols did not invade the heartlands of Song China until 1271 under the leadership of Khubilai Khan, it was more than evident to the Japanese in the 1250s and 1260s that they were a formidable threat and that it would likely not be long before Mongol sights were set on Japan.

In addition to making Japan's rulers keenly aware of the need for Buddhist institutions firmly committed to supporting— and not competing with or contesting—the state, the continent-spanning military predations of the Mongols also seem to have encouraged increasing numbers of Chinese monks to immigrate to Japan. One of the most renowned of these was the Chan monk Wuan Puning (1197–1276). While he was a student of Wuzhun in the 1230s, Wuan had met Enni and perhaps had been favorably impressed by Enni's accounts of Japan and its readiness for the transmission of Chan. At any rate, without an official invitation, he made the dangerous journey to Japan in 1260. There he was warmly welcomed by Hōjō Tokiyori, who was pleased to meet and debate with one of the most widely respected and accomplished of Wuzhun's Dharma heirs.

The relationship had profound effects for both men. Tokiyori accepted Wuan as his primary teacher, and after sending Lanqi to Kyōto to spread Rinzai teachings there, Tokiyori asked Wuan to assume the leadership of Kenchōji. Under Wuan's tutelage, Tokiyori's practice deepened. After a breakthrough realization, he was granted confirmation of enlightenment and given transmission as one of Wuan's Dharma heirs—the first Japanese warrior to be accorded this honor. Shortly after Tokiyori passed away in 1263, Wuan returned to China, and rumors began to spread— perhaps from Tendai headquarters at Enryakuji—that Wuan and Lanqi were Mongol agents. Lanqi eventually regained the trust of the Kamakura elite in 1278, including that of Tokiyori's son, Hōjō Tokimune (1251–1284), who had assumed the regency in 1268.

Tokimune's assumption of the regency occurred the same year that the first Mongol emissary arrived in Japan to "request" Japan's submission as a vassal state. Although the emperor and the court in Kyōto were inclined to accede to this wish, Tokimune and the rest of the Hōjō inner circle elected to refuse this and subsequent requests made in 1269, 1271, and 1272. Instead, they began preparing for war. Like his father, Tokimune was an ardent practitioner of Zen and a generous sponsor of Chan monks emigrating from China to Japan, and it came to be widely believed that it was his skill in *zazen* that enabled him to lead with calm and clarity even in the face of Mongol attack. At the very least, his affiliation with Chinese Chan monks and his sponsorship of a growing network of Rinzai Zen communities across Japan were important factors in stimulating an amplification of Buddhist efforts to ritually assist in the protection of Japan.

Khubilai Khan began his invasion of the Song in 1268, laying siege to the city of Xiangyang to establish a foothold in the Yangzi River valley and gain entry to the Chinese heartlands. The siege lasted five years, and within two years of the fall of Xiangyang, the Empress Dowager Xie officially surrendered. A year later, while still consolidating control in southern China—which would not be complete until 1279—Khubilai ordered the invasion of Japan. Arriving in Hakata Bay in November 1274, the Mongol forces were better armed, better trained, and more battle hardened than the Japanese. The initial engagement went disastrously for the Japanese, and it was doubtful whether any amount of reinforcements would have been able to turn back the Mongol force in a second day of battle. Tokimune is said to have succumbed to an almost debilitating fear and on the advice of his Zen teacher entered into *zazen* practice, experiencing an awakening that steeled his resolve to resist the Mongols and attain victory. But in fact it was the *kamikaze*, or "divine wind," caused by an intense winter storm that played the decisive role in ending this first invasion. Near sundown, the horizon blackened with a rapidly approaching storm, and the Mongol leader, fearful of being stranded on land without supplies if their ships sank or were scattered during the storm, ordered his troops to go back aboard. This proved to be a fatal choice. Roughly three-quarters of the fleet sank that night, and the force that remained afloat the next day was easily dispatched by the Japanese navy.

Four years later, in 1278, Lanqi died, and Tokimune sent two monks to China to bring back a suitable replacement just as the final centers of Song resistance against the Mongol occupation of China were crumbling. In the midst of this final stage of China's defeat, the head monk at one of Mount Tiantong's key Chan monasteries, Wuxue Zuyuan (1226–1286), agreed to assume the abbacy of Kenchōji and arrived in Kamakura in 1279. A staunch loyalist to the Song, Wuxue was a powerful advocate for preserving Japanese sovereignty and for committing Rinzai Zen ritual resources to achieving this end.

The second Mongol invasion occurred in the spring and summer of 1281. Although this was a much larger force, with more than one hundred thousand soldiers on thousands of ships, the Japanese were able to keep the Mongols from progressing inland. Once again, the turning point came with a storm—a massive typhoon—that destroyed most of the Mongol fleet. As an expression of gratitude for the assistance rendered by the Rinzai community and as a memorial to all those who gave their lives during the battle, Tokimune commissioned the construction of a large monastic complex, Engakuji, and installed Wuxue as the founding abbot in 1282. Two years later, Tokimune fell suddenly ill and before dying asked to be ordained as a Zen monk. In the space of just a few days, Wuxue conducted both Tokimune's ordination and funeral ceremonies.

The regency was assumed by Tokimune's son, Sadatoki, who continued the practice of patronizing Rinzai Zen and became a student of yet another Chinese Chan monk, Yishan Yining (1247–1317). Yishan arrived in Kamakura in 1299 as an emissary of the Mongol Yuan dynasty. Like Wuxue and Lanqi before him, Yishan was initially suspected of being a Mongol spy, but he soon impressed his Japanese hosts with his sincerity, intelligence, and cultural acumen and was successively appointed abbot of Kenchōji and Engakuji in Kamakura, as well as Nanzenji in Kyōto, where at Emperor Go-Uda's request he served from 1313 until his death in 1317.

Importantly, Yishan was not only a well-trained Buddhist monk; he was also extraordinarily well versed in the Confucian and Daoist traditions, including Song neo-Confucianism, and highly skilled in the most current elite Chinese literary and artistic practices. As a skilled writer, a superlative calligrapher, and a connoisseur of Chinese painting—including the ink landscape painting tradition—Yishan was a model for the combined embodiment of spiritual intensity and cultural refinement.

This new approach to Rinzai Zen was so attractive both to lay patrons and Buddhist monks that Engakuji was soon filled to capacity, and Yishan instituted an "entrance exam" that tested prospective students' abilities to demonstrate their understanding of and commitment to Zen in Chinese-style poetry. From this point forward, Zen came to be increasingly associated with a unique combination of monastic asceticism and secular aestheticism—an association of meditation and the arts that would become a signal feature of Japanese culture from this point forward.

One of the young Japanese monks who passed Yishan's entrance exam was a ninth-generation descendant of Emperor Uda, Musō Soseki (1275–1351). Like many of the early leaders of Rinzai Zen, Musō was originally trained in Tendai and Shingon and is said to have developed an interest in Zen after he dreamed of traveling to China and being given a portrait of Bodhidharma. Although Musō was in large part self-trained, undertaking long periods of meditation in remote locations, he also studied both with Yishan and with Kōhō Kennichi (1241–1316), a son of Emperor Go-Saga (1220–1272), who himself had first studied with Enni and then with the Chinese masters Wuxue and Wuan. Musō thus realized a unique balance of independent practice and strong connections with the émigré Chinese monks heading many of the foremost Kamakura Zen temples, their warrior patrons, and their key first-generation Japanese Dharma heirs, many of whom had roots in Kyōto's aristocratic and imperial circles. As such, he was poised to play a prominent role in the rapid development of the *gozan* or "five mountains" system of officially sponsored Zen monasteries in the early fourteenth century. [2]

THE *GOZAN* SYSTEM: THE INSTITUTIONALIZATION OF ZEN MONASTIC HIERARCHIES

Although nominally hearkening back to the "five mountains and ten temples" (*wushan-shicha*) system in China—a state-supported network of public monasteries—the *gozan* system was in many ways uniquely Japanese. As noted earlier, in China, the Song government instituted a network of publicly supported monasteries, the abbots of which were peer selected on the basis of both their spiritual gravity and administrative skill. Although the state retained the right to veto any particular selection, the network was intended to be a self-governing system of state-supported and state-supporting Buddhist institutions. In principle, the installation of abbots at public monasteries was strictly a matter of religious merit and organizational promise, not political alliance.

The system that emerged in Japan was different, first, in being inseparable from the political, social, and cultural aspirations of individual sponsors. Like the "private" or lineage-based monasteries that complemented state-sponsored public institutions in China, the Zen monasteries that came to serve as the organizational nodes of the Japanese *gozan* system were in practice locally and not state funded, and leadership succession in them tended to be "internally" managed through a combination of lineage considerations (as in China) and the personal and familial interests of individual patrons. This is not to deny that authentic spiritual aspirations played important roles in the elite sponsorship of temples and in decision making regarding monastic leadership. It is, however, to acknowledge that the authority that was both granted to and exercised by *gozan* monasteries had a very complex pedigree.

Some sense of this complexity can be gleaned from the fact that in 1307 the Emperor Go-Uda had to request permission from Hōjō Sadatoki to have Nanzenji, a major Kyōto monastery, designated as an "associate *gozan*" (*jun-gozan*) temple. In spite of constituting a clear challenge to what had until then been a Hōjō monopoly on the concept of an elite system of Zen monasteries, this request was approved—a sign, perhaps, of fractures opening up in the Hōjō family capacity for autocratically expressing its dominance. Immediately thereafter, however, a reciprocal request was forwarded by the Kamakura government, asking the imperial court to award the Hōjō-sponsored temples of Kenchōji and Engakuji the status of "imperially sponsored monasteries" (*jōkakuji*). In short, decisions about which monasteries were ranked as top-tier institutions were inseparable from negotiations about the relative power of aristocratic court society (*kuge*) in the "ancient capital" of Kyōto and that of the warrior society (*bushi*) in the "garrison town" of Kamakura. Being accorded *gozan* status certainly was in part a matter of recognizing the charisma and the religious and cultural capital of immigrant Chan masters and their Japanese Dharma heirs; but it was also in part a competitive measure of the political and economic capital of warrior patrons in Kamakura and aristocratic/imperial patrons in Kyōto.

By the beginning of the 1320s, competitions for authority between the Kamakura shogunate and the imperial court in Kyōto were no longer restricted to matters of ranking Zen monasteries and reached new levels of complexity. In the half century after the founding of the Kamakura shogunate, the Hōjō alliance had managed to strip the imperial family of virtually every vestige of real political power and had established a practice in which the emperorship alternated between two branches of the imperial family. This arrangement was tolerated for a time, but when Go-Daigo assumed the throne in 1318, he claimed exclusive succession rights for his own branch of the royal family and openly set his sights on wresting political power from the shogunate and restoring the rule of Japan to the imperial throne.

In a move that set a precedent for challenging the *gozan* rankings that to that point had been a Hōjō privilege, Go-Daigo invited Musō—already widely regarded as a leading Rinzai master of his generation—to assume the abbacy of Nanzenji in Kyōto in 1325. Musō agreed but managed to remain relatively neutral in the brewing status dispute by departing after a year to open a new temple in his native province of Ise and then returning to Kamakura the following year.

When Go-Daigo's political aspirations became too apparent to continue to ignore, the *bakufu*, or military government, banished him from Kyōto to the relatively remote coastal province of Hoki, where he immediately set about gathering samurai disaffected with the Kamakura rulers and building his own army. In response, the Hōjō sent the warrior Ashikaga Takauji (1305–1358) to quell this threat. Unexpectedly, Takauji switched allegiance to side with Go-Daigo. In 1333, Go-Daigo and his army defeated the forces of the Kamakura *bakufu*, and Go-Daigo returned to Kyōto. After resuming the throne and officially reestablishing imperial rule, one of Go-Daigo's first acts was to place three Kyōto monasteries at the top of the *gozan* system—Nanzenji, Tōfukuji, and Kenninji—effectively displacing the previously top-ranked, Kamakura monasteries of Kenchōji and Engakuji. To add insult to this injury, he then ordered Musō to return to Kyōto to serve as the institutional architect of a reconfigured *gozan* system.

Due perhaps to Go-Daigo's lack of administrative skill, and perhaps due to emerging political aspirations among various provincial warrior groups, his "Kenmu Restoration" lasted only three years. Among those who deposed Go-Daigo were many who had helped usher him into power, including Ashikaga Takauji. Go-Daigo was exiled to Yoshino where he set up a so-called Southern Court and spoke out in open denial of the legitimacy of the "Northern Court" of Emperor Kōmyō, whom Takauji had placed on the throne strictly to reign and not to rule. Although the rivalry between the Southern and Northern courts would persist until nearly the end of the fourteenth century in the midst of newly emerging local and regional power structures across Japan, the new military government that was formed by Takauji was stable enough for the period of rule by the Ashikaga or Muromachi (a district in Kyōto) shogunate from 1336 to 1573 to be later characterized as among the most culturally innovative in Japanese history.

It was a time of explosive growth for Rinzai Zen. Takauji and his brother, Ashikaga Tadayoshi (1306–1352), both had strong ties to Zen and upon assuming power brought Musō back to Kyōto to serve as their special adviser and Zen teacher. It would seem that Musō did his best to make use of his close ties to the Ashikaga leadership to spread and deepen appreciation for Zen, and to promote the restoration of national unity. An indication of Musō's skill as a broker of national unity is that he was able to remain in close relations with the exiled Go-Daigo, even though Go-Daigo's Southern Court contested Ashikaga authority and the legitimacy of the Northern Court. Indeed, in an open display of honor and affection, when Go-Daigo passed away in 1339, Musō built a commemorative temple and garden in Kyōto for him, Tenryūji, which soon became one of Japan's most important Zen temples. Over the last fifteen years of his life under the Ashikaga, Musō was able not only to work with over a thousand lay and ordained disciples, but he also played crucial roles in consolidating and reshaping the *gozan* network and helping to spread Rinzai Zen throughout Japan.

As sources of both prestige and protective power, leading Zen monasteries functioned as symbolic repositories of both religious and political capital. Given this, the social and political dynamics surrounding *gozan* status were very highly charged. Although governmental power ultimately rested with the Ashikaga shogunate, the *gozan* system that Musō helped to build evidenced a balance-seeking spirit of compromise consistent with Musō's engagements with the Ashikaga *bakufu*, those loyal to the Southern Court, and those who had been allied with the deposed Kamakura shogunate.

Among Musō's early accomplishments along these lines was to convince Takauji and Tadayoshi to sponsor the expansion of Zen through construction of a system of "Temples for National Pacification" (*Ankoku-ji*) and "Pagodas Dedicated to the Welfare of All Sentient Beings" (*Rishōtō*)—a system that spanned all of Japan's sixty-six provinces. Connected with this was the first formal articulation, in 1341, of a national *gozan* system that paired leading monasteries in Kyōto and Kamakura for the first and second ranks, and designated one monastery for each of the third (Kamakura), fourth (Kyōto), and fifth (Kyōto) ranks. Over succeeding decades, this system would gradually shift in the direction of full parity between Kamakura and Kyōto. The final articulation of the system in 1386 accorded equal status to parallel sets of five top-tier monasteries—Tenryūji, Shōkokuji, Tōfukuji, Kenninji, and Manjuji in Kyōto, and Kenchōji, Engakuji, Jufukuji, Jōchiji, and Jōmyōji in Kamakura—with a single highest monastic "peak" in Kyōto, Nanzenji, presiding administratively over them all.

Below this top level of monasteries were the so-called "ten temples" or *jissetsu*. Set outside the imperial and shogunal power centers, there were initially ten such midlevel Zen monasteries. In keeping with the 1386 formalization of parallel sets of *gozan* temples, this was expanded into separate Kyōto *jissetsu* and Kantō (Kamakura) *jissetsu*, each with ten monasteries. At the lowest level of the *gozan* system were the *shozan* or "many mountains." By the beginning of the fifteenth century, there were over two hundred *shozan* monasteries across Japan and nearly three hundred monasteries in the entire *gozan* system. Not surprisingly, given the circumstances of the system's origins, the vast majority of these monasteries were associated with either the Shōichi (Enni Ben'en) or Musō Rinzai lineages, with just a handful associated with Sōtō lineages.

As skilled as he was as an organizational architect and in maintaining effective political neutrality, Musō was no less skilled in carrying forward the legacies of immigrant monks like Yishan and Wuxue who had affirmed the "unity of the three teachings" of Confucianism, Daoism, and Buddhism, and who had strong literary and artistic inclinations and talents. Renowned for his garden designs, poetry, and calligraphy, Musō brought a distinctive aesthetic character to the teaching and practice of Rinzai Zen, establishing an association of Zen and the arts that would remain powerful through the modern era, including *chanoyu* or tea ceremony, *nō* and *kyōgen* drama, ink landscape painting, and poetry.

Reflecting the revitalization of Rinzai Zen that resulted from the influx of Chinese masters in the thirteenth and early fourteenth centuries, *gozan* monasteries were also characterized by a strong emphasis on facility in reading and writing Chinese. In part this was a function of communicative necessity. Most immigrant Chan teachers arrived knowing no spoken Japanese, and even those Japanese monks and lay practitioners who could read and write Chinese often were not fluent enough in spoken Chinese to engage in the conceptually rich and rhetorically charged conversational exchanges that were crucial to Linji Chan. As a result, much of the teaching and learning taking place in Rinzai monasteries had been conducted through what was known as "brush talk." Lanqi's entrance exam of being able to write fluently enough in Chinese to compose reasonably refined Chinese poetry was thus not a matter of Chinese cultural arrogance; it was a practical measure of the likelihood that a given individual could in any effective degree ever be his student. This set a precedent for fluency in Chinese as a general entry barrier for practicing in a *gozan* monastery.

Yet true to the earthiness of Linji's teaching style and the sensibilities of his Japanese Zen teacher, Kōhō Kennichi, Musō was not constrained by his penchant for refined artistic expression. His most widely read work, the *Muchū Mondō-shū*, or "Conversations in a Dream," is a dialogue in which he responds to questions posed by Ashikaga Tadayoshi (translated in Kirchner, 2010). In one key exchange, Musō urged Tadayoshi to resist the idea that Zen enlightenment is something special that depended on extensive study and book learning. On the contrary, he insisted, enlightenment is realized simply by doing whatever is needed to see our own original nature—an experience he compared to that of coming back to one's senses when the effects of drinking too much alcohol suddenly wear off.

This use of ordinary life experiences as analogies would have been appealing for warriors and others living outside of traditional Japanese aristocratic cultural circles. The warrior sponsors of Rinzai during the Kamakura and Ashikaga shogunates clearly appreciated being introduced to elite Chinese cultural practices and artifacts as a means to acquiring cultural capital commensurate with their political authority—an important factor in establishing their rights to rule in the eyes of aristocratic and imperial elites. But they would not have been entirely comfortable engaging in extensive "brush talk." And in fact, while many warrior sponsors like the Ashikaga brothers seem to have had relatively strong interests in sitting meditation—a calming and concentrating of attention being as useful in military and political battles as in the pursuit of Zen realization—few seem to have been equally interested in the scholarly approach to *kōan* study that became the norm in *gozan* monasteries.

It is perhaps a reflection of both his commitment to effective communication and his own discomfort with using Chinese cultural forms that Musō's own artistic efforts and communicative style were at times resolutely Japanese in flavor. He was, for example, an acclaimed master of the indigenous Japanese forms of *waka* and *renga* poetry. Indeed, what would come to be called Five Mountains Literature (*gozanbungaku*) and its characteristic use of humor and ordinary life experiences can be seen as a distinctive hybrid of Chinese and Japanese aesthetic sensibilities. As was the case for medieval Japanese more generally, the Zen aesthetic ideal was to express sensitivity to the exquisite and often delicately lonesome beauty of the unadorned present moment—a quietly celebratory appreciation of rustic naturalness, simplicity, and transience. In the context of this aesthetic and its central values of *wabi* (rusticity and simplicity) and *sabi* (ephemeral beauty), the mark of literary success was expressing in spoken or written language the "mindful heart" (*kokoro*) of a given situation—the longingly expressed revelation of *this* moment as a uniquely experienced participation of all things.[3]

THE *RINKA* MONASTERIES AND THE PROVINCIAL SPREAD OF ZEN

Not all Rinzai monasteries were part of the *gozan* system, however, and not all Rinzai monks agreed with Musō's accommodative approach and what could be regarded as an inadequate commitment to practicing "pure" Song Chinese Chan on Japanese soil. Other monks were simply not inclined toward participating in the socially and politically complicated affairs of the leading metropolitan monasteries, whether affiliated with Zen or with the Tendai headquarters on Mount Hiei. Some followed the precedent set by Shinichi Kakushin (1207–1298). After studying Chan in China under the tutelage of Wumen Huikai—the author of the *Wumen Kuan*, or "Gateless Gate," a compilation of forty-eight "public cases" (Ch: *gongan*; J: *kōan*) of enlightening encounters that became part of the core curriculum of both Rinzai and Sōtō Zen—Kakushin returned to lead a reclusive life of practicing *zazen* and *kōan* study in remote mountain temples. Others, including some who had extensive training in *gozan* monasteries, resonated more strongly with the ideal established in Baizhang's Chan monastic code of a communal life centered on daily group meditation practice and shared labor.

In some cases, these "disenchanted" monks managed to find elite sponsorship that enabled them to build significant monastic communities around the ideal of a "simple" and "pure" approach to Zen. Over time, these monastic communities came to be known as *rinka*, or "below the grove," monasteries in contrast with those belonging to the *gozan* "grove" (*sōrin*). Two of the most important monks who chose to build viable *rinka* Zen communities were Shūho Myōchō (more commonly referred to as Daitō Kokushi, 1282–1338) and Kanzan Egen (1277–1360). Like Musō, both managed to sustain good relations with both the Southern and Northern courts, but otherwise they removed themselves from the thicket of ties between the religious and political spheres. With imperial support from both Emperor Hanazono and Emperor Go-Daigo, Daitō and Kanzan were able to found two of the most important non-*gozan* temples: Daito-kuji and Myōshinji, respectively. From these *rinka* communities there emerged a Rinzai lineage—the so-called Ōtōkan line—that would eventually eclipse the lineages of Enni and Musō to become the only Rinzai lineage that continues to the present day.

Ironically, part of the eventual success of the *rinka* communities was their emphasis on a "pure" Chinese form of Rinzai that focused on *zazen* and *kōan* study in a strictly disciplined, relatively austere, and (in social and political terms) remote monastic environment. For Daitō and Kanzan, Musō's Zen— like that of Enni and Eisai before him —was a synthetic blend of Chinese and Japanese cultural elements, of Chan meditation and esoteric rituals, and of what might be termed monastic and metropolitan ways of life. And, much as the English word "synthetic" can connote not only productive combination, but also something that is artificial or inauthentic, Daitō and Kanzan found much to criticize in the kind of Rinzai Zen that was being promulgated through the *gozan* system. For them, *gozan* efforts to exemplify a productive "harmony" of Chinese Chan and Japanese cultural norms and aesthetic sensibilities might charitably be seen as a matter of using "skillful means" to attract warrior and aristocratic patronage. But like offering sweets to gain the cooperation of children, this approach could easily result in the equivalent of spiritual "cavities"— the eventual decay of the Zen teachings, practices, and institutions for which these "skillful means" were intended to gain support.

From the perspective of its founders, the Ōtōkan approach to Rinzai that they were spearheading "below" the *gozan* "grove" was a necessary corrective based on a reassertion of the centrality of communally practiced *zazen* and the embrace of rustic simplicity, not as an aesthetic ideal celebrated in richly appointed aristocratic and warrior palaces and on lavishly endowed monastic estates, but rather as a quality of day-to-day life in secluded settings suited to the single-minded pursuit of awakening to one's true nature (*kenshō*). At the same time, however, the line of demarcation between those in the *gozan* "grove" (*sōrin*) and those below it (*rinka*) was not drawn on purely normative grounds, but also on very practical ones.

Many of those who ended up practicing Zen in *rinka* monasteries did not do so for ideological reasons, but because they lacked the literary skills to be able to engage in the kind of scholarly study and cultural practices required in *gozan* temples. For example, while *kōan* study was part of the monastic curriculum in both *rinka* and *gozan* institutions, this meant quite different things in the two contexts. In both settings, Wumen's forty-eight case compilation, the *Wumen Kuan* (J: *Mumonkon*), was used as a standard core curriculum for *kōan* study. Successfully navigating through this curriculum was understood as requiring great confidence, great tenacity, and great doubt—a total body-mind commitment to the practice of seeing and demonstrating one's true nature. Students were expected to meditate on and deeply investigate a given case, presented in Chinese, and to develop an appropriate response to it—a "capping phrase" (*jakugo*) that expressed both one's personal realization of the significance and relational force of the case, and one's familiarity with the discourse records of Chan masters, the Buddhist canon, and Chinese literary classics.

In *gozan* settings, the process of investigating a case and developing a response to it would often include scholarly study of Chinese texts, and it was expected that responses would be phrased in ways that demonstrated insight, full familiarity with commentaries on the case, a broad and profound understanding of Chinese literary resources, and sufficient literary skill to be able to "cap" the *kōan* in a spirit of "deft play." In *rinka* settings, it was often the case that students lacked the linguistic ability to do more that memorize standard Chinese formulations of *kōan*-generated questions and responses to them.

Moreover, while in both *gozan* and *rinka* contexts the aim of *kōan* study was to drill sufficiently deeply into the protective shield of one's intellectual, emotional, and bodily habits to bring about a breakthrough experience (*kenshō*), this was not understood as a matter of breaking into one's innermost and essential core, but rather as a breaking out into freely responsive relational virtuosity. The resulting demands were very different, however, for those dedicated to embodying wisdom and compassion in the midst of the relational dynamics of *kuge* and *bushi* society—interacting with aristocrats, members of the imperial family, and warrior elites—and those dedicated to doing so in provincial towns and rural settings, among merchants, local samurai, and farmers. In terms developed somewhat later, Zen awakening (*satori*) through combined *zazen* and *kōan* practice is not best understood as the end or purpose of practice, but rather as a "gateless gate" through which one passes to engage in "long nurturing the sacred fetus" (*shōtaichōyō*)—a protracted process of nurturing oneself as an embryonic Buddha. Only through appropriate nurture would one be able to go beyond just sitting and speaking like a Buddha to acting like one.

For Daitō, nurturing the capacity to conduct himself like a Buddha or bodhisattva reputedly took the form of living with beggars under a bridge in Kyōto for twenty years; for Kanzan it is said to have consisted of spending eight years in the mountains, tilling the soil and tending cattle. For those inheriting the "metropolitan" approach to Rinzai forwarded by Enni and Musō, this nurturing was undertaken in the midst of medieval Japanese urban life and in zones of cultural difference where responsive virtuosity entailed improvising both *with* and *within* changing canons of cultural refinement and appreciation.

RINZAI IN THE LATE MUROMACHI AND EDO PERIODS

Zen flourished during the roughly 250 years of the Muromachi period. When the rule of the Ashikaga shogunate came to an end in 1573, in addition to roughly three hundred temples included in the three tiers of the *gozan* system, there were several thousand subtemples and branch monasteries included in the system, the vast majority of these affiliated with Rinzai lineages. There were also a similar number of *rinka* temples, including temples affiliated with the Ōtōkan lineage, and several thousand Sōtō temples. In short, by the close of the Muromachi period, Rinzai Zen had spread throughout Japan, and though not as popular in farming communities as Sōtō Zen, Rinzai institutions were nevertheless a powerful presence in the lives of a majority of the Japanese people.

An Era of Unrest: From the Ashikaga to the Tokugawa

The relatively rapid spread of Rinzai was not without its problems. The *gozan* system had been built up largely through the patronage of the Ashikaga shoguns, but this came at a significant cost: all of the external affairs of the system were overseen by secular officials. In effect, a parallel system of authority was built into the *gozan* system which ensured that activities undertaken within its temples accorded both with the religious needs of the temple community and with the secular needs and aims of the patronage network. The resulting close connections between the "sacred" and "secular" spheres proved conducive to a gradual drift from strict discipline and the centrality of communal *zazen* and labor toward increasing temptations to benefit materially from sponsorship relations— especially with newly wealthy provincial samurai and merchants. As increasing numbers of nobles and warriors sent their sons to study in *gozan* temples for cultural and political reasons, the character of life within monastic walls did not remain unchanged.

Although the Ashikaga shogunate was theoretically the center of political power in Japan, the ongoing battle between the Southern and Northern imperial courts added an element of instability to the political, social, and economic life of Japan until roughly the end of the fourteenth century. At the same time, Japan was undergoing a profound economic transformation as a combined result of its transition to a monetized market economy and rapidly expanding trade with China. These conditions opened considerable new opportunities for generating and accumulating wealth. But they also made possible significant upward social mobility for perhaps the first time in Japan's imperial history. Over time, these changing economic and social circumstances resulted in much more complicated power dynamics, enabling a significant change in relations between central and outlying provinces.

Up until the rule of the third Ashikaga shogun, Yoshimitsu (1358–1408), the shogunate was able to function as a relatively effective central government. But from the beginning of the fifteenth century, the Ashikaga shoguns were of very uneven quality. This led to increasing autonomy in the provinces and intensifying needs for the central government to renegotiate the terms of cooperation with various newly wealthy and powerful warrior families in provincial areas. These *daimyō* (literally, "great names") had acquired enough economic and military might to build virtually independent domains that were centered on their heavily fortified castles and landholdings. Often their armies were larger and better equipped than those of either the shogunal headquarters or the imperial guard.

Under these conditions, a dispute between two leading families about who would succeed the childless shogun, Ashikaga Yoshimasa (1435–1490), escalated into a decadelong civil war (from 1467 to 1477) that eventually involved hundreds of thousands of warriors from across Japan. Because of the close ties between warrior and aristocratic families and the leading Zen temples, the major *gozan* temples were obvious targets of rival factions. Virtually all of the major Zen temples in the metropolitan areas of Kyōto were plundered and burned to the ground during the civil war. In a ten-year period, the thriving economies that had centered on the *gozan* temples were laid waste, and although many of these were eventually rebuilt, the *gozan* system itself never fully recovered.

In the aftermath of the so-called Ōnin War, Kyōto was rebuilt, and samurai culture and the arts were once again able to flourish. Daily life resumed. But the hostilities that had erupted in Kyōto were never entirely quelled, and the result was a century dominated by low-intensity but continuous conflict among "warring states barons" (*sengoku-daimyō*) carving out and consolidating their own spheres of influence. During this "warring states" period, patronage of *gozan* system temples by Ashikaga elites in Kyōto and Kamakura was considerably diminished as the business and benefits of Japanese trade with Ming China shifted away from Japan's metropolitan core to *daimyō* based on the island of Kyūshū and in the coastal provinces along the Inland Sea. The rising fortunes of these newly powerful provincial warrior and merchant families were used to support Zen temples, but primarily from the Myōshinji and Daitokuji lines. These *rinka* temples were amenable to working with new and rising "peripheral" powers, and they understood the benefits of spreading Zen among the common people by blending Zen with local popular beliefs, conducting prayer ceremonies aimed at material benefits, and officiating at funerals. In sum, although Rinzai Zen was intimately involved in the burgeoning of era-defining Japanese cultural practices in poetry, drama, and tea ceremony, over the final decades of the sixteenth century, in both *gozan* and *rinka* settings, Rinzai headed into dilution and decline.

The ultimate demise of the Ashikaga shogunate was set in motion when one of the claimants to control of the shogunate enlisted the help of an ambitious warrior from a relatively minor *daimyō* by the name of Oda Nobunaga (1534–1582). A talented military strategist, Nobunaga was successful in performing this tactical service. But from the time he took control of Kyōto in 1568, it was clear that his sights were set on personal-ly ruling a unified Japan. Before his murder in 1582, he was able to conquer roughly a third of the hundred and twenty *daimyō* who under weakening Ashikaga rule had turned Japan into a patchwork of indepen-dent domains. Japan was fully unified in 1590 by Toyotomi Hideyoshi (1536–1598), one of Nobunaga's most able and ambitious generals.

Hideyoshi came from a peasant family and rose quickly through the ranks in part due to his unwavering loyalty and legendary ruthlessness. This combination proved effective in gaining the allegiance of every *daimyō* in the land. But it also enabled him to justify burning the monas-tic complex of Mount Hiei to the ground in retaliation for its complicity with one of his main rivals, and to coldly order thousands of Pure Land Buddhists (including women and children) to be put to the sword for openly contesting his right to unify Japan. Following Hideyoshi's death from old age in 1598, control of Japan fell to one of his key allies, Tokugawa Ieyasu (1543–1616), who in 1600 formally established the Tokugawa shogunate, under which Japan would be ruled through the middle of the nineteenth century.

Foreign Influences and the Changing Fortunes of Rinzai

Japan's turbulent transition from Ashikaga rule to the founding of the Tokugawa shogunate had a profound if largely indirect effect on the development of Rinzai Zen. A significant factor in this was Japan's in-creasing interaction with European missionaries and traders. The Jesuit missionary Francis Xavier landed in Japan in 1549 and was an active broker of accelerated trade and cultural exchange between the Japanese and Europeans. Jesuit priests played crucial roles in the development of port facilities and in the 1571 founding of the trade city of Nagasaki. Nobunaga in particular seems to have been favorably impressed with Jesuit-led introductions of Japan to European science, technology, and culture. But while Nobunaga, Hideyoshi, and Ieyasu all recognized the benefits of expanding trade with Europeans and clearly made effective use of firearms modeled on European designs, Hideyoshi and Ieyasu also recognized the potentially destabilizing effect of sustained interactions with outsiders and the spread of European religion.

Hideyoshi was concerned enough about the impacts of European re-ligion to place formal restrictions on the practice of Christianity in

1587—a concern that Ieyasu came to share in spite of initially affirming the value of global trade and working to develop his capital, Edo (modern-day Tokyo) into a major port. Ieyasu eventually came to see a European presence and the spread of Christianity in Japan as a political and cultural threat. Beginning in 1612, he placed increasingly severe restrictions on both the trading and missionary activities of Europeans, including a number of mass executions in 1622 and 1629. In 1635, he promulgated an edict that prohibited Japanese from traveling abroad and limited contact with Europeans to a single, artificial island located in the harbor of Nagasaki. Finally, in response to the Shimabara Rebellion of 1637–1638 that was mounted by Japanese samurai who had converted to Catholicism, Ieyasu executed the Portuguese diplomatic mission and outlawed Christianity.

As a way of ensuring at least the formal retraction of Christian adherence, he instituted a system whereby every Japanese family was required to register all of its members at a Buddhist temple. The primary purpose of this so-called *terauke* system was to compel all Japanese subjects to formally affirm their political loyalty to the Tokugawa shogunate by legally becoming members of a Buddhist temple—in effect forcing the renunciation of any ties they might have had with the "sedition-brewing" Christian religion. The impact on Rinzai temples was an increase of political backing and stature, greater integration into local communities, and new sources of income. The unintended consequence of this was a notable increase in monastic materialism and lax discipline. By the latter part of the seventeenth century, the disparity between ideals and realities in Rinzai temples was pronounced enough to become a topic for novelistic treatment, with writers like Ihara Shikaku (1642–1693) crafting highly popular fictional exposés of the social machinations and sexual exploits of Buddhist monks.

Perhaps in response to the resistance offered by some True Pure Land groups during Hideyoshi's unification campaign, another Tokugawa innovation was the institution of the main temple/branch temple, or *honmatsu*, system in which a relatively small number of main temples were each granted responsibility for overseeing the actions of all their own branch temples. This hierarchic system enabled both a remarkable degree of centralized government surveillance and a mechanism for disseminating governmental directives. Among these was a restriction on critical scholarly activities undertaken at Buddhist institutions, including the promotion of conservative scholarship that downplayed sectarian differences and was in basic agreement with neo-Confucian teachings that were being spread with great vigor at the time.

Although ostensibly aimed at promoting social order and political security, these Tokugawa measures gradually brought about substantial enough changes in the life of Rinzai communities that many Rinzai monks came to be convinced of the need for a revolutionary, internal or countercultural critique.

RINZAI REVISION AND REVIVAL IN THE TOKUGAWA

One of the more notable of those to act on convictions that Rinzai was due for internal critique was Takuan Sōhō (1573–1645). Renowned for his Buddhist philosophical works, his literary and artistic endeavors, his knowledge of Daoist and Confucian traditions, and his martial arts skills, Takuan was strident enough in his criticism of Tokugawa meddling in religious affairs to be banished to the far north in 1629. Three years later, however, as part of a general amnesty, he was allowed to return to Edo. There, he was introduced to the shogun, Tokugawa Iemitsu (1604–1651), by a noted sword master who proclaimed that the secret to his own martial virtuosity was his study of Zen with Takuan. The shogun developed such positive rapport with Takuan that he asked him to head the Tokugawa family temple.

In Takuan's view, Rinzai had become ossified by the predominance of people who confused *zazen* with bringing the mind to a stop and who identified the purity of Rinzai practice with rigid adherence to formal monastic discipline. He insisted that while the neo-Confucian thinking then being embraced by many in positions of power properly emphasized "seriousness" and "allegiance" as core values, Buddhists should realize that these are useful only at the very beginning stages of practice. Zen enlightenment had nothing to do with slavish adherence to specific teachings, to the precepts, or even to bringing the mind to a stop through "one-pointed sitting." Drawing on his own martial arts training, Takuan spoke a language that samurai would understand, insisting that formal discipline and training were useful only as ways of breaking through one's mental and physical habits. Zen awakening is realizing what it means to not be "stuck" on anything—activating a mind of responsive virtuosity that demonstrates uninhibited clarity, flexibility, and spontaneity.[4]

Another important "countercultural" Rinzai voice was that of Bankei Yōtaku (1622–1693). Bankei felt that Rinzai institutions had, on one hand, become too withdrawn from the day-to-day affairs of people, and on the other hand too completely immersed in personally gratifying but socially unproductive aesthetic pursuits. His approach to Zen practice was one of radical deconditioning aimed at realizing what he referred to as the "unborn" (mushō)—one's own mind or nature prior to imprinting by social, cultural, intellectual, and emotional customs and habits.

For Bankei, the unborn mind was not a hidden metaphysical essence that required elaborate rituals or special occasions to reveal; it was a quality of attention that could manifest at any moment in the midst of daily life. In contrast with most Rinzai teachers, Bankei focused his efforts on working with the common people rather than aristocratic, imperial, or warrior elites. Even more radically, he readily included women among his students and explicitly stated that realizing one's unborn Buddha-mind was possible for both men and women, and that in terms of spiritual potential there was no difference at all between them. Although this was a position with a long history in Chan and Zen, and although a majority of Rinzai sponsors throughout the Muromachi period had been women, it was not a position granted practical attention in early Tokugawa Rinzai institutions. Against the view that a woman could only become enlightened in a future life born as a man, Bankei insisted that enlightenment "in this very body" was possible regardless of whether one's body was male or female, noble or common.[5]

In spite of the efforts of revisionists like Takuan and Bankei, however, Rinzai was undergoing what is generally characterized as a period of decline. Because the Ashikaga shogunate had kept Zen institutions from developing the armed defense forces (sōhei) that made Tendai and Shingon temples so difficult to control, Zen temples had proved to be easy targets for military attacks, looting, and pillaging during the Ōnin War. Thereafter, during the warring states period, sponsorship was erratic at best, leaving many Rinzai temples scraping by for survival. Even after general order had been established by the Tokugawa and some income was guaranteed to Buddhist temples as a result of the mandatory household registration system, continued factionalism resulting from disputes over monastic succession, the "sale" of enlightenment certificates and abbacy titles, and moneylending practices made Rinzai temples increasingly visible targets for moral attack. Moreover, it is at this time that neo-Confucianist teachings emphasizing "returning to the ancient order" (*fukko*) were being blended with new Shintō movements based on celebrating its indigenous origins, creating conditions for the eventual emergence of an ideology of National Learning (*Kokugaku*) that called into question the twin-like nature of Japanese and Buddhist identities.

The Arrival of Ming Buddhism and the Advent of Zen Sectarianism

In this volatile mix of conditions, the arrival of Chan Buddhist monks from Ming China—again after a period of relative Japanese isolation— had a particularly profound effect. Prior to the mid-seventeenth century, factional distinctions within Rinzai and Sōtō were in some ways more prominent and important than distinctions between them. The *gozan* and *rinka* systems included both Rinzai and Sōtō temples, many monks learned from teachers in both traditions, and both organized Zen practice around *zazen* and *kōan* study. For reasons we will explore later, Sōtō had penetrated much more deeply into Japanese society than Rinzai, but this was largely a function of Sōtō openness to rituals and practices that appealed to farmers and laborers. In other words, there was a relative absence of what could be termed sectarian divisions between these two "branches" of the Zen family tree.

This changed with the arrival in Nagasaki of monks from the Huangbo-Linji Chan lineage—monks who brought with them a legacy of sectarian dispute about the relative authenticity of the Linji and Caodong schools. The seriousness of these disputes can be gauged by the fact that they eventually warranted a legal case being heard by the Ming imperial court. Perhaps the most important of these monks arriving in Japan was Yinyuan Longqi (1592–1673). Arriving in Japan in 1654, Yinyuan brought a form of Chan that carried on the Huangbo or Ōbaku lineage. But in sharp contrast with the Song era Chan that had been brought to Japan in the late twelfth and thirteenth centuries, the Ming era form of Linji Chan that Yinyuan represented was a syncretic blend of Chan and Pure Land that attracted the interest of many of the merchants in the Nagasaki area, as well as patronage by the Tokugawa *bakufu*, perhaps as a bulwark against Rinzai temples and their close ties with the imperial court.

The claim that this "hybrid" of Chan and Pure Land was the "true" expression of Linji Chan did not sit well with many in the Rinzai community. Consistent with the general affirmation of a return to ancient ways, monks affiliated with the Ōtōkan lineage of Kanzan Egen and Daitō Kokushi advocated a return to Zen's true origins. One manifestation of this was an increase of efforts to clearly distinguish among Zen traditions, not only in terms of the purity of their lineages—something characteristic of Zen from its beginnings—but also in terms of the purity of their commitments to the practices and disciplines associated with the Song dynasty Chan schools from which Rinzai and Sōtō ultimately derived their authority. As a result, in both Rinzai and Sōtō communities through the beginning of the nineteenth century, there had been mounting emphasis on discourses of uniqueness and superior authenticity.

In the Rinzai tradition, the various currents flowing toward a critical and conservative return-to-origins came into powerful and fruitful confluence in the teachings of Hakuin Ekaku (1686–1768), to whom the successful "reform" of Rinzai is traditionally credited, and to whom all Rinzai teachers today trace their lineage. Content to live and teach in an area distant from the centers of Tokugawa power, Hakuin undertook a restoration of the core Chan practices of daily labor and meditation, extensive meditation retreats (*sesshin*), and one-to-one interviews between master and student (*dokusan*) in a markedly simpler and more serious temple environment. He also is renowned for developing what is said to have been the first systematic Zen curriculum for *kōan* study. Here, too, his emphasis was on a return to a style of practice rooted in Rinzai's ancestral lineage of Linji Chan, especially the *kanna* (Ch: *kanhua*) approach advocated by the Song dynasty master Dahui.[6]

Like Dahui, Hakuin worked with significant numbers of lay students and argued that, properly understood, *kōan* practice was not only possible in the midst of daily-life activities but was actually more effective when carried out within them. In contrast with the scholarly approach to *kōan* study in *gozan* temples and the memorization approach taken in *rinka* temples, Hakuin's method was to set the body, breath, and mind in proper relationship and undertake what he called "meditation work" (*kufū*; Ch: *gongfu*) focused on the continual cultivation of "great doubt." The aim of this "work" was not some sort of intellectual realization or the rehearsal of encounter dialogues and commentaries by ancient Chinese masters; it was to demonstrate the presence of a fully embodied "vitality pertinent to all situations"—a virtuosic capacity for engaging others.

Hakuin's *kōan* curriculum was not fundamentally a means of "testing" the insight of students or of bringing about a sudden insight into one's own nature (*kenshō*). It was formal insurance against becoming complacent with the experience of awakening (*satori*) and resting content with the mere dawning of insight into nonduality. For Hakuin, the purpose of Rinzai Zen was not to "arrive" at the point of enlightenment but to develop capacities for continuously "going beyond" (*kōjō*)—an unrelenting commitment to the "post-awakening practice" (*gogo no shugyō*) of embodying awakening in all situations.

Hakuin insisted that this was not easy. Meditation work is hard work. It was in part for this reason that he found fault with Bankei for promulgating a form of Zen suited to those content with just experiencing a single moment of awakening, and whose own enlightenment, perhaps importantly for Hakuin, had been certified by an Ōbaku monk from China. Hakuin's approach eventually proved to be decisive in altering Rinzai's descending trajectory. As successive generations of his students further articulated his *kōan* method and exemplified the merits of dedication to the ongoing "work" of Zen, his lineage flourished to the point that by the end of the nineteenth century, Hakuin's Rinzai lineage had absorbed all others.

5

SŌTŌ ZEN

The Sōtō tradition of Japanese Zen is generally regarded as having been founded by one of the most intellectually audacious monks associated with premodern Zen, Dōgen Kigen (1200–1253). Like the majority of monks in his and the previous generation of those drawing inspiration from Song dynasty Chan Buddhism, Dōgen first encountered Zen through the teachings, practices, and institutional frameworks articulated by Nōnin and Eisai in their own efforts to root Linji Chan traditions within the social, cultural, political, and economic landscapes of Kamakura Japan. Dōgen differed from his predecessors, however, by not aligning himself with the ancestral tradition of Rinzai Zen but rather with the alternative Chinese tradition of Caodong Chan. Although initially slower to develop a broad institutional base than Rinzai, by the middle of the Tokugawa period there were more than 17,500 Sōtō temples across the country; and by the end of the nineteenth century, the Sōtō Zen system was the largest religious institution in Japan. [1]

Like Nōnin and Eisai, Dōgen was first ordained in the Tendai tradition and underwent initial monastic training on Mount Hiei. Also like them, he found that his most searching questions were left unanswered by his Tendai teachers and that life on Mount Hiei did little to slake his spiritual thirst. While still a teenager, Dōgen embarked on a search for more complete Buddhist instruction that ended three years later—at age seventeen—with his decision to study Zen with Myōzen (1184–1225), one of Eisai's Rinzai Dharma heirs. In 1223, after six years of study and practice, he traveled with Myōzen to China and eventually met his second Zen teacher—the Caodong Chan master Tiantong Rujing (1163–1228). In a short two years, he received transmission from Rujing as a lineage holder in the Caodong Chan tradition.

When Dōgen returned from China in 1227, he brought with him not only Rujing's pithy identification of Chan with realizing the "dropping off of 'body' and 'mind'" (*shinjindatsuraku*) through "just sitting" (*shikantaza*); he also brought a strong conviction that it was the Caodong tradition that carried on the legacy of the great Tang masters and afforded the most complete access to the roots of Buddhist awakening. If Rinzai originated in a "countercultural" spirit of reform from within the Tendai establishment, Dōgen's articulation of Sōtō can be seen as a further "countercultural" response to Eisai's syncretic approach to Zen and Rinzai's institutional deference to Tendai authority. Not unlike Nōnin, Dōgen took the more radical approach of seeking full institutional independence for the Caodong or Sōtō Zen lineage in Japan.

In Sōtō histories written during the Tokugawa period of reform—influenced, perhaps, by the intensification of Zen sectarianism in connection with the arrival of Ōbaku Chan—the form of Zen that Dōgen introduced to Japan was modeled on his training under Rujing: a "pure" Zen stripped of all Tendai esotericism and rooted instead in the primacy of *zazen*, regular public Dharma talks, private interviews with students, communal labor, and strict monastic discipline. After Dōgen's death, adherence to this "pure" form of Zen practice reportedly deteriorated as his disciples scrambled to secure financial support by, for example, performing rituals in support of potential patrons' health, wealth, and political interests. This process is said to have culminated in a "third-generation schism" (*sandaisōron*), after which Sōtō both spread with great rapidity and became increasingly diluted with popular religious practices and esoteric Tendai rituals.

The idea that Dōgen's Zen was "diluted" and eventually "split" by his third- and fourth-generation disciples seems, however, to be grounded more in the narrative preferences of later Sōtō historians than in the actual dynamics by means of which the Caodong lineage took root in Japan. Indeed, it would seem that a more accurate description might be that Dōgen's various disciples—through their karmically informed entanglement (*kattō*) with Dōgen in the master–student relationship—simply amplified different aspects of Dōgen's quite complex approach to practicing Buddhism in community with others.

Relatively little is known of Dōgen's activities in the first years after his return from China. But in 1230, he took up residence in Gokurakuji, a small and somewhat rundown temple on the outskirts of Kyōto that had previously been dedicated to the Bodhisattva Kannon (Ch: Guanyin). From his writings that survive from this period—including a letter to the Zen nun Ryōnen, a short meditation manual, and *Bendōwa* (A Talk on Pursuing the Way)—it is clear that Dōgen gathered a considerable number of students, both ordained and lay. The central message of *Bendōwa* was that practicing *zazen* is not a means to an end, an effort aimed at some future attainment; rather, *zazen* is actively demonstrating the non-dualism of body and mind as a dynamically embodied expression of unshakable poise. As Dōgen insisted, Zen enlightenment was not available only to a few monks and a smattering of exemplary noblemen and warriors; it was available to all, whether high ranking or common, male or female. And in fact, for much of the first decade after his return from China, the majority of his sponsors were women.

From the relative ease with which Dōgen was able to fund the addition of a Chinese-style monks' hall to the temple—renamed Kōshōji in 1236—it is evident that during this period he established strong and positive relations with a number of powerful figures in the environs of Kyōto. Among them were two of the most powerful men at the imperial court—Konoe Iezane (1179–1243) and his son, Kanetsune (1210–1259)—to whom Dōgen is likely to have been introduced by a rugged, one-eyed warrior from the relatively isolated province of Echizen, Hatano Yoshi-shige (d. 1258). Yet, during his time at Kōshōji, Dōgen also seems to have come somewhat controversially to the attention of both the Tendai establishment and such prominent Rinzai teachers as Enni Ben'en.

In all likelihood, the primary point of controversy was Dōgen's desire to establish Sōtō as a completely independent Buddhist lineage, free to conduct its own ordinations and establish its own practice regimes and organizational structure. Dōgen presented his refusal to remain under the umbrella of Tendai authority or to accept affiliation with Rinzai as a matter of commitment to Chan authenticity. This clearly would not have sat well with those whose own sponsorship relations depended on being seen as offering access to cutting-edge cultural and religious develop-ments in Song China. But the animosity expressed toward Dōgen and his small community may also have had to do with the welcome that he extended to third-generation members of the Darumashū—the "heterodox" Zen lineage that many in Kyōto decried as a renegade Buddhism espousing freedom from monastic precepts and social constraints and thus as a potential threat to social and political order.

Indeed, one of Dōgen's most senior disciples and his eventual successor, Koun Ejō (1198–1280), had first ordained in the Tendai school and then gone "on the road" while still a teenager, studying first with a Pure Land teacher before apprenticing himself to Nōnin's Dharma heir, Kakuan (d. 1234?). Apparently sensing the imminence of his own death, Kakuan directed Ejō to continue his Zen studies with Dōgen, whom he joined in 1234. The connection between them was immediate and apparently quite strong. Not long after joining Dōgen, Ejō took on primary responsibility for compiling his new teacher's lectures and written essays and quickly became Dōgen's closest disciple.

Perhaps with Ejō's encouragement, a number of Darumashū monks entered Dōgen's community at Kōshōji in 1241. Headed by one of Kakuan's senior disciples, Ekan, this group was apparently fleeing violent disputes with both Tendai and Rinzai authorities in Echizen, where there was a relatively large Darumashū community. Dōgen's welcome of this group would likely have been perceived by Tendai and Rinzai authorities in Kyōto as a provocation. Although Ekan integrated well into the community, this seems not to have been the case for all of these Darumashū monks. From roughly the time of their arrival, Dōgen's writings evidence a significant shift. Instead of presenting Zen in terms that had appeal across the socioeconomic and political spectrum, he turned toward conducting highly detailed examinations of Chinese Chan texts that also included direct criticisms not only of Rinzai and Darumashū approaches to Zen in Japan, but also of what he lamented as the lax practices and conceptual muddles characterizing many of the Linji Chan communities he had visited in China.

This shift in the subject matter and style of Dōgen's writings seems to have been directed toward establishing the distinctive identity and superior authenticity of the Caodong lineage, toward promoting the value of voluntary poverty, and toward establishing clear Chinese precedents for strictly adhering to monastic precepts. Whether this change of orientation was a response to challenges posed by the new Darumashū members of his community is not clear. It did, however, coincide with the Kōshōji community being subject to increasingly pointed Tendai and Rinzai critique. Whether due to these escalating conflicts or to escape metropolitan distractions, Dōgen effectively pulled up stakes in 1243 and moved his community from the outskirts of Kyōto to the Hatano family domain in Echizen, settling in a mountainous and relatively isolated stretch of coast along the Sea of Japan.

Over the next few years, as Dōgen slowly reconditioned and expanded the modest family temple he had been granted, he led a small community of monks in a resolutely ascetic life centered on the strict observation of Chan monastic regulations, daily lectures on *kōans* and illustrative local events, and rigorous practice of *zazen*. On completing the renovation work, he christened the new temple Eiheiji, the "Temple of Eternal Peace," and claimed that as the head temple of the Sōtō lineage in Japan it would become a cousin of the great Chinese temple complex at Mount Tiantai: a national treasure for the authentic propagation of Buddhism.

The move to Echizen had an enormous impact on Sōtō's evolution. To begin with, it effectively cut off the possibility of securing any significant sponsorship from either the aristocratic or warrior elites in Kyōto and Kamakura, forcing Dōgen to rely entirely on rural warrior families and villagers for support. Although the move insulated his community from the power struggles occurring in the major metropolitan areas, and from the temptations that attend interacting with social, cultural, and political elites, it also made material poverty an inarguable matter of fact, not a matter of choice. Judging from Dōgen's recorded talks during this period, not all the monks who had moved with him from Kōshōji were enamored with their new circumstances, especially since even basic subsistence needs for food and clothing were often in painfully short supply. On occasion, internal rifts within the community were severe enough for Dōgen to banish dissenting members, and despite his considerable charisma, Eiheiji's population fluctuated widely and remained relatively small.

Yet Dōgen's insistence that his monks comport themselves properly when conducting ritual practices and interacting with local community members, his personal acceptance of a simple and austere communal lifestyle, and his community's reputation for intensive and effective meditation practice all resonated well with Japanese conceptions of embodied spirituality. In a relatively short period, Eiheiji acquired a reputation for being imbued with both spiritually and materially efficacious power—a "field of merit" (*fukuden*) to which offerings could be made in full confidence that they would bear positive fruit.

Contrary to the Sōtō historical narratives that became dominant in the Tokugawa period, the records we have of life at Eiheiji under Dōgen's leadership do not support his depiction as a radical Zen purist who refrained from ritual practices of any sort. Like daily life in the Song dynasty Chan monasteries that Dōgen took as his institutional model, daily life at Eiheiji did center on vigorous *zazen* and *kōan* practice. But it also included group chanting, sutra recitations, prostrations, offerings of incense and water, repentance ceremonies for monks and laypersons, lay precept recitations, and other ritual activities that had been part of Buddhist monastic practice in China (and in India and Central Asia) for over a thousand years. Dōgen's remark that there is no such thing as "Zen" was, among other things, a forceful denial of Zen exceptionalism. For him, Zen was simply Buddhism returned to its original core practices, respect for the interdependence of the monastic and lay communities, and recognition of the need to create the conditions for their sustained and effective mutual contribution.

SUCCESSION MATTERS

In spite of Dōgen's insistence on strict adherence to monastic rules, it is perhaps not surprising that different approaches to carrying on his lineage appeared in the years immediately following his death in 1253. He was by all accounts a powerfully charismatic person, and there would likely have been little expectation that any one person could effectively "replace" him. An additional factor would have been that many of Dōgen's students had first trained in Tendai, Rinzai, and Darumashū contexts, and that Dōgen himself had held dual lineage transmissions—in Linji Chan or Rinzai Zen through Myōzen, and in Caodong Chan through Rujing. On top of this, there is the fact that Dōgen's essays and lectures, and his commentaries on Chan and other Buddhist texts, were remarkably innovative and displayed a rhetorical virtuosity and conceptual brilliance that would have made them extraordinarily difficult to master.

Dōgen's appointed successor, Ejō, was by all accounts a thorough but conservative trustee of his teacher's legacy. Others among Dōgen's first- and second-generation disciples tackled the task of interpreting and commenting on Dōgen's writings—most notably Senne (n.d.) and his student Kyōgō (n.d.), who were among the first to explicitly identify themselves as Sōtō monks and engage in direct criticisms of other Zen (Rinzai and Darumashū) teachers. No one had as complete a command of Dōgen's writings and recorded lectures as Ejō, but it seems that Ejō lacked the kind of vision and personal charisma that would have been needed to do more than simply preserve Dōgen's literary and institutional legacies. Under his leadership, Eiheiji gradually fell into decline, its cultic aura fading.

There is some indication that Dōgen himself recognized the tradeoff between effective conservation and creativity that would accompany Ejō's assumption of the abbacy at Eiheiji. Prior to his death, he is said to have taken one of Ekan's Darumashū disciples, Tettsu Gikai (1219–1309), into his confidence and expressed a wish that Gikai should one day lead Eiheiji and carry on the work of spreading Dōgen's Zen lineage throughout Japan. In the eyes of some within the Eiheiji community, this meant that Gikai had just as strong a claim to the abbacy as Ejō. Tensions mounted, and in 1259 Gikai departed for a three-year tour of China, including periods of study with a range of Chan and other Buddhist teachers. On his return, Gikai made use of local contacts that he had developed while still a member of the Darumashū temple in Echizen, pulling together funding to complete the construction of the temple complex at Eiheiji in keeping with the latest designs being used in monastic construction in China. Ejō placed Gikai in charge of the work, and upon its completion in 1267 he acceded to requests by powerful patrons in the Hatano and Fujiwara clans, turning over the abbacy to Gikai.

The impressive new buildings and increasingly warm interaction with local lay sponsors were celebrated by some within Eiheiji, but criticized by others as marking a definitive and mistaken departure from Dōgen's commitments to a simple and frugal way of life. Some even charged Gikai with including esoteric Shingon practices in the ceremonial practices at Eiheiji in total disregard for what they felt was Dōgen's unwavering commitment to "pure" Zen. In 1272, Ejō was asked by a majority of the community to come out of "retirement" and to resume leadership of Eiheiji. He did so, and remained abbot until his death in 1280.

Significantly, Ejō did not name a successor prior to dying, and contention arose about who should assume control of Eiheiji. Gikai had returned to nurse Ejō during his last days and felt that he should resume the abbacy. Initially, the faction supporting his return prevailed over those supporting the other main candidate, a slightly older monk by the name of

Gien (d. 1313), who had first studied under Ekan and then received transmission from Ejō. Fatefully, Gikai's return to Eiheiji coincided with anticipations of a second Mongol invasion, and he embraced the governmental request that all Buddhist temples perform esoteric ceremonies for the safety of the nation. For his opponents, this was undisguised evidence of Gikai's intent to steer Eiheiji irreversibly away from Dōgen's pure Zen. Dissent within the community intensified, led by supporters of Gien and a Chinese monk, Jakuen (1207–1299), who had managed memorial services at Eiheiji under Dōgen and who had also become one of Ejō's main disciples.

In 1287, Gikai once again left Eiheiji, this time moving to the nearby coastal province of Kaga where he eventually converted a small temple, Daijōji, which had been built for the purpose of esoteric (Shingon) worship of Dainichi. Among those who joined Gikai at his new Zen temple was Keizan Jōkin (1268–1325), around whom all the issues surrounding the so-called third-generation schism eventually coalesced. Eiheiji was placed under the guidance of Gien, who remained abbot until his death and was succeeded by one of Jakuen's Dharma heirs, Giun (1253–1333). Like his teacher, Giun stressed Sōtō's Chinese heritage and especially the teachings of the early-twelfth-century Caodong master, Hongzhi. Enjoying positive relations with the Hatano family, Giun was able to refurbish the buildings at Eiheiji and restore some of its spiritual vibrancy.

Keizan and the Expansion of Sōtō Religiosity

But it was Keizan who is best seen as having set the institutional trajectory of Sōtō, and who by the end of the Tokugawa period came to be recognized retrospectively as the "mother" of Sōtō, second in prestige only to the tradition's "father," Dōgen. Keizan seems to have been destined for a monastic Buddhist life. His grandmother, Myōchi, had been among Dōgen's earliest sponsors, and his mother, Ekan, ordained as a nun and eventually became the abbess of an important Sōtō convent. As a child, Keizan became a novice monk under Gikai and after a period of formal study with Ejō embarked on a religious journey, in the course of which he studied with Rinzai and Tendai masters. He then apprenticed himself briefly to both Jakuen and Gien before finally returning to Gikai. A few years later, he received Dharma transmission from Gikai and was shortly thereafter awarded the abbacy of Daijōji.[2]

After Gikai's death in 1309, however, key warrior sponsors decided that the abbacy of Daijōji should be assumed by a Rinzai monk. Keizan made the most of this adverse situation, heading north up the coast to Noto Province where he was granted land and a promise of noninterference by a nonsamurai patron, Shigeno Nobunao, and his wife, Sonin, both of whom eventually became Keizan's lay students. There, he eventually built two Zen temples, Yōkōji and Sōjiji, and developed an approach to Zen that combined monastic rigor with expanding attention to the needs of the local community—an approach that would become normative for Sōtō during the Muromachi and Tokugawa periods. Like Dōgen, Keizan saw Zen as marking a restoration of the original complexion of Buddhist practices centered on cultivating wisdom, attentive mastery, and moral clarity, with the aim of liberating all sentient beings from suffering. But the tenor of Keizan's own Buddhist journey was such that he was open to including a much wider range of religious experiences than seems to have been true for Dōgen and many of his heirs.

Although Keizan clearly valorized the Zen practices of *kōan* and *zazen* training, he also brought other Buddhist practices into the lives of the monastic and lay communities he initiated at Yōkōji and Sōjiji, founded respectively in 1317 and 1324 during the increasingly turbulent final years of rule by the Kamakura shogunate. Perhaps influenced by his mother and grandmother's experiences, he built shrines for practicing devotion to Kannon, the highly popular Bodhisattva of Compassion, as well as other Buddhist "deities," and he championed the rights of women to enjoy the full spectrum of Zen practices. In fact, he was the first Zen teacher in Japan to grant full Dharma transmission to a woman, the Sōtō nun Ekyō. Alongside relatively exoteric practices like sutra recitation and chanting the names of Buddhas (*nembutsu*), Keizan also embraced relatively esoteric practices like chanting *dhāranīs* (or energy-infused incantations), aimed at creating, for example, extraordinary conditions for healing or protection. Monks at Yōkōji and Sōjiji regularly conducted prayer ceremonies for the purpose of fulfilling the wishes of the lay community. And, perhaps as a result of his own experiences of what might be called shamanistic dreaming, he advocated bringing local spirits (*kami*) into the Buddhist fold and affirmed the efficacy of conducting propitiatory ceremonies for them.

This model of Zen practice proved to be very powerful. Over the same period that Rinzai was achieving unquestioned dominance through the elite-sponsored *gozan* system, Keizan's Sōtō lineage rapidly spread across Japan, putting down deep root in towns, villages, and more remote rural areas. By the sixteenth century, Sōjiji was at the head of a multi-branched system of several thousand temples and vied with Eiheiji for recognition as the head temple of the Sōtō tradition.

Post-Dōgen Dynamics: Competitions, Crossings, or Complementarities

The rhetoric of the "third-generation schism"—a construct of Zen historians from the fifteenth century and later—paints a picture of intense and acrimonious lineage competitions regarding primacy in passing Dōgen's Zen on to future generations. Yet, there is good evidence to suggest that what was occurring is better described as a diversification of fundamentally complementary approaches to Zen. For example, it is difficult to square the picture of acidic recrimination across lineages with the fact that Keizan, one of the key fourth-generation players affected by the so-called schism, studied under and remained in respectful and affectionate relationships with all of the other major third-generation actors. In addition, the sharp line between those who conservatively carried on Dōgen's vision of "pure" and spiritually focused Zen practice and those who innovatively expanded that vision to include materially oriented, esoteric ceremonies and prayers seems to have been drawn in either ignorance or denial of the broad range of activities mandated by Dōgen for his communities at Kōshōji and Eiheiji.

What seems certain is that Dōgen and his Dharma heirs were drawing on an extraordinarily rich array of both Chinese and Japanese Buddhist traditions and religious sensibilities in their efforts to realize vibrant patterns of communal relations rooted in shared convictions about body-mind nonduality and the intrinsic capacity of all beings to demonstrate enlightenment. Rather than signaling disputes about Zen orthodoxy (or correct doctrine), the differences that emerged among the first generations of Dōgen's successors seem to have centered on issues of orthopraxy (or correct practice), including practices related to monastic succession.

This focus on practical rather than doctrinal differences accords well with the broader medieval Japanese propensity toward argument by relegation rather than by refutation. And it is especially apt in the context of the complex lineage crossings that characterized early Sōtō history. Whatever claims later historians might make about the purity of Dōgen's Zen, the fact is that virtually all of the major players in the first three generations of Sōtō had studied in a number of Buddhist traditions and had received transmission through both Caodong (Sōtō) and Linji (Rinzai or Darumashū) lineages. What seems to have been in dispute was not what practices to exclude or include, but rather how best to rank their centrality and priority.

At any rate, by the end of the first quarter of the fourteenth century, as the Kamakura period was coming to a close, Sōtō had developed five distinct branches: the communities led by Jakuen and Giun at Hōkyōji and Eiheiji; the community led by Gikai and Keizan at Daijōji, Yōkōji, and Sōjiji; the Yōkōan community near Kenninji led by Senne and Kyōgō; and the geographically distant Daijiji community in Kyushu led by Giin. Over the course of the Muromachi period, however, not all these communities proved equally adaptable to the changing political, economic, social, and cultural conditions across Japan. By the end of Ashikaga rule in 1573, the monastic systems headed by Eiheiji and Sōjiji were firmly ascendant.

INSTITUTIONAL EXPANSION AND POPULARIZATION

By the mid-fourteenth century, monks from the Gikai-Keizan line who styled themselves as itinerant "men of the Way" (dōnin) had succeeded in establishing small temple footholds in roughly half of Japan's provinces, ranging from the far north of the main island in the Japanese archipelago, Honshū, to the southern tip of the island of Kyūshū. By this time, virtually every village in Japan had a small, general-purpose religious building that was maintained by the village elders and was used to host an eclectic range of Buddhist and other religious activities. When traveling Sōtō monks arrived in a village, it was apparently not uncommon for them to take up informal residence in or near these modest structures and establish a daily regimen of intensive meditation practice that served to impress the local populace with their sincerity and ascetic vigor. Once a positive rapport had been established, they would then offer basic Zen instruction and perform rituals for material benefits of the sort desired by agricultural communities, including rituals for rain and successful harvests. All of this served to attract the attention of village leaders, land-owners, and local samurai families or *daimyō*. Perhaps at first simply wishing to ingratiate themselves to the population at large, these relative-ly powerful actors would often offer the itinerant monk a more permanent home, sponsoring the conversion of the village chapel to a Zen temple.

In the major metropolitan areas of Kamakura and Kyōto, a major dimension of the appeal of Zen sponsorship and the dynamics of institu-tional expansion was that Zen monks provided uncommon access to the latest literary, artistic, and fashion developments in China. In the rural, often mountainous, and geographically isolated communities in which Sōtō monks were trying to establish themselves, brokering access to Chi-nese culture had no particular appeal. In that context, possibilities for institutional expansion rested on earning the trust and sponsorship of these communities, responding to their specific needs and interests.

Sōtō Religious Substance

Charismatic Presence

Perhaps the single most important factor in the success with which Sōtō spread throughout rural Japan was the way in which Sōtō emphases on ascetic vigor and strict meditation practice resonated with the Japanese religious imagination. From very early in Japanese history, mountain as-cetics and meditation masters (*zenji*) came to be strongly associated with the possession of supramundane powers. Although we might today refer to these as "mystical" powers, with the implication that they were some-how "supernatural," in the medieval Japanese worldview, abilities, for example, to heal, to imbue objects (talismans) with protective power, or to affect the weather were not seen as evidence of having achieved some sort of break from the natural world, but rather as evidence of intensified and more efficacious connections with it. The feats accomplished by those who had cultivated such abilities were evidence that they—like *kami*—were at the center of a field of extraordinary, but nevertheless natural, relational energies. Reverently entering such a field was a way of altering one's fortunes.

But unlike traditional mountain ascetics, the religious charisma of Sōtō monks was distinguished by their participation in a complex of personal and institutional relationships that extended throughout Japan, stretched across the sea to China, and ultimately reached even to the fabled West in which the Buddha had lived and taught. The precincts of efficacy surrounding these monks thus projected well beyond the local environment. But, even apart from the new scales of possible connections resulting from the arrival of charismatic Sōtō monks, in a much more immediate way their arrivals opened mediating spaces in which competing local claims for authority could be placed in conversation—spaces that encouraged cooperative support for an institution that could powerfully and positively affect everyone's fortunes.

Sufficiently impressed with the efficacy of Zen practice as exemplified by the monks in their presence, many men and women were moved to adopt lay Buddhist precepts, to engage in precept recitation ceremonies and annual celebrations of Buddha's birthday, and in some cases to begin practicing simple attention training and meditation practices. Moreover, in keeping with the Sōtō conception of Zen practice as the simultaneous exemplification of wisdom, attentive mastery, and moral clarity, Sōtō monks served to heighten community concerns about morality, often through public lectures featuring stories easily understood and appreciated by rural folk lacking any formal education.

Funeral Rites

In addition to their role as mediums for favorably transforming various this-worldly dimensions of connectivity, Sōtō monks also offered rituals by means of which it was possible to affect the individual and familial fates of the departed. From quite early in the spread of Buddhism in Japan, there were a number of different rituals being used to ensure the honor and tranquility of the deceased, especially for high-ranking monks. By the eighth century, as wealthy imperial and aristocratic elites came to understand Buddhist teachings on karma and the transfer of merit, they saw the value of investing in having these rituals performed for their family members. Building on Chan monastic funeral rites, Rinzai and Sōtō Zen developed a highly elaborate and integrated set of ceremonies for high-ranking monks and especially important patrons, as well as simpler ceremonies for ordinary monks that emphasized their posthumous liberation from suffering through the intercession of Amida Buddha (Amitābha).

Japanese Buddhist funerals for laypeople, modeled on those for ordinary monks, became more widespread over time, as did the Japanese innovation of conducting ritual ordinations of the dead (and those for whom death was imminent), thus enabling them to be treated to full monastic funeral rites. A crucial element in Sōtō's rapid expansion throughout Japan was that Sōtō monks introduced both the purposes and possibility of Zen funerals to the general populace in areas previously lacking the trained monks and financial resources needed to ritually assist their loved ones toward freedom from suffering. By the end of the fifteenth century, not only were most Sōtō Zen funerals conducted for commoners rather than members of ruling elites, but most of the funding that kept Sōtō temples operating came from donations made in connection with funeral rites performed for the common people living nearby. Significantly, a majority of the funerals conducted for commoners were performed for women—a fact that, unfortunately, is likely to say something about the low status of nuns in the institutional hierarchy of medieval Sōtō Zen and the correspondingly scant incentives that existed for religiously inclined women to seek full ordination.

Ritual Support

Sōtō monks traveling throughout rural Japan brought with them religious practices and concepts new to the general public and to many of those wielding local authority. They also encountered existing religious practices that were crucial to the communal identities of those on whom they would ultimately depend for their livelihoods. A distinctive feature of the evolution of Sōtō Zen as it spread across the Japanese archipelago was the readiness of Sōtō monks to accept the importance of these indigenous beliefs and practices. Rather than denouncing local customs as unsophisticated superstitions or forbidding the worship of local *kami* as antithetical to Buddhist teachings, Sōtō monks worked to supplement locally prevailing spiritual and religious beliefs and practices by placing them within a more comprehensive Buddhist framework, enhancing their efficacy rather than seeking to suppress or supplant them.

As a result, rather than Sōtō ritual structures being imposed on local ones, they were effectively interwoven with them, enabling Sōtō Zen to become part of the fabric of daily life in the local community, rather than a foreign presence within it. The often-repeated saying that "Zen is nothing special"—a saying that can be traced back at least to Tang dynasty China and Chan master Mazu's assertion that "ordinary mind is Buddha-mind"—can in many ways be seen as a statement about the skill with which Sōtō monks infused Zen into the communities in which they lived. Through their efforts, Zen became "nothing special" in the sense of being a natural part of people's day-to-day lives.

It should be kept in mind that the spread of Sōtō throughout the Japanese countryside occurred in a period when rural living conditions were both rough and uncertain. Traveling on foot and relying on the kindness of strangers for food and shelter was not a comfortable, vacation-like trek. The "men of the Way" who left the relative safety and certainties of established communities of like-minded monks to carry Zen into the lives of ordinary people would have required remarkable commitment to fusing wisdom and compassion and would have needed extraordinary confidence. This confidence might be attributed to a spirit of self-reliance, leading to an image of these monks as intrepid explorers. But in actuality their travels were conducted in the spirit of both offering and entrusting themselves to others, and it is likely much closer to the truth to say that their successes were related less to their capacities for independence than to their demonstration of a spirit of transformative interdependence.

Institutional Structures

It must also be kept in mind that the Japanese countryside through which Sōtō monks were traveling in the late fourteenth and fifteenth centuries was neither peaceful nor centrally governed in any significant sense. This was an era dominated by low-intensity but continuous conflict among "warring states barons" (*sengoku daimyō*) who were predatory in their bids for control over economic resources and ruthless in their efforts to consolidate political power. While much of the support that sustained the day-to-day workings of Sōtō temples came from commoners and from locally ambitious village leaders and samurai, there was no ultimate security—or even freedom of movement—without the favor of regionally powerful warriors.

Realizing favorable relations with warrior clans came with certain costs. For a temple aligned with an ascendant *daimyō*, each new military conquest resulted in both opportunities and imperatives to establish branch temples in newly acquired territories. The accelerating pace of military engagements, especially from the Ōnin War onward, was thus paralleled by increasingly rapid growth of Sōtō temple networks. But the entrainment occurring between the dynamics of military conquest and that of the geographical spread of Sōtō went beyond just growth rates; it came to include mutually reinforcing structural dynamics so that the hierarchies evident in head and branch temple relations in Sōtō institutional networks increasingly resembled the pyramidal structure of military alliances among *daimyō*. In practical terms, this meant that the degree of prestige enjoyed by various warrior families was paralleled by the relative prestige of the temples for which they were primary sponsors.

A second structuring force operating during this period was the normalization at key Sōtō temples of a succession system based on "rotating abbotship" (*rinjū*). Unlike the great public monasteries in China in which new abbots were selected competitively without regard to the lineages to which candidates belonged, the abbacies of Japanese Zen temples and monasteries were handed down from one generation to another of a given lineage. They were, in effect, "Dharma family" temples or "lineage cloisters." Only if no lineal descendants existed or if patrons insisted on a break in succession—as was the case when the major patrons of Daijōji bypassed Keizan to award the abbacy to a Rinzai lineage holder—would the administrative control and spiritual leadership of a temple or monastic complex pass to another Zen lineage. Many of the factional disputes associated with early Sōtō temples originated from the lack of clear instructions as to which disciple in a given generation should succeed a deceased abbot.

The formalization of the *rinjū* system addressed this problem by specifying that all of an abbot's first-generation disciples would sequentially share the abbacy of the temple, progressing in order from the most senior monk to the least. Because many of the most powerful and effective Sōtō teachers had many Dharma heirs, this system led to a rapid and regular transfer of authority at leading temples. One result of this was a proliferation of former abbots of high-prestige temples, who would then found new temples of their own. Over the course of several generations, this generated expansive hierarchies of head and branch temples that took the form of nested pyramids of prestige and influence.

Because of the ways in which these nested systems were aligned through sponsorship practices with shifting complexions of political allies and competitors, the institutional dynamics of Sōtō could scarcely avoid becoming increasingly competitive. But just as importantly, it was part of the *rinjū* system that when one was granted the honor of serving as abbot, one incurred a debt of gratitude to those who made this possible. The payment of this "debt" typically took the form of economic offerings to the head temple of the lineage—a burden not always easily discharged by those without extensive sponsorship networks of their own, or by those who were compelled to serve repeated terms as abbot of the same temple. In response, there developed a practice of allowing "exemptions" to taking part in the rotation system for those without the financial means to meet the obligations associated with assuming an abbotship.

This led, however, to a measure of insecurity for major temples and monasteries, the economic solvency of which was effectively linked to the ability of lower-level temples to appoint new monks as abbots. The cumulative effect of abbacy exemptions was that some monasteries, like Sōjiji, would at times find themselves unable to recruit the numbers of new monks they needed to sustain the required rotation of abbots. To attract sufficient numbers of new monks, some major monasteries developed the practice of offering special honors to those who committed fully to the system for example, the provision of distinctive robes and titles indicating high rank within the lineage.

With greater long-term impact, another practice was to offer initiations that enabled monks entering the system to perform rituals that would otherwise be beyond their training and authority. Key to this practice was access to secret initiation documents (*kirikami*) and other Zen texts—especially the teachings and lectures of famous Zen masters like Dōgen and Keizan—that were effectively off limits to ordinary monks. Because the value of these initiation documents and texts was a function of restricted access, there developed what amounted to lineage-specific bodies of "esoteric" Zen literature. And since abbots could not refer to these documents or texts in their public talks or published writings, the lectures and essays of the most highly regarded Zen teachers were effectively taken out of circulation. Rather than commenting on or drawing upon their own Japanese forbears, over the course of the fifteenth and sixteenth centuries Sōtō teachers came to focus their public talks and teachings almost exclusively on older, Chinese-language texts. By the early sixteenth century, texts like Dōgen's seminal *Shōbōgenzō* had assumed the status of talismans—relics imbued with power that suffused the monasteries in which they were guarded—rather than resources for furthering the personal practice of Zen.

This shift of emphasis from Japanese teachers and their writings and lectures to Chinese forebears had an impact on the Sōtō use of *kōans* in monastic training. In contrast with many of the Rinzai monks in leading *gozan* monasteries, the majority of Sōtō monks did not have the Chinese-language skills needed to engage in the scholarly study of *kōans* or to compose the kinds of verse and prose responses that were normative in Rinzai settings. By allowing Japanese-language lectures and essays by leading masters to be taken out of circulation, Sōtō institutionally steered *kōan* study in an increasingly formulaic direction in which standard sets of answers to an established set of *kōans* in stereotypical Chinese would simply be memorized. Whereas Rinzai Zen followed the precedent set by Dahui in focusing *kōan* study on generating sufficiently "great doubt" to *bring about* a sudden breakthrough to "seeing one's nature" (*kenshō*), Sōtō Zen used *kōan* study to provide monks with an idealized language for *expressing* enlightenment. Like *zazen*, *kōan* practice came to be understood not as a means-to awakening, but rather as a way of demonstrating the meaning-of Buddhist enlightenment.

SŌTŌ DEVELOPMENTS UNDER THE TOKUGAWA

All forms of Buddhism, including Sōtō Zen, were subject to great and often violent disruption during the final decades of the sixteenth century as the Ashikaga shogunate was being undermined and then overthrown. During the 1570s, Oda Nobunaga's military conquests in Echizen led to the destruction of many temples in the Sōtō heartlands, including Eiheiji and Yōkōji. But due to its less close association with the major power brokers in Kamakura and Kyōto, and the fact that the vast majority of its temples served small rural communities, Sōtō suffered less damage than the more metropolitan forms of Buddhism. In fact, after peace was restored in the early 1600s, a number of the policies established by the Tokugawa *bakufu* worked substantially in favor of Sōtō's continued institutional development and heightened economic security.

The first of these measures, mentioned already in connection with Rinzai, was the household registration system put in place by the Tokugawa government. In formal terms, this required every family to register with a Buddhist temple, affirm that no one in the family was associated with either Christianity or the banned Nichiren form of Buddhism (both of which were, for various reasons, regarded as threats to political and social order), and engage in conduct befitting members in good standing with the temple. In practice, this required registered families to maintain the temple through regular donations associated with attending annual and seasonal rituals, conducting funerals, and so on—a set of responsibilities aptly summarized by the term used to designate temple members: *danna*, or "those who offer." Since the vast majority of the Japanese population was rural, and since most rural communities had but a single, typically Sōtō temple nearby, this governmental regulation resulted in a period of economic stability and growth for Sōtō temple networks.

Second, consonant with its efforts to centralize control over especially religious traditions in light of Christian-led insurrections, the Tokugawa government declared in 1615 that the heads of the two largest networks of Sōtō temples—Eiheiji and Sōjiji—were to have equal status. These temples would be responsible for ensuring the quality of religious conduct at all Sōtō temples, but also the orderly conduct of all Sōtō monks. A particularly stringent requirement was that those authorized to offer Dharma instruction must have committed to a minimum of thirty years of study. This spurred the development of major Sōtō academies that often had up to a thousand students and offered a quality of education equal to that offered in government-sponsored academies. New scholarly approaches being developed in the early Edo period in connection with burgeoning Confucian and Native studies movements were appropriated by Sōtō monks, resulting in a decisive turn toward textual and historical studies.

The Impact of Ōbaku Zen

Much like their Rinzai counterparts, many Sōtō monks were inspired to rethink their own traditions in light of the institutional forms and practices brought from China in the mid- to late seventeenth century by representatives of the Ōbaku or Huangbo lineage of Chan. Although the impact on Rinzai was perhaps more dramatic, even for Sōtō Zen monks the arrival of Chinese counterparts whose approach to discipline and practice differed significantly from their own forced confrontation with issues of historical contingency. This helped usher in an almost modern degree of critical self-consciousness in Sōtō circles.

At one level, the Ōbaku stress on strict monastic discipline and its incorporation of Pure Land practices like chanting the names of the Buddha gave warrant to themes then current in Sōtō intellectual discourse and resonated well with the inclusive nature of the Sōtō Zen practice. This was especially true in small rural communities where distinctions among different Buddhist traditions were often indistinctly drawn. But on another level, encounters with Ōbaku Chan begged a new kind of attention to Sōtō traditions and their origins, adding significant weight to questions being raised by Sōtō monks who had followed the lead of Confucian and Nativist scholars and turned back to their own "ancient texts" for inspiration in addressing contemporary concerns. Monks like Dokuan Genkō (1630–1698) and Manzan Dōhaku (1636–1714) broke with the tradition of using Dōgen's writings purely for talismanic purposes and began reading them for insight into the meaning of "restoring the past" (*fukkoundō*) and reviving Sōtō's original vision.

Among the central concerns of Manzan and other Sōtō reformers of his generation were the confusing and often unapologetically pecuniary practices that had come to surround monastic succession. Over the Muromachi period, it had become common to recognize two kinds of Zen monastic transmission: one based on a direct teaching relationship and the other on a transfer of title to the abbacy of a temple or monastery. Based on his reading of Dōgen's *Shōbōgenzō*, Manzan argued that the seal of succession can be received from only one master, based on having engaged in an actual master–disciple relationship, and that so-called temple transmission was not true to the founding vision of Sōtō Zen. This was a direct attack on the practice of monks acquiring transmission documents from Zen teachers simply to forward their own careers, jumping from one lineage to another in pursuit of increasingly prestigious temple affiliations. After several years of failing to bring about succession reform from within the Zen community, Manzan took the case to the Tokugawa *bakufu*, which ruled in his favor in 1703.

This ruling was greeted with generally wide support. However, there were those who felt that Manzan erred in placing his greatest emphasis on the ritual form of the master-disciple relationship rather than on its spiritual content. Tenkei Denson (1648–1735) was among the most outspoken of this group, arguing on the basis of his own readings of Dōgen that the heart of Zen is realizing enlightenment, and that this might occur in the course of a long relationship with a single teacher or it might not. Simply having a personal relationship with a Zen teacher was, in his view, neither a necessary nor sufficient condition for being granted transmission. Tenkei's view remained in a minority, but it continued to inform institutional dynamics in Sōtō through the end of the Edo period.

The reappraisal of early Sōtō texts was not restricted to the task of finding precedents useful in addressing current institutional concerns. Many Sōtō monks also sought philosophical and religious inspiration in these texts, particularly those of Dōgen. The most prolific writer among this group was unquestionably Menzan Zuiho (1683–1769), a monk who combined scholarship with rigorous meditation practice, including an extraordinarily challenging thousand-day solo retreat in honor of his teacher's death. The author of several hundred works on different themes, Menzan's greatest legacy was perhaps his decisively religious and historical engagement with Dōgen's formal writings, lecture notes, daily discourse records, and poetry. This sparked a renaissance of appreciation for Sōtō's uniquely Japanese origins in the literary and philosophical innovations of its founder.[3]

SŌTŌ BEYOND THE TEMPLE DOORS

This summary of changes brought about in Sōtō Zen by policies of the Tokugawa shogunate might suggest that, during the Edo period, Sōtō was on the whole becoming increasingly scholarly and bureaucratic. But Sōtō's roots remained sunk deeply in remote mountain temples and rural communities. Although the rise of Zen scholarship and the sedimentation of new institutional forms were important factors in shaping the public face of Zen as Japan gradually transited from medieval to modern ways of life, Sōtō continued to be sustained by and responsive to the Japanese people.

For example, although Tenkei was deeply involved in academic disputes about the nature of Zen transmission, wrote erudite *kōan* commentaries, and was often invited to speak in elite circles, he was also a firm advocate of spreading Zen teachings and practices among the common people. Very much like Bankei, the Rinzai monk who proclaimed that everyone could realize their "unborn mind," Tenkei insisted that everyone possesses a mind of enlightenment that is only waiting to be unveiled. For many of the tens of thousands of Sōtō monks and nuns living in small rural communities, this was not an abstract claim about some deep, metaphysical core; it was a truth that could be actualized in the course of one's daily-life activities. Taking seriously the assertion made by Chan luminaries like Bodhidharma and Huineng that true meditation can be practiced whether sitting, standing, lying down, or walking, many Sōtō monks went so far as to insist that—performed with the right kind of attention and intention—any activity from working in the fields to building homes to cooking or weaving could be the practice of "*zazen*."

Perhaps the most outspoken and famous of those affirming the possibility of practicing Zen in the midst of daily life was Suzuki Shōsan (1579–1655), a samurai who renounced his life as a warrior to become a Buddhist monk. Like the Rinzai sword master Takuan, Shōsan denied that there was any ultimate dividing line between the sacred and the secular. Enlightenment is not something to be attained only by retreating from the world and entering the monastery. Enlightenment is attained through wholeheartedly and joyously doing one's work, whatever that happens to be. In apparent acknowledgment that increasing numbers of Japanese people were involved in commercial activities, Shōsan explicitly stated that this was true not only for farmers, artisans, and warriors, but even for merchants. As long as those in business pursued profit without being caught by clinging forms of desire, their work could also be a form of bodhisattva action. Without exception, he claimed, every form of work can become the work of the Buddha.[4]

This nondualistic understanding of the relationship of the sacred and secular was, of course, an entailment of widespread Japanese Buddhist convictions about "original awakening" (*hongaku*). In the context of Zen practice, this understanding underlay Dōgen's claim that *zazen* is not a means to enlightenment, but rather the embodied expression of its meaning. But it also served to give religious warrant to artistic endeavors. If all things are originally and thoroughly suffused with Buddha-nature, creating works of art can also be doing the work of the Buddha. In this sense, the Zen transmission of Chinese cultural practices to Japan was not just a way of earning elite support. Engaging in poetry, calligraphy, painting, and garden design demonstrated that cultural production could also be enlightening—an enactment and refining of the truth of nondualism.

Zen continued to be associated with the arts throughout the Edo period, directly through the artistic endeavors of aesthetically gifted monks and nuns, and indirectly by serving as a source of inspiration for secular artists. As is true today, explicitly artistic pursuits were most common in Japan's urban centers. The capital of the shogunate, Edo (contemporary Tokyo), had a population of over a million people (larger than either Paris or London) in the early eighteenth century and was a center for the production of popular arts and culture. The imperial capital, Kyōto, had a population of over four hundred thousand and was the epicenter of elite art activity. Many of the Edo period Zen masters with considerable artistic leanings like Hakuin (1685–1769), Torei Enji (1721–1792), and Sengai Gibon (1750–1837) were from the Rinzai tradition and were well known in urban elite circles.

Among those devoted to both the monastic life and artistic excellence associated with Sōtō Zen, none were as well loved and committed to living among the common people as Daigu Ryōkan (1758–1831). A literal translation of Ryōkan's full name would be the "great fool of positive abundance"—a name that he certainly lived up to over the course of a life spent largely in the countryside, dwelling in a humble hermit shack, begging for his food, and cavorting with village children with uninhibited and infectious joy. Yet Ryōkan managed also to gain a national reputation as a poet capable of combining an appreciation for the latest poetry coming from China with an ability to express the aesthetic spirit of the "golden era" of Heian period Japanese arts. Famous for saying that he did not like poetry by poets or cooking by cooks, Ryōkan embodied an ideal of meditation in action that was expressed in the Buddha's identification of mindfulness with the realization of "seeing" in the absence of either a "seer" or anything "seen"—the realization of being present without-self (*anatman*). For him, everyday relationships with other people and with nature were the ultimate canvas for expressing the "Zen" aesthetic values of irregularity (*fukinsei*), simplicity (*kanso*), unpretentious naturalness (*shizen*), tranquility (*seijaku*), and freedom from convention (*datsuzoku*).⁵

By the end of the Edo period, as Japan was opening fully again to global interactions and beginning a self-conscious process of modernization, Sōtō Zen was the most widely practiced Buddhist tradition. Although generalities can be overdrawn, if Rinzai had become the Zen of warrior and aristocratic elites, Sōtō had become the Zen of the common people.

6

ŌBAKU ZEN

By the Edo period, Zen narratives about the origins of Rinzai and Sōtō traditions typically began with the arrival of Chan teachings, practices, and institutions and then charted the evolution that they underwent as they took root and flourished in Japan. But while the Chinese origins of Chan were crucial to Rinzai and Sōtō expressions of their own religious identities, the primary significance of Zen's Chinese derivation was that it enabled tracing a direct line of person-to-person transmissions back to the historical Buddha. The religious authenticity of Rinzai and Sōtō Zen did not rest on being Chinese, but on being "purer" expressions of Buddhism than other forms of Japanese Buddhism.

The dramatic embrace of Ōbaku Zen was in contrast inseparable from its being culturally Chinese and from the questions its arrival compelled about the purity or authenticity, not of other kinds of Buddhism in Japan, but of Japanese Zen.[1] As already noted, the arrival of Chinese monks associated with the Ōbaku (Ch: Huangbo) line of Linji Chan stimulated and helped to nurture a new kind of critical self-consciousness within both the Rinzai and Sōtō communities. But the impacts of Ōbaku institutions and practices extended well beyond monastic discussions about issues of lineage authenticity.

Within a century of its arrival in Japan, Ōbaku Zen was being practiced at over a thousand temples in Japan. To give a sense of the rapidity of its growth, while there were only ten Dharma heirs produced in the second generation after Ōbaku's arrival in the mid-seventeenth century, in the third generation there were 123, and in the sixth generation over one thousand monks were recognized as Ōbaku Zen masters or lineage holders. This rate of growth signals an extraordinary interest in Ōbaku within the Zen monastic community, but also an impressive degree of interest from among those able to sponsor new temples and sustain growing monastic communities. Indeed, the vast majority of Ōbaku monks and lay practitioners were from samurai and aristocratic families, and Ōbaku had significant support from both the Tokugawa shogunate and imperial circles.

A partial explanation for the rapidity with which Ōbaku established itself in Japan is the timing of its arrival during a period when many leading Rinzai thinkers were increasingly critical about the quality of practice taking place in Japan and were actively advocating a "return to ancient ways." The Ōbaku stress on the strict observation of precepts and textual study resonated well with this movement for Rinzai reform. But Ōbaku also appealed to members of the Sōtō community, as well as to laypeople with no immediate interest in issues of monastic discipline or in the study of Chinese-language texts. This suggests that Ōbaku Zen offered something timely, not just in terms of the historical trajectory of the Rinzai Zen tradition into which it was eventually absorbed, but also in terms of the religious needs of the Japanese people.

HISTORICAL CONTEXTS

The arrival of Ōbaku Zen in Japan occurred in the 1650s, a little more than a decade after the Tokugawa shogunate effectively closed Japan to foreigners following a peasant rebellion led by Christian converts. The new Tokugawa rulers, while appreciative of some aspects of accelerating trade with China and Europe, had been skeptical about whether a globally connected Japan offered the best prospects for maintaining social order and political control. A series of political incidents linked to the activities of Christian missionaries led to a ban on foreign travel by Japanese subjects in 1635. And a few years later, a large-scale rebellion led by Christian converts on the Shimabara Peninsula seemingly confirmed Tokugawa fears that continued foreign contacts would ultimately be destabilizing.

In 1639, the Tokugawa *bakufu* closed all but one of Japan's ports: Nagasaki. Foreigners were evicted from Japanese soil, and trade with

Europeans was allowed only through Dutch intermediaries (who were perceived as having purely secular interests), and then only on a two-acre artificial island in the middle of the Nagasaki harbor. Chinese and other Asian traders and merchants, however, were allowed to enter the city and maintain warehouses, shops and residences. With several thousand residents, the Chinese community in Nagasaki was able to support Confucian and Buddhist temples—including three Zen/Chan temples—and enjoyed a steady stream of visiting merchants, craftsmen, monks, scholars, and artists from China.

The cultural vitality of the Chinese community in Nagasaki was at least partly a function of events on the continent. Over the course of the 1630s, Ming China lost virtually all of its lands north of the Great Wall to a Manchu-led coalition of Mongol and other nomadic peoples. Beset by both internal strife and invading forces, the Ming could not hold on to the capital of Beijing, and in 1643 the emperor committed suicide. In 1644, invading Manchu forces claimed the empire as their own. Although armed resistance would persist until 1683, especially along China's southeastern coast, China had once again fallen under foreign control.

Much as had happened when the Mongols conquered China in the thirteenth century, the founding of the Manchu Qing dynasty triggered significant emigration from China. Among those who made the dangerous sea crossing to the Japanese islands were a number of relatively well-regarded Chan monks. The first of these, Daozhe Chaoyuan (1602–1662), actively taught in Nagasaki from 1651 to 1658 before returning to China. During his stay, he attracted quite a large following of Japanese monks who were favorably impressed with his strict approach to monastic discipline and the obvious depth of his Buddhist understanding. Among his students were many Sōtō monks, but also the Rinzai monk Bankei, who received Dharma transmission from Daozhe and was part of his community in Nagasaki for several years before leaving to live in retreat near the ancient capital of Nara.

The second important monk to arrive in Nagasaki was Yinyuan Longqi (1592–1673). A well-known lineage holder in the Huangbo (J: Ōbaku) line of Linji Chan, it is not clear what led Yinyuan to leave Fujian Province at the age of sixty-two and make the arduous journey to Japan. The fact that he was invited to assume the abbacy of Kōfukuji—one of the three Chan temples in the Chinese community in Nagasaki—would hardly have been compelling since at the time he was leader of the prestigious home temple of his lineage's founder. The political turmoil associated with the overthrow of the Ming and ongoing armed resistance—a substantial amount of it emanating out of Fujian—may also have factored into his decision. But given his stated intention of staying in Japan for just a few years, this seems not to have been a major consideration. The strongest evidence, perhaps, is that his primary considerations may have been connected to acrimonious lineage disputes in which he had apparently become embroiled.

Chinese Lineage Disputes and the Arrival of Ōbaku Zen in Japan

The last century of the Ming dynasty is often associated with a significant revival of interest in Chan Buddhism, fueled by fresh engagement with Tang and Song dynasty Chan discourse records, and by critical interest both in the biographies of eminent monks and the genealogies of their Dharma transmissions. Ironically, this surge of attention to Chan texts and genealogies triggered disputes about Chan identity that, for present purposes, can be seen as culminating in a 1654 lawsuit brought by Caodong monks against Yinyuan's master, Feiyin Tongrong (1593–1662). According to his Caodong accusers, Feiyin had "fudged" his data to produce a Chan genealogy that asserted the preeminence of his own lineage and effectively denied the existence of a legitimate Caodong line after the death of Rujing (Dōgen's teacher) in the early thirteenth century. Feiyin lost the lawsuit, and the original printing blocks for his Chan transmission record were burned. It was earlier that same year that Yinyuan left for China with thirty other monks. Within three years, Yinyuan had arranged for Feiyin's banned book to be printed in Japan and for copies to be carried back to China.[2] Whether Yinyuan's decision to travel to Japan was informed by his master's difficulties or not remains speculative. What is not a matter of speculation is that his arrival was widely anticipated, and that it coincided with intensifying Japanese concerns about the authenticity of Zen Dharma transmissions and with the rise of "sectarian consciousness" (shūtōishiki)—the emergence of discourses about religious identity that invoked the existence of relatively sharp and exclusive boundaries between schools or traditions.

The fanfare surrounding Yinyuan's arrival in Nagasaki was considerable. Since the wave of émigré Chan monks from China that had occurred in connection with the Mongol conquests of the thirteenth century, Japanese Zen had developed largely on its own. Although travel to and from China had continued, including travel by Buddhist monks, there is no indication that this resulted in any major impacts on Zen's development. In both Rinzai and Sōtō settings, textual study had remained focused on Chan discourse records and *kōan* collections from the Song and early Yuan periods when Chan was being actively imported into Japan, and on the writings of eminent Japanese Zen teachers. In terms of practice, Zen had remained conservatively committed to a combination of sitting meditation (*zazen*) and *kōan* study. In short, Zen had remained contentedly unaffected by changes taking place in Chan on the Chinese mainland.

Stimulated in part by neo-Confucian discourses that stressed the need to look afresh at the core Confucian canon, in part by efforts among certain Japanese elites to revitalize engagement with Japan's own ancient traditions, and in part by a growing sense that Zen had lapsed into a period of protracted stagnancy, many mid-seventeenth-century Zen monks were ready for an infusion of new energy and thinking. With the Tokugawa ban on travel beyond Japan's borders, interacting with Chinese monks in Japan was particularly appealing—a practical alternative to exiting Japan illegally to study abroad in China. Through monks like Daozhe and others in the Chinese community in Nagasaki, it was known that there was an ongoing boom of Chan scholarship in China, including new editions of the Buddhist canon and of important Chan texts.

As a leading Chan master of the day whose written works had recently been brought to Japan, Yinyuan's arrival was much anticipated. A relatively large number of high-level Rinzai and Sōtō monks visited him during his first years in Nagasaki, and many were positively impressed. His stress on the strict observation of Chan monastic rules and on the necessity of face-to-face teaching relationships had a powerful appeal for Rinzai and Sōtō reformers who felt that Japanese Zen had become overly lax and formalistic.

Among the Rinzai monks most favorably disposed toward Yinyuan were Jikuin Somon (1611–1677) and Ryūkei Shōsen (1602–1670). As a former abbot of Myōshinji, the leading Rinzai temple of the day, Jikuin's endorsement of Yinyuan as a leading exemplar of Linji Chan and as a guiding light for the revitalization of Zen in Japan set a tone of open and productive engagement in Rinzai circles. Jikuin was instrumental in having the *bakufu* ban on Chinese traveling outside of Nagasaki lifted in Yinyuan's case, and in setting up the latter's initial trip to Kyōto. But it was Ryūkei who worked most wholeheartedly on Yinyuan's behalf, eventually becoming Yinyuan's first Japanese Dharma heir. As the abbot of Ryōanji (a Kyōto temple famous for its exquisite sand and rock garden) and as someone who twice held the abbacy of Myōshinji (in 1651 and 1654), Ryūkei was particularly well connected both in Rinzai circles and with *bakufu* officials and imperial elites. Through the joint efforts of Jikuin and Ryūkei, Yinyuan was permitted to take up residence in Kyōto and—after a personal meeting with the governor—to travel somewhat freely outside of the city. He was also introduced to the retired emperor, Go-Mizunoo, with whom he developed a particularly strong rapport.

In 1658, Ryūkei arranged for Yinyuan to have a personal audience in Edo with the reigning shogun, Tokugawa Ietsuno. This meeting set in motion a sequence of events that culminated a year later, when the *bakufu* granted Yinyuan twenty-two thousand acres of land outside of Kyōto to build a major Zen temple, along with a guarantee of annual support for up to four hundred resident monks. With additional donations of gold from shogunal officials, Yinyuan was able to begin construction of a new temple—a turn of events that seems to have helped convince him to remain in Japan rather than returning to China. Making use of the latest Ming dynasty architectural designs, he oversaw the construction of Ōbaku Zen's head temple, Manpukuji, which opened in 1663. Just ten years later, Manpukuji presided over twenty-four branch temples located throughout Japan.

A Mixed Reception

Not every Rinzai monk was as favorably impressed as Jikuin and Ryūkei with Yinyuan and his Ōbaku style of Zen. Yinyuan's arrival in Japan came at a time when support for Rinzai was not as robust as many would have liked, when the once-dominant *gozan* temple system was in apparent decline, and when the Tokugawa government took a generally controlling attitude toward Buddhism. In this context, the extraordinarily positive reception that was granted to Yinyuan by the shogunate served to crystallize concerns that had been circulating about Yinyuan and his entourage of Chinese monks since shortly after their arrival in Nagasaki.

One set of concerns centered on what some Japanese monks experienced as the cultural arrogance of the Chinese monks accompanying Yinyuan. At the Zen temples in Nagasaki's Chinese quarter, every aspect of daily life had an unmistakably Chinese flavor, including the food that was served, the manner in which meals were eaten, the kinds of robes and hairstyles worn by the monks, the music played during rituals, and of course the language spoken in both formal and informal settings. This was to be expected. Since these temples served an immigrant Chinese community, it was natural for Chinese cultural elements to be prominent in them. It was neither expected nor appreciated, however, that Yinyuan's students would engage their Japanese hosts with what seemed to be an air of unquestioned superiority.

It is certainly possible that the charges of "cultural chauvinism" leveled against Yinyuan and his students were based in relatively innocent failures to adjust to Japanese manners and customs in the initial period after their arrival. But nothing changed appreciably, even after Yinyuan had relocated to Kyōto. No adjustments were made to the character of temple life at Manpukuji even when Japanese monks there far outnumbered those from China. In fact, both Yinyuan and the Tokugawa *bakufu* apparently did not see Manpukuji as a Japanese Rinzai temple, but rather as a "purely" Chinese temple built on Japanese soil: an autonomous refuge of authentic Linji Chan practices and institutional protocols. Instead of being forced by the government to be placed within one of the existing Zen temple hierarchies—something required for all new Rinzai and Sōtō temples—Manpukuji was allowed an ambiguous and yet undeniably privileged, independent status.

In addition to their Chinese customs, Ōbaku monks from China also seem to have brought with them distinctly Chinese sectarian sensibilities. In keeping with Feiyin's reconstruction of Chan transmission genealogies, the members of Yinyuan's émigré community had no hesitation in regarding themselves as being at the historical pinnacle of Linji Chan: the current generation's legitimate representatives of Chan orthodoxy and orthopraxy. And there clearly were Japanese who were ready to embrace this as fact. Since Yinyuan was a direct descendant of Huangbo, Linji's grandfather in the Dharma, he was at least the equal of the present generation of Rinzai lineage holders in Japan. But because his line had been continuously Chinese, it was at least conceivably more direct and pure than those in Japan where adaptations to local conditions had taken place.

This was apparently the view of Yinyuan's most steadfast advocate, Ryūkei, who brought tensions surrounding the Ōbaku presence in Japan to a critical head by suggesting that Yinyuan be granted the purple robes

of a preeminent Rinzai master and installed as abbot of Myōshinji. As the
head temple of the dominant Ōtōkan lineage that had been built by the
lineage founder, Kanzan Egen, on the grounds of the former palace of
Emperor Hanazono, this would have symbolically granted leadership of
the most vibrant Rinzai Zen community to a foreigner. This proposal was
rejected outright by such well-respected Rinzai authorities of the day as
Gudō Tōshoku (1577–1661) and Daigu Sōchiku (1584–1669). But the
fact that it was forwarded seriously by Ryūkei is a powerful indicator
both of the degree to which some Rinzai monks were longing for real and
significant change, and of the depth of their skepticism about the prospects of such a change coming from within the Japanese Rinzai community.

It does not seem that Yinyuan himself aspired to a "takeover" of
Rinzai authority. He seemed, instead, more interested in simply consolidating Ōbaku's presence while at the same time ensuring its distinctively
Chinese character. As part of its founding mandate, the abbacy of Manpukuji was to be given only to qualified Chinese monks, and even at the
Ōbaku branch temples headed by native Japanese, it was clear that the
material and cultural character of Ōbaku communities were to remain
explicitly Chinese. In fact, the first appointment of a Japanese monk to
the abbacy of Manpukuji would not occur until the fourteenth generation,
almost a hundred years after Yinyuan's arrival. In short, Ōbaku temples
were designed to function as outposts of Chinese Chan in Japan, not to
compete with those associated with Rinzai.

This might have been acceptable if Ōbaku presented no challenge to
Japanese Rinzai hierarchies. But this was not entirely the case. Reservations about Yinyuan and his community intensified over time, especially
in connection with issues surrounding the role of monastic precepts in
Zen and the sectarian boundaries asserted by Ōbaku expressions of their
own identity in relation to Rinzai. The group at Myōshinji that was most
opposed to Yinyuan held that observing the precepts should not be undertaken slavishly in accordance with a literal reading of the monastic code,
but in a spirit of spontaneous, responsive genius characteristic of the heart
(*kokoro*) of Zen awakening. Although a revitalization of Rinzai surely
entailed a restoration of sincere observation of the precepts, the route to
this was not externally imposed discipline but internally generated realization.

In addition to the way the Ōbaku sharpened existing Rinzai debates about the proper approach to precept observation, disparities in how Ōbaku was viewed in relation to Rinzai posed still deeper identity challenges. The issues involved were epitomized in the terms used to refer to Ōbaku from outside and from within. The official phrase used by outsiders through the Edo period was *Rinzaishū Ōbaku ha*, or the "Rinzai lineage, Obaku branch." Ōbaku monks, however, referred to themselves as members of the *Rinzaishōshū*, or "True Linji lineage," implying that only they had legitimate claim to being Linji's Dharma heirs. Especially at a time when government and elite support for Ōbaku was growing, effectively drawing resources away from Rinzai, this could not simply be dismissed as a purely semantic matter. In a society that was literally closed, in which support for Zen was finite, and in which the growth of Japanese Zen was legally restricted, the spread of Chinese-led Ōbaku was more than just a curiosity; it was an institutional threat.

One of the most vocal and relentless critics of Ōbaku was Jikuin's Dharma heir, Mujaku Dōchū (1653–1744). Dropping any pretense of "argument by relegation," Mujaku directly attacked Yinyuan and his heirs with the aim of refuting their claims to being the most authentic representatives of Linji Chan. Making use of an array of stories from those who had expectantly met and then become disenchanted by Yinyuan, Mujaku painted a very unflattering picture of Yinyuan as a fame-seeking and morally deficient example of Chan chicanery, not authenticity. In addition, he undertook a critique of Yinyuan's Ōbaku monastic code, published in 1673, countering it with his own Rinzai monastic code—a code that was later embraced by Hakuin as part of his reform efforts, and which remains in use to this day. Often referred to as the father of modern Zen scholarship, Mujaku was a fierce advocate for restoring Rinzai to its true origins. And based on his extensive study of Chan texts and commentaries, he concluded that they offered no support for taking Yinyuan as a guide for such a restoration.

Ōbaku Syncretism: Rinzai Reservations

Among the troubling elements in Yinyuan's codification of the Ōbaku Zen monastic regimen were instructions for using Pure Land Buddhist sutras in the daily practice of sutra recitation, and instructions that monks enter and exit the practice hall chanting the *nembutsu*, formally invoking the support of Amida Buddha. While some of the first Rinzai monks to participate in the traditional Zen summer and winter retreats held in Yinyuan's Nagasaki temple described the overall approach to Zen there as "Pure Land on the outside, Zen on the inside," roughly a century later, Hakuin, the prime architect of Rinzai reforms, derisively described Ōbaku practice as "Zen on the outside, Pure Land on the inside."

The blending of Pure Land and Zen practices and texts was not unheard of in Japan. But by the time of Yinyuan's arrival in Nagasaki, it was almost universally considered by Rinzai and Sōtō monks to be a mistake—at least for any but the least serious or capable practitioners. The culture of Zen practice was based on the conviction that enlightenment could be realized and expressed only on the basis of one's own sincere effort. Although eminent Chan masters like Huineng might speak about birth in the Pure Land, they explicitly used this as a metaphor: the "Pure Land" was not some distant place; it was one's own mind. As the Pure Land (*Jōdo-shū*) and the True Pure Land (*Jōdo-shinshū*) traditions had developed in Japan, they expressed the opposing view that in an age of the decline of the Dharma (*mappō*) it was impossible to attain liberation through any means other than the *nembutsu*; liberation could be attained only by relying on the saving grace and power of Amida. Indeed, according to the Pure Land and True Pure Land founders, Hōnen and Shinran, undertaking any other practices would be harmful.

When Yinyuan stepped off the boat in Nagasaki, then, he unexpectedly stepped into a fractious opposition of Zen reliance on self-power (*jiriki*) and Pure Land reliance on other-power (*tariki*). The possibility of combining Chan and Pure Land practices had been entertained with varying degrees of seriousness from very early in the development of Chan as a distinctive Buddhist tradition in China. The general view through the Tang and Song dynasties was that although combined practice was possible, the advantages were at best modest, with a much greater potential for it proving problematic. But the idea that Chan and Pure Land practices and teachings might complement one another became widespread over the latter part of the Yuan and into the Ming dynasty. For Yinyuan and his Chinese contemporaries, as long as *nembutsu* was practiced to realize the nonduality of subject and object, there was no conflict between it and either *zazen* or *kōan* practice. Especially for lay practitioners, the *nembutsu* could be effectively used as the focus of *kanhua* practice—using the *nembutsu* as a kind of *kōan*: "Who, right now, is chanting Amida's name?"

By the time of Hakuin's mid-eighteenth-century reforms, this very limited combination of Zen and Pure Land in the form of the "*nembutsukōan*" was generally considered acceptable in Rinzai circles. What was not acceptable was the mandated use of the *nembutsu* as part of the daily rituals associated with monastic training. This had always been at the core of Rinzai charges of Ōbaku syncretism, but over the first half of the eighteenth century it became a major focus of anti-Ōbaku polemic.

ŌBAKU'S SUCCESS AS AN INDEPENDENT ZEN TRADITION

The foregoing account of Yinyuan arrival and the initial receptions of his approach to Zen might give the impression that Ōbaku was treated skeptically at best by the Zen establishment. But that would be a mistake. Over the first decades of Ōbaku presence in Japan, there were many from within Rinzai and Sōtō monastic circles who energetically embraced Yinyuan's articulation of authentic Chan practice. Primary among this group were seasoned monks who believed that only a resolute commitment to strictly observing monastic precepts would enable a systemic revitalization of Zen in Japan. Many of them left their home temples, in effect giving up the possibility of receiving (or retaining) Dharma transmission in their original lineage. Making such a decision is evidence of a very sincere level of commitment to what was still a very small Zen community with a quite uncertain future.

One source of appeal was the Ōbaku stress on the scholarly study of the Buddhist canon and of Chan texts in particular. While Japanese Zen training made use of compilations of *kōans* that had been excerpted from much longer encounter dialogues and often stressed rote memorization of responses in Chinese over insight, Yinyuan and his Ōbaku Dharma heirs made use of the full texts of a wide range of encounter dialogues. Ōbaku masters were also known to "invent" new *kōans* in response to specific students' needs and to engage in lively interaction that included real shouts and kicks—one of the hallmarks of Feiyin's style of Chan. These differences were perceived as evidence of a flexibility and rigor that were very attractive when contrasted to some of the formulaic approaches to Zen training that had become accepted norms in Japan.

One of the earliest Japanese monks to commit to Ōbaku was Tetsugen Dōkō (1630–1682). Originally ordained in the True Pure Land tradition, Tetsugen was among Yinyuan's first students and worked closely with Yinyuan's most senior Dharma heir, Muan Xingtao (1611–1684), who would become the second abbot of Manpukuji and a primary force for the institutional expansion of Ōbaku. Tetsugen was more interested in scholarly work than institution building, however. His major contribution to Ōbaku's positive reputation in Japan was his editorial work that led to the first publication in Japan of the entire forty-eight-thousand-page Ming dynasty version of the Chinese Buddhist canon—an effort that entailed commissioning the carving of over seven thousand individual woodblock plates.

Another of Yinyuan's early "converts" to Ōbaku was Chōon Dōkai (1628–1695). Whereas Tetsugen was by nature reclusive and scholarly, Chōon was a gifted and, it would seem, charismatic speaker. Although he was an avid student of Buddhist texts, Chōon also was interested in Confucianism and Shintō, and this gave him a wide and very effective angle for approaching members of the samurai and aristocratic classes. He was the founding abbot of several Ōbaku temples and over the course of his career added more than twenty temples to the Ōbaku network.

Chōon was among the first generation of Japanese Ōbaku monks to travel throughout Japan with the expressed intention of bringing Ōbaku Zen to the common people and others living outside of Japan's major urban areas. This was not a simple matter since the absence of a nationwide system of Ōbaku temples at the time meant that a traveling monk would have nowhere to take shelter or practice while on the road. Some monks would find an abandoned temple or hermitage to use as a temporary shelter; others would stay in the homes of supportive laypeople (a practice that invited the scorn of other Zen monastics). Having done so, they would interact with the local population much as Sōtō monks had during the days of Sōtō Zen's national expansion in the fourteenth and fifteenth centuries—finding ways of presenting Zen that would be relevant in the lives of farmers, villagers, and small-town samurai.

One of the common practices undertaken by Ōbaku—as well as both Rinzai and Sōtō—monks was to offer laymen and laywomen the opportunity to participate in precept-taking ceremonies. These might be ceremonies that would commit a layperson to following basic monastic vows regarding both moral and material conduct for a specific period of time. Or they might consist in taking lay precepts that would identify them as having made a religious commitment to Zen, often in connection with efforts to make merit and affect the karma of their families and villages. Over the course of his career, Chōon is said to have bestowed precepts on more than one hundred thousand laypeople, an extraordinary indication both of his own charisma and the appeal of Ōbaku Zen.

In interacting with commoners and those without the Chinese-language skills needed to engage in textual or *kōan* study, offering *nembutsu* practice as an initial entry point for Zen practice is likely to have been an advantage for Ōbaku monks. *Zazen* is a relatively simple practice requiring little in the way of ritual accoutrements—just a cushion of the sort common in a culture accustomed to sitting on the floor and a relatively quiet space. But it also requires not being otherwise involved in mundane activities—a relative luxury for the vast majority of the population. One of the appeals of Pure Land Buddhism among the common people had been that its core practice—the *nembutsu*—could be carried out virtually any place, at any time. The "synthetic" Zen offered by Ōbaku enabled many people who otherwise would not have been able to undertake Zen practice to do so in earnest. In fact, one of the distinguishing features claimed for their own approach to Zen by Ōbaku practitioners is that it was "universal"—a Zen that was not just for the landed and wealthy elite, but everyone.

Another important dimension of Ōbaku efforts to engage a wider public was the remarkable willingness, exhibited even by many senior monks, to engage in practical work on behalf of the common people, including building bridges, clearing canals, and providing food and shelter to those impacted by natural disasters. This willingness, by itself, is likely to have had a profound and positive impact on those unaccustomed to being given more than passing consideration by those enjoying higher social, economic, and political status. The fact that Ōbaku monks were not just passing through but making an effort to put down roots in the local community would have generated a sense of shared purpose that is likely to have been missing in their encounters with monks associated with already-established systems of Zen temples. In a very real sense, although Ōbaku monks had "left the home life" by taking monastic vows, they were nevertheless looking to make homes for themselves among the people.

All of this was possible, of course, because Ōbaku also had the support of the Tokugawa *bakufu*. As part of their efforts to restrict the political power of Buddhist institutions, the Tokugawa government placed a ban on the construction of new temples and required all Zen temples to be affiliated with one of a small number of hierarchic, government-recognized temple networks. The exceptions to policy that allowed Yinyuan to build Manpukuji and that allowed temples from other Zen networks to be "removed" and placed under the jurisdiction of the growing Ōbaku system were, in fact, extraordinary. And in all likelihood, these exceptions were granted less out of religious appreciation for Ōbaku than in an effort to counterbalance the power of existing Zen institutions. Since Chinese could only enter Japan through the explicit permission of the *bakufu*, the government was in a position to exercise considerable control over who would serve as abbot at Manpukuji. It was also in a position to deny travel rights entirely should there be any question of Ōbaku monks or temples engaging in politically threatening activities.

At the same time, Tokugawa shoguns, elite samurai, and members of the aristocracy were interested in keeping abreast of the latest cultural developments in China. Chinese Ōbaku monks were well known for their cultural acumen, and many were very accomplished calligraphers, painters, and poets. The fact that the Tokugawa *bakufu* was effectively able to control the circulation of this "cultural capital" is also likely to have been a factor in their ongoing support of Ōbaku.

These practical reasons for endorsing and supporting the spread of Ōbaku need to be seen against the backdrop of Ōbaku's appeal both to the common people at one end of the social spectrum, and to the imperial family and members of the court at the other end. The retired emperor Go-Mizunoo had a serious personal interest in Zen and enjoyed a very close relationship with Yinyuan's first Japanese Dharma heir, Ryūkei. Beginning with invitations for Ryūkei to lecture on Zen for the imperial family and courtiers, this relationship eventually became a true master–student relationship. Go-Mizunoo studied Zen with Ryūkei until the latter's death—a period of over nine years, in the course of which he attained enlightenment and was granted Dharma transmission.

Even though his role as retired emperor made it impossible for him to undertake the duties typical for Zen masters, Go-Mizunoo clearly regarded Ryūkei as his master and took responsibility for ensuring the survival of his line. This was complicated since Ryūkei had not designated any other Dharma heir—a fact that in Ōbaku, with its focus on face-to-face transmission, would have meant an end to Ryūkei's line. Instead, Go-Mizunoo used his considerable influence to arrange (somewhat controversially) for the warrior-led government to allow an exception so that a suitable monk could be awarded Ryūkei's posthumous certification as Dharma heir. Aside from illustrating the power of the imperial family, even under Tokugawa military rule, this incident also offers evidence of Ōbaku Zen's transformative contribution to Japanese religious life.

Zen Family Matters: The Status of Ōbaku within Japanese Zen

Seen from a purely institutional perspective, Ōbaku became an independent Zen tradition in Japan at the point that Yinyuan was granted permission to construct Manpukuji and was exempted from Tokugawa policy that would have required placing Ōbaku temples and monks within an existing Rinzai temple network. It has maintained this status throughout its history, with the exception of a brief period during the 1870s when the Meiji government classified it as a branch (*ha*) of Rinzai. From the opening dedication of Manpukuji in 1663, there have been three "members" in the Zen family or ancestral lineage (*zenshū*), each living in their own separate institutional "homes."

Seen from a religious perspective, matters are not quite so clear cut. The complexion of Ōbaku practices and monastic regulations, with its affirmative inclusion of Pure Land elements, sets Ōbaku clearly apart from both Rinzai and Sōtō. But the border space separating it from these other traditions is not sharply defined. Even in the case of Hakuin, who vehemently denied Pure Land practices any official place in Rinzai monastic life, an attitude of accommodation was taken toward laypeople making use, for example, of *nembutsu* recitation as a meditative technique. Ōbaku's religious "syncretism" places it at an indeterminate distance from Rinzai and Sōtō. A useful analogy might be that in terms of practice regimens, the three members of the Zen family all have the same basic "diet," but Ōbaku practitioners regularly and happily partake in limited Pure Land fare while those in Rinzai and Sōtō do so only irregularly and with a certain amount of misgiving.

The claim that Ōbaku Zen carried on the "true lineage" of the Chinese Chan master Linji—the ninth-century Chinese ancestor shared by Ōbaku and Rinzai—is more complicated since it raises issues of inheritance and "purity" in relation to Rinzai. But there seems not to have been any systematic attempt by Ōbaku monks to alter Rinzai's status within the Zen family. Instead, Ōbaku's claims in relation to it carrying on the "true lineage" of Linji seem to have been aimed at ensuring the legitimacy in Japan of its own, culturally Chinese approach to Zen.

Ultimately, the differences among Ōbaku, Rinzai, and Sōtō are not a function of doctrinal disparities but of practical emphases. That is, they are differences about correct practice, not about correct teachings. As such, questions about their statuses relative to one another are answerable in terms of what is most effective or least effective, rather than what is true or false. Whereas questions of truth are often assumed to have answers of universal relevance, questions about what is effective necessarily point us in the direction of further questions—effective for whom, in what circumstances, for which purposes? The fact that in less than a hundred years, Ōbaku grew from a small community of immigrant monks to a nationwide system of over a thousand temples suggests that for many Japanese it provided convincingly apt answers to these more existentially framed questions—offering sufficiently distinctive religious sustenance for Ōbaku to remain a vibrant part of the Zen family.

7

ZEN IN A MODERNIZING JAPAN

The Tokugawa *bakufu* generally aimed to limit the political influence of religious institutions. While the government's stance toward Zen was fairly supportive and its household registration policy helped to ensure the financial stability of Zen temples, the government also exercised considerable control over both the internal dynamics of Zen communities and their relationships with the general public. The overthrow of the shogunate in 1868 and the restoration of direct imperial rule had a dramatic and complex impact on Zen as Japan opened to global influences and began embracing modern ideals and institutions.

The Tokugawa regime had carefully circumscribed Zen's religious authority and made sure that Zen's public presence remained consonant with maintaining social order and state security. Later generations of Buddhist historians predominantly came to see this relationship as having brought about the spiritual stagnation of Zen. From such a perspective, it might be imagined that the overthrow of the regime would result in a restoration of spiritual vitality as Zen communities were released from shogunal regulations and policies. In actuality, the conditions that made the Meiji Restoration possible were not conducive to a new "golden age" of Zen. Along with other Buddhist traditions, Zen found itself in much greater jeopardy.

ANTI-BUDDHIST FALLOUT OF THE MEIJI RESTORATION

The sequence of events that culminated in the dissolution of the Tokugawa *bakufu* began more than a decade and a half earlier, in 1853, when American warships entered the harbor at Edo (modern-day Tōkyō) with the intent of pressuring Japan to open its ports to American traders. An open-port treaty was signed the following year when Commodore Matthew Perry returned with eight ships, precipitating a storm of controversy. Since the political legitimacy of the shogunate was rooted in its supposed military prowess, the fact that the government could not prevent the entry of just a handful of foreign warships gave considerable warrant to those who questioned the shogun's right to rule and sought to place the emperor back in direct political power.

Although the general ban on foreign travel to and from Japan had remained in place since the 1640s, access to foreign books—especially military treatises, scientific texts, and technical manuals—had been permitted since the latter part of the eighteenth century. By the mid-nineteenth century, Japanese were well aware of the Industrial Revolution and the way it was reshaping patterns of global power. China's humiliating defeat at the hands of the British in the so-called Opium War and the forced opening of increasing numbers of Chinese ports were lessons not lost on the Japanese. China's cultural achievements, its Confucian model of moral rule, and the ritual protections offered by its Buddhist institutions were no match for European and American industrial and military power.

Questioning the Past and Nation Building

The crisis of confidence in Tokugawa rule and accelerating demands for a restoration of imperial rule did not occur in a vacuum, however, and they were not caused entirely by external forces. In the early part of the eighteenth century, Japanese thinkers were already beginning to rationally dismantle the medieval Japanese worldview that had been built with Buddhist and Confucian conceptual resources imported from China. Among the earliest and most insightful of these thinkers was Tominaga Nakamoto (1715–1746), who developed a theory of historical layering or sedimentation to explain the development of cultural traditions and the worldviews expressed through them. Making use of an almost "postmodern" method, Tominaga undertook a meticulous deconstruction of not only Buddhist and Confucian, but also Shintō, cosmologies and claims to truth. In each tradition, he argued, truth claims were not grounded in careful reasoning or in experientially validated facts, but rather in texts and narratives that were historically contingent artifacts that expressed "truths" relative to specific times, places, and peoples. Whatever these traditions might claim about their texts and narratives, their contents were neither universally nor eternally valid. [1]

Inspired by Tominaga's critique of Confucianism and Buddhism, "Native Studies" (*Kokugaku*) thinkers like Motoori Norinaga (1730–1801) took the underlying thesis that truths are specific to peoples, times, and places and began looking to Japan's past as a source of truths for the reconstruction of Japanese society in accord with essentially Japanese values and concepts. As works of Western philosophy, history, and science made their way into Japan, influential Native Studies and "Ancient Ways" thinkers like Hirate Atsutane (1776–1843) somewhat ironically made use of modern scientific discourses to externally validate the universality and ultimate superiority of Japan's ancient traditions—a view that became a rallying cry for later nineteenth-century exponents of state Shintō. [2] By the time of the Meiji Restoration, Japanese Buddhism was in general on the defensive. For many of those clamoring for change, Buddhism was a foreign religion that had mired the Japanese people in superstition and drained national resources for over a thousand years. The Meiji Charter Oath, issued in 1868 by the emperor when he resumed the throne as the ruler of Japan, stated in no uncertain terms that all "evil customs of the past" would be severed at their roots and no expense spared in seeking the world over for knowledge relevant to strengthening the Japanese nation. Less than a year later, the Meiji government issued the first of a series of "separation edicts" that mandated the separation of Buddhist temples and Shintō shrines. In a direct attack on the financial solvency of Buddhist institutions, the government also mandated that Shintō shrines take responsibility for conducting household registrations and funerals.

This national blow would have been bad enough, but a number of local and regional movements to eradicate all debilitating foreign influences began issuing violence-condoning calls to strengthen the nation by "discarding Buddhism and destroying Shakyamuni (Buddha)" (*haibutsu-kishaku*). Although these abolitionist movements were never a truly na-

tional phenomenon or fully endorsed by the state, the result was nevertheless stunning. From 1868 to 1874, tens of thousands of Buddhist temples
were either closed or destroyed, and perhaps as many as a fourth of all
Buddhist monks and nuns were forced to return to lay life.

This period of outright attack on Buddhist institutions lasted only half
a decade. But the Meiji government policy of national strengthening had
long-term and dramatic impacts on Buddhism. Taking inspiration from
European and American models, national strengthening in Japan was
understood as grounded, first, on rapid industrialization and modernization, and, second, on constructing and celebrating an essentially Japanese
national character (*kokusui*). The summative effect was a dual embrace of
rational universalism and of Japanese particularism—an uneasy fusion of
openness to learning from global exemplars mixed with deepening cultural exceptionalism. In this new political and intellectual climate, it became apparent to at least some in the Zen community that the tapestry of
medieval Buddhist rituals and concepts needed to be rewoven or it would
irreversibly unravel.

ZEN AND MODERNITY

Three broad currents of change in Zen emerged over the course of the late
nineteenth and early twentieth century in response to the effects of modernization, especially the changes brought about by the combination of
nation building, industrialization, and globalization. Two of these currents focused primarily on redefining Zen's contribution to Japanese
identity in the context of Japan's commitments to "self-strengthening"
through nation-state development and industrialization. The third current
developed in response to global engagements with issues of universality
and religious identity, transposing Zen teachings and practices into transnational frames of reference as a Japanese contribution to world culture.

Strengthening the Nation: Zen as Collaborator and Critic

Officially approved efforts to alienate Buddhist institutions from the political and social order were curtailed by the mid-1870s. The consensus
vision of new government leadership was that both Shintō and Buddhist
traditions should be drafted into service as part of Japan's self-strengthen-

ing and nation-building initiatives. A Ministry of Doctrine was created to promote loyalty to the emperor and the popular embrace of Meiji commitments to transform Japan into a powerful nation destined for global greatness. Shintō and Buddhist teachers were invited to become founding members of a Great Teaching Academy (Daikyōin), which had the primary purpose of serving the nation by designing and implementing educational projects focused on moral indoctrination and the inculcation of modern, nationalist values.

A number of Rinzai and Sōtō monks embraced this task. Some went so far as to acknowledge that Zen had become too self-serving over preceding generations and that it had deserved much of the harsh criticism it suffered during the first years of the Meiji Restoration. But even apart from those associated with the Great Teaching Academy, a significant number of Zen teachers in this period committed to serving the public good by actively supporting the government's nation-building and modernization efforts. Many in the Sōtō community did so by working to update the traditional educational role of Zen temples as places where people could learn to read and write, gain basic proficiency in arithmetic, and other useful life skills. Sōtō temples were actively turned to the task of participating in the government's aim of building a universal basic education system, and by the 1890s the curriculum at many Zen temples included not just reading and writing in Japanese (and Chinese), but also instruction in Confucian ethics, mathematics, science, medicine, and even English. Rinzai and Sōtō monks were sent to study abroad, and the first Zen-sponsored universities were established: Komazawa University (Sōtō) and Hanazono University (Rinzai).

Alongside these educational contributions to nation-building efforts, conferences and courses directed to the needs and interests of laypeople also became increasingly common, giving a new public face to Zen. Monks who had received academic training in the West—especially after the early 1890s—brought back with them new ways of thinking about religion in the public sphere, including the roles of religiously affiliated charitable societies. Some also brought back skills in the early Buddhist languages of Pali and Sanskrit, sparking both new intellectual interests in early Buddhist teachings and efforts to critically assess the history of Japan's Mahāyāna traditions. Zen monks began traveling to parts of Buddhist Asia where Theravada traditions predominated at the same time as the first Zen teachers were taking up residence and beginning to teach in Europe and the United States.

Other Zen teachers went far beyond efforts to educationally support Japanese modernization and nation building. From the 1890s onward, some Zen teachers began openly and enthusiastically endorsing Japan's imperial aspirations. Perhaps the most outspoken of these Zen teachers was the Sōtō master Iida Tōin (1863–1937), who proclaimed the nonduality of the Japanese imperial "wind" and the Buddhist "sun" as forces for bringing about "enlightening" change in the world. Some of those who espoused this "Imperial Way Zen" even went so far as to suggest that since Japan's military campaigns in China, Russia, and Korea were part of a "just war" to bring about a truly harmonious sphere of Asian co-prosperity, no ill karma would be made by those who fought and killed on behalf of the emperor and the nation.[3]

Troublingly, this particular current of Zen response to modernity persisted through the Second World War in both monastic and lay circles. Although it cannot be claimed that most Zen teachers embraced the radical nationalism of Imperial Way Zen, neither can it be claimed that the majority of Zen teachers and practitioners took an openly adversarial stance toward it. In the context of the Japanese government's increasing militarism and its ever more authoritarian approach to pursuing its expansionist goals and maintaining public order, it is perhaps understandable that Zen leaders were mostly silent in regard to the country's war efforts. As Japanese military aggression accelerated and expanded abroad, those who voiced objections at home—from both monastic and lay Buddhist perspectives—were subject to increasingly swift and severe repression. But the fact remains that the silence of the majority was politically and morally ambiguous, and a number of leading Zen monks and Zen-affiliated academics (especially those in the so-called Kyōto School of philosophy) did publicly endorse Japan's imperialism, even after a point in time when ignorance of atrocities being committed on the continent could not easily have been claimed.

These facts eventually led to some members of the monastic and lay Zen communities feeling that Zen itself was in need of explicit and profound self-criticism. Among the first to voice this perspective in the aftermath of Japan's defeat were the famous Kyōto School thinkers Nishitani Keiji (1910–1990) and Tanabe Hajime (1885–1962). And as will be discussed later, roughly a generation later, proponents of "critical Buddhism" in the 1980s would take this perspective to its logical conclusion by questioning whether the sociohistorical record of Zen was even consistent with referring to Zen as Buddhist. Yet these more radical efforts to expose the shortcomings of Imperial Way Zen can be seen as historically rooted in Buddhist activist movements that had already begun emerging in the final decades of the nineteenth century.

One of the early leaders of Buddhist activism, Furukawa Isamu (1871–1899), argued from a progressive humanist perspective that Buddhism needed to engage Japan's new social realities in ways that were freed from medieval superstitions and loyalties. Like many of the more critically minded Buddhists of his generation, Furukawa felt that the Meiji government's pursuit of industrial and military power did not represent a sustainable vision for realizing a just society, but also that the Buddhism of Japan's past did not speak with sufficient clarity to modern issues. He and other progressive Buddhists attempted to develop an alternative vision of a modern, Buddhist Japan, speaking out against Meiji authoritarianism and speaking out for a New Buddhism (*Shin Bukkyō*) capable of guiding Japan toward peaceful self-transformation.

As Japan's regional stance became more aggressive and its domestic policies more repressive, New Buddhist activists became correspondingly more pacifist and liberal. Some, like Inoue Shūten (1880–1945), placed Zen and Theravada Buddhism in conversation with the egalitarian ideals of European and American socialism. Drawing on experiences gained from travels in South and Southeast Asia and from contacts with the activist Chinese Chan teacher Taixu (1890–1945), Inoue contested both government policy and the "Imperial Way" identification of Zen with *bushidō* or the "warrior's way." As a result, like many other New Buddhist activists, he was subjected to increasing government surveillance, especially after the infamous Kōtoku Incident in 1910 when the government foiled a socialist-anarchist plot to assassinate the emperor—a plot implicating at least one Zen monk with whom Inoue had enjoyed close ties. This incident resulted in mass arrests of socialists and other political activists, as well as an amplification of government restrictions on freedom of speech and thought. Politically oriented Buddhist activism persisted, but with considerably less visibility and with almost no effect on Japan's headlong rush to stake imperial claims in East and Southeast Asia.[4] As mentioned earlier, some Zen thinkers responded to Japan's eventual defeat after the 1945 atomic bombings of Hiroshima and Nagasaki by calling for a revival of the self-critical approach of early-twenti-eth-century Buddhist activists and an explicit assessment of Zen's impli-cation in Japan's war efforts. During the period of Japanese reconstruc-tion, however, most Zen teachers and communities turned their energies primarily to helping the Japanese people grapple with the aftermath of defeat. For the first time in its history, Japan was occupied by invading forces. Most major urban areas had been bombed into rubble, rural com-munities had been stripped almost entirely of a generation of young men who had lost their lives overseas, and transportation infrastructure was in a shambles. Daily life was inseparable from working through the effects of severe physical, psychic, and social trauma.

During this period, it was natural for Zen thinkers like Hisamatsu Shin'ichi (1889–1980) to focus attention less on using Buddhism to en-gage issues of structural injustice than to address the daily-life sufferings of the Japanese people. For Hisamatsu, Zen had become too monastically focused and the Buddhist ideal of jointly realizing compassion and wis-dom had been compromised by an almost exclusive focus on practices aimed at achieving *satori*, or the personal experience of awakening. Zen could contribute to the transformation of society, but doing so required the inseparable fusion of liberating insight with compassionate action.[5]

It was not until decades later, in the 1980s, that the seeds of Zen self-criticism sown in the early twentieth century came into full flower. This was spurred by a radical claim made by two Sōtō tradition academics, Hakamaya Noriaki and Matsumoto Shirō. Arguing that Buddhism is fun-damentally critical in nature, they claimed that Japanese Zen did not qualify as a truly Buddhist tradition. For Hakamaya, Matsumoto, and others spearheading the "critical Buddhism" (*hihanbukkyō*) movement, Buddhism consists in the practice of critical investigation informed by rational commitments to realizing a just and ethical way of life. They argued that Japanese Buddhist teachings about "original enlightenment" and "Buddha-nature" had no basis in the earliest strata of the Buddhist canon and were also not products of either critical investigation or ethical engagement. Instead, they claimed that these concepts were the result of troubling, culturally specific forms of imagination that had been used historically to exempt social, political, and economic institutions from critical examination, resulting in the "justification" of rampant inequal-ities and untold suffering.[6]

This provocative and harsh "deconstruction" of Zen set off a storm of largely academic controversies related to Zen's complicity in the suffering wrought through Japanese militarism, the historical treatment of minorities in Japan, and the persistence of other forms of structural injustice. For many of those teaching and practicing Zen in the last decades of the twentieth century, this effort to "prune the *bodhi* tree" helped clarify the need to stress that there is no Zen practice in the absence of actively embracing the Buddhist ideal of suffusing one's environment with compassion, loving kindness, equanimity, and joy in the good fortune of others. But the idea that Buddha-nature, for example, is a "heterodox" concept has been less readily embraced and has itself been deconstructed as expressing an errant and essentialist (rather than relational) construction of Buddhism. From this perspective, critical Buddhism has the liability of resulting in a kind of Buddhist "fundamentalism" that would mandate not just pruning some branches of the Buddhist family tree, but cutting off some of its deepest spiritual roots.

In spite of this danger, however, it is perhaps useful to engage the critical Buddhist claim that Zen is not Buddhist as a historical *kōan*—one that recalls and reframes Dōgen's claim that there is no such thing as a Zen tradition and that our primary concern as practitioners is not to transmit legacies of past masters but to personally *exemplify* Buddhist awakening. As Dōgen himself so powerfully demonstrated, this can clearly include exemplifying wisdom in the form of superlative abilities for thinking and communicating. But Buddhist awakening has from earliest times also been conceived as the joint realization of wisdom and compassion, and this suggests that rational criticism has to be paired with responsive creativity—a fusion of universally valid insights with situation-focused actions aimed at responding to the needs of others in whatever ways needed to ease suffering and bring about increasingly liberating relational dynamics.

Transnational Zen: The Globalization of Buddhism as a World Religion

In addition to the currents of collaborative and critical engagement with Japan's modernization, there also emerged in the late nineteenth and early twentieth centuries a creative current of Zen response that attempted to marry Zen's uniquely Japanese character with a global religious vision. A key factor in this move to "globalize" Zen was the participation of Rinzai and Sōtō monks and laypersons in the 1893 World's Parliament of Religions.

Held in Chicago in conjunction with the World Columbian Exhibition—a forerunner of the World's Fairs—the World's Parliament of Religions was the first formal gathering of leaders representing both Euro-American and Asian religious traditions. The purpose of the gathering was to explore commonalities and share approaches to addressing such important issues of the day as education, labor rights, temperance, and poverty. In light of the stated priority of articulating a unified vision of progress for all of humankind, an implicit aim of the parliament was to express universal religious truths that could be delinked from the specificities of culture and ethnicity. With this goal in mind, the organizers invited representatives from what they determined to be the ten great "world religions"—Christianity, Judaism, Islam, Zoroastrianism, Hinduism, Jainism, Confucianism, Daoism, Shintō, and Buddhism—as well as from "new religions" like Bahá'í and Theosophy.

The representatives of Zen at the parliament included the Rinzai master Shaku Sōen (1859–1919) and his lay student and translator, Suzuki Daisetsu (1870–1968), who is more commonly known in the West as D. T. Suzuki. Sōen was himself a Dharma heir of Kōsen Sōon (1816–1892, also known as Imakita Kōsen)—a Rinzai master who was among the first to forward a "progressive" vision of Zen that made use of both Confucian and Western texts, and that gave significant attention to the needs of lay practitioners in a time of rapid and unpredictable change. In addition to his Rinzai training in Japan, Sōen had spent three years studying Theravada Buddhism and living the life of a wandering monk in Sri Lanka. On returning to Japan, he followed his teacher, Kōsen, in advocating for a new and more modern form of Zen that emphasized the importance of lay practice.

Sōen's participation in the World's Parliament of Religions served, among other things, to confirm his conviction that Zen should be spread throughout the world as a universal guide to life in an era of scientific and technological revolution. At the parliament, he delivered a paper on karma as a distinctively Buddhist concept and spoke on behalf of arbitration as an alternative to war. But unlike Inoue Shūten, Furukawa, and others advocating a new Buddhism for the modern age, Sōen was not an absolute pacifist. He subsequently defended Japan's military engagement with

Russia as a defense against foreign aggression that served to protect innocents, claiming that it could be seen as a just war. In addition, he openly identified the samurai spirit as having played a key and positive role in Japan's extraordinarily rapid and successful modernization. These views would later lead critics of Zen to see him as troublingly aligned with Imperial Way Zen. But seen in a more transnational context, his greater legacy consists in his conception of Zen not as a purely Japanese religious phenomenon but as a distinctive Japanese contribution to world culture.

Sōen spent nearly a year in the United States in 1905 and 1906, teaching and delivering lectures that were translated by his student D. T. Suzuki. After studying first with Kōsen and then with Sōen over an intense period of roughly four years, Suzuki had attained a spiritual breakthrough (*kenshō*) in 1897. Later that year, Sōen recommended him for a translator position in the United States at a relatively new publishing house dedicated to the academic exploration of religion and global spirituality. Over the next decade, in addition to translating Buddhist and Daoist texts, Suzuki undertook extensive reading in Western religious thought and intellectual history and began writing about Buddhism in English. After serving as translator for Sōen's tour of the United States, he spent nearly two years in London studying the works of the Christian mystic Emmanuel Swedenborg before returning to Japan in 1910 with his American bride to pursue a teaching career and his interest in presenting Buddhism to the West. In 1927, Suzuki founded the English-language journal *The Eastern Buddhist* and published the first of a three-volume series, *Essays on Zen Buddhism*. This series was followed by further books aimed at introducing Zen to a global audience, culminating in his 1959 book, *Zen and Japanese Culture*.

Writing over a period of modern history that included the First World War, the Great Depression, the Second World War, and an accelerating nuclear arms race between American and Soviet power blocs, Suzuki became the primary spokesperson for Zen in the West, eventually earning sufficient respect to be offered visiting teaching posts at such elite institutions as Columbia University and Harvard. His modernist vision of Zen as a means to directly experience reality—freed from the limitations of the individual ego and logic-bound rationality—appealed profoundly to a generation forced to bear global witness to the tragic consequences of personal cravings for power and the unenlightened uses (or abuses) of science and technology. Suzuki was not only an advocate for a "united Buddhism" (*tsūbukkyō*), suited to the needs of a rapidly changing Japan; he was also an advocate for globally embracing Zen as an antidote to the paroxysms of modernization—a means of disentangling oneself from the world's increasingly complex webs of social and cultural conditioning and personally realizing the timeless source of all authentic spirituality.

Consistent with his vision, Suzuki presented Zen as an ideal tradition unbounded by historical or institutional trappings—a universally valid religion of charismatically communicated personal transformation. At the same time, he presented Zen as an expression of uniquely Japanese propensities for naturalness and spontaneity tempered by almost warrior-like capacities for loyalty and trust. For Suzuki, the conceptual tension between presenting Zen as offering intimate access to the universal truth of all religions and as embodying uniquely Japanese cultural traits was itself a reflexive expression of the trans-rational nature of Zen. Viewing this tension as evidence of a contradiction was, in his view, a function of attachment to an either/or logic that blocked opening to the central Buddhist truth of nonduality.

Charitably understood, Suzuki's efforts to present the distilled "essence" of Zen—a Zen from which ritual and cosmology had been almost thoroughly jettisoned—were appropriately responsive and creative. Like contemporaries who were presenting science and democracy as global human achievements and not as products of Western European and American invention, Suzuki was intent on making Zen a part of the heritage and future of all humanity, not just the Japanese people.

Suzuki's Zen of almost mystically realized pure experience was not universally embraced. For example, fellow New Buddhist Inoue Shūten came to criticize Suzuki for his acceptance of the "necessity" of state censorship and his endorsement of the possibility of being both a good Buddhist and a good soldier. For Inoue, no legitimacy could be granted to state curtailments of freedoms of thought and speech, and no practicing Buddhist could with good conscience kill as a matter of obedience to military dictates. Others, like the renowned Chinese scholar of Chan Buddhism, Hu Shi (1891–1963), vehemently objected to Suzuki's imagination of a Zen stripped of history, culture, rituals, institutions, and sectarian divisions. Indeed, the mid-1950s debates between Hu and Suzuki mark a watershed both in the academic study of Chan and Zen and in the global development of Buddhist studies.

Deciding whether Suzuki was a key transmitter of Zen to the West or a purveyor of invented spiritual ideals that he labeled "Zen" is, however, perhaps less important than recognizing the importance of a transnational current of Zen responses to modernization and globalization over the last century. Monks like Imakita Kōsen and Shaku Sōen, activists like Inoue Shūten, and writers like Hisamatsu Shin'ichi and D. T. Suzuki were not "representatives" of Zen as it was understood and practiced by the majority of Japanese. But their efforts to actively reinvent Zen in response to emerging realities offered significant alternatives to approaches that reinforced what amounted to exclusive appeals to Japanese culture and nation.

In some ways, the efforts of these exponents of modern Zen can be seen as kin to those of the first generations of Japanese monks who sought to create the spiritual, intellectual, ritual, and institutional conditions needed for Chan to take root and flourish in Japan. But instead of being primarily concerned with enabling Zen to put down roots in new places, they focused on placing Zen into productive global circulation. In these terms, they were evidently successful. Centers affiliated with Rinzai and Sōtō lineages can now be found on all the inhabited continents, blending Zen meditation, ritual, and narratives in ways keyed to addressing the challenges and spiritual needs of those living contemporary and increasingly postmodern lives. The public face of Zen is now undeniably global.

Part III

Personal Zen

The public dimensions of Zen have been shaped by complex sets of processes as Japanese first adopted Chinese Chan institutions, teachings, and practice regimens and then adapted them in response to changing political, economic, social, and cultural conditions. As a "public" phenomenon, the development of Zen gradually transformed the daily lives of the Japanese people. Most visibly, Zen reconfigured the material landscape as tens of thousands of Zen temples and monasteries were built throughout the archipelago—a reconfiguration that could not have occurred without significant transformations of Japanese political and economic relations. As these temples and monasteries became focal points for Japanese religious and cultural practices—ranging from village funerals to the artistic endeavors and aspirations of imperial, aristocratic, and warrior elites—no less significant "personal" transformations were taking place.

By the mid-twelfth century, when Japanese monks began turning actively to Chan teachers, teachings, and institutions for inspiration in transforming Japanese Buddhism, Chan self-consciously distinguished itself from other Chinese Buddhist traditions by claiming to be based on a direct transmission from "heart-mind to heart-mind"—a transmission made possible by refusing to rely on "words and literary culture" and engaging instead in continuous meditation-in-action, expressing enlightenment through participating in the unprecedented immediacy of truly liberating relationships. As such, Chan presented itself as returning to the origins of Buddhism in the daily-life encounters of the Buddha and his students. Chan masters were not just talented individuals like those featured in the biographies of eminent monks that had been written and circulated in China since at least the sixth century—individuals who excelled in *scholarly* activities like memorizing and explaining Buddhist texts or engaging in intellectual debates; in *ascetic* activities that involved living beyond the norms in terms of food, sleep, sex, clothing, and physical exertion; or in *miraculous* activities like predicting the future, reading minds, or generating protective/productive fields of "sympathetic resonance" (*ganying*). As epitomized by granting the title of "sutra" to the collection of Huineng's lectures, Chan masters were presented and revered as nothing short of "homegrown" Chinese buddhas. What Chan offered was not just new sets of teachings or monastic rules; it offered a new ideal of exemplary Buddhist personhood.

Recognizing this is crucial to understanding what motivated the embrace of Zen as an alternative to other Buddhist traditions—either those like Pure Land and Nichiren that were emerging, along with Zen, during the early Kamakura period, or those that had flourished during the preceding Nara and Heian periods. A partial explanation for the embrace of Zen has already been offered. After centuries of virtually no contact with the continent, Japanese monks traveling to China in the mid- to late twelfth century found a radically transformed cultural and religious landscape. During the centuries that Japan had severed contacts with the continent, considerable "evolutionary drift" had occurred between the various schools of Japanese Buddhism and their ancestral traditions in China. Most dramatically, the Chan tradition—some techniques and teachings of which had been transmitted to Japan in the eighth and ninth centuries and absorbed within Tendai—had risen to wholly unexpected prominence.

The eminence of Chan in imperial and elite literati circles in China would naturally have attracted the interest of Japanese monks who had journeyed to China convinced that Buddhist institutions in Japan had grown spiritually and culturally moribund. In search of inspiration for a revitalization of Buddhism at home, these monks could scarcely have failed to be impressed with Chan as a model for reforming Japanese Buddhism. In the context of the medieval Japanese worldview, Chan's unexpected eminence would have signaled much more than just a new religious "fashion" in China; it would have signaled the emergence of a new kind of creativity—a new religious "technology" for transforming personal, communal, and imperial fortunes.

Medieval Japanese did not understand the cosmos as shaped solely by the interaction of objective material forces. They were not ignorant, of course, of the effects of gravity and of the presence of various forms of physically manifest energy. Japanese architectural achievements and their constructions of dams and reservoirs evidence a formidable grasp of engineering principles, the quality of their swords and ceramics attests to their skill in materials manipulation, and their forest management and sophisticated cuisine leave no doubt as to their deft possession of ecological and biological understanding. But these practical achievements were not grounded in a framework of knowledge that could be called scientific in the modern sense of the term—an explanatory framework of abstract relations among generically existing entities and forces. On the contrary, the Japanese viewed their world as thoroughly dramatic or karmically conditioned.

In keeping with the Buddhist teachings of interdependence and impermanence, medieval Japanese saw themselves as bound together with all things in an ongoing dance choreographed from within as a function of their own feelings, thoughts, speech, and actions. Rather than seeing their life circumstances and experiences as imposed by natural law, chance, or divine will, they saw both their present and future lives as generated by the force of their own intentions, values, and conduct. Much as we consider it natural to work for a secure and healthy old age by saving in the present and eating and exercising well, it was natural for medieval Japanese to act in ways that they believed would positively alter their life prospects—not only in this present life, but in lifetimes still to come.

Through the Nara and Heian periods, although Buddhism did spread among the general populace, the power to significantly transform personal, familial, and imperial fortunes was generally assumed to be the privilege of the educated elite—a power gained through textually transmitted knowledge and personally transmitted ritual practices. Monks and (to a lesser extent) nuns were seen as skilled intermediaries for the reconfiguration of karma, and the ultimate proof of their efficacy was seen as manifest in the improving fortunes of their sponsors as well as in more widely shared experiences of societal flourishing. Conversely, the experience of widespread and persistent natural calamities, famines, fires, and economic turbulence were seen as evidence of ongoing inappropriate conduct, especially by powerful elites. This was certainly true in the final decades of the Heian period. Part of the appeal of the so-called Kamakura schools of Buddhism—Pure Land, Nichiren, and Zen—was that they made available relatively simple "single practice" methods of effecting changes in one's own karma, without relying on religious, social, or political elites as intermediaries.

In the case of Japanese Pure Land traditions, the turbulent conditions of the late twelfth and early thirteenth centuries were framed as proof of the onset of *mappō*, or the age of the decline of the Dharma, and thus as evidence of the need to resort to personal practice as a means of altering one's life prospects. By depicting the decline of material conditions both as inexorable and as resulting from/in a relentless erosion of moral and spiritual capabilities, Pure Land Buddhism presented medieval Japanese with two alternatives: resignation or reliance on the salvific power of the cosmic Buddha Amida (Skt: Amitābha). Although vehemently opposed to the Pure Land "solution" to the onset of *mappō*, Nichiren offered a no less simple way of directly and personally transforming one's karma: the continual recitation of homage to the *Lotus Sutra* as the supreme and unchallenged vehicle of Buddhist truth.

Zen presented itself as a restoration of the Buddhist path of not relying on anything—including other persons, specific deities, or texts—and offered a starkly contrasting response to the experience of deteriorating material, moral, and spiritual conditions. For reform-minded Japanese monks traveling to the continent in the late Heian and early Kamakura periods, the merits of Chan's method of nonreliance would have been readily apparent in the factual pairing of Chan's unquestionable preeminence and the social, economic, and political vitality of Song China. Chan was clearly working. But just as importantly, whereas the "other-power" (*tariki*) approaches of Pure Land and Nichiren Buddhism effectively affirmed one's subordinate status as a beneficiary of the Buddha's realization and teachings, the "self-power" (*jiriki*) approach espoused by Chan affirmed one's capacity for realizing one's own Buddha-nature, here and now. Chan insisted that it was possible to replicate—and not just refer to or revere—the Buddha's enlightening expression of boundless wisdom and compassion. For those aiming to reform Japanese Buddhism, the exemplary *personal ideals* championed by Chan were no less important than its modeling of new *institutional realities*.

8

PRACTICING ZEN

Practicing Zen is a profoundly personal endeavor. The central Zen practice of sitting meditation, or *zazen*, cannot be undertaken abstractly or through an exercise of the imagination. It cannot be undertaken by proxy or outsourced. Performing *zazen* requires us to be wholly and readily present. And although there is always the possibility of merely "going through the motions" of Zen, in the absence of total body-mind commitment, these motions will not make us Zen practitioners. Practicing Zen means personifying Zen.

Yet precisely because practicing Zen is *personal*, it is *not individual*. Almost all of Zen's greatest Japanese proponents have said that Zen practice is a function of realizing enlightenment "with this very body." If my body belongs exclusively to *me* as the most readily manifest proof of *my* individuality, it follows that practicing Zen is ultimately something that *I* undertake as an individual. When Zen was taking root in Japan, however, none of these assumptions about the relationship between the body and personhood were predominant.

Presenting Zen practice as exemplifying enlightenment with this very body recalls, of course, the shared conviction of Saichō and Kūkai, the founders of Japanese Tendai and Shingon: practicing Buddhism involves more than intellectual study of Buddhist teachings or reducing one's karmic debts through various merit-making activities. Insisting on the possibility of realizing enlightenment "with this very body" is a way of declaring that awakening does not need to be put off until some future moment when enough texts have been read or enough rituals performed, whether in this lifetime or another. Since all beings have/are Buddha-nature and are thus already endowed with "original enlightenment" (*hongaku*), even the "grasses, trees, mountains, and rivers" can express the meaning of awakening. What, then, could prevent each and every one of us from doing so as well? Awakening can be realized here and now, without transcending either the body or its present environs. As Kūkai emphatically stated, enlightenment can be realized right now with "the body given to you by your parents."

Importantly, however, for medieval Japanese whose worldview was significantly shaped by Confucian thought, the body that I am given by my parents is *not* exclusively "mine." For people living in societies shaped by the ideals of modern liberalism, the body is an index of our individuality—it is that which differentiates us most fundamentally from every*body* else. Our bodies are ours and ours alone. But from a traditional Confucian perspective, our bodies are entrusted to us by our parents and ultimately belong to them. It is through our bodies that our families extend themselves into the world, and it is our obligation to make good on our parents' trust, treating our bodies well and returning them whole to our ancestors when our lives end. Although medieval Chinese and Japanese were well aware that the pleasures and pains of *this* body belong to it alone, and that our bodies in some sense distinguish us, their emphasis was on seeing the body as a focus of life-enabling relationships. For Kūkai, realizing enlightenment in this very body meant illuminating the body *as* a unique locus for the interdependence and interpenetration of all things.

This view of the body implies that neither the considerations involved in committing to Zen practice nor the benefits accruing from it should be understood as fundamentally individual. Whether as a monk, as a nun, or as a dedicated layperson, engaging in Zen practice affects one's family and the complexion of relationships through which it is sustained and flourishes. The fortunes of a particular family, of course, are implicated in those of other families, the community at large, the state, and ultimately the cosmos as a whole. And from this medieval Japanese perspective, it is hardly surprising that when Eisai returned from China and set about establishing the Linji/Rinzai Zen lineage in Japan, rather than first circulating texts proclaiming the superior individual benefits of Zen practice, one of his first publications was a document titled "Promoting Zen to Protect the Country" (*Kōzen Gokokuron*).

In this document, Eisai argued that although all Buddhist institutions have the mission of enhancing the welfare of the community and ensuring the security of the state, Buddhist institutions in Japan had ceased doing so effectively. This, he claimed, was not due to any shortcomings of their specific methods, but rather to the shortcomings of their members in accurately and fully *personifying* the ideal of truly Buddhist conduct. As a result, the rituals performed at these institutions were only minimally effective, and realizing deep and sustained social and political harmony had become little more than a distant goal. Zen temples were different, Eisai insisted, not because they had different purposes or ritual technologies, but because they were organized to serve as beacons of uncompromising moral radiance.

PERSONAL DISCIPLINE AND RITUAL EFFICACY

Eisai's claims on behalf of the greater efficacy of Zen temples in promoting the ancestral ideals of harmony, prosperity, and security were in part warranted by the collective discipline observed therein. In addition to the ten major and forty-eight minor "bodhisattva" precepts that were peculiar to Mahāyāna traditions and that had been deemed sufficient for Tendai monks, Zen monks were required to observe all of the 253 *bhiksu* precepts that had been required for full ordination during the Buddha's lifetime. This requirement of observing the *bhiksu* precepts would have carried considerable force among Eisai's intended readers, who were well aware of the divisiveness and at times militant corruption rampant at many Tendai temples. While the bodhisattva precepts are aspirational in nature, the *bhiksu* precepts prescribe in considerable detail the proper conduct of monks both within the temple and in their interactions with the public, establishing a comprehensive and detailed set of behavioral forms (*kata*) that exemplified the determination and dignity proper to those living in intimate community with the Buddha himself. Zen monks could be relied upon to demonstrate moral rectitude.

Understanding the importance and effectiveness of this argument requires an appreciation of the widespread East Asian correlation of concentrated moral force with achieved celestial and earthly harmony. Among the legacies of Confucianism throughout East Asia was the prevalence of convictions that appropriate ritual conduct (*li*) was crucial to achieving personal and communal flourishing, the prosperity and peace-fulness of the state, and the harmonious interplay of the ancestral, spiritu-al, human, and natural realms. Far from being dismissed as essentially empty formalities or customs, rituals were understood as providing a grammar of interaction that enabled meaningful relationships to be real-ized among the members of a family, within a community, with one's ancestors, and with both celestial/spiritual and natural forces.

Yet as Confucius himself had been intent on pointing out, effectively conducting a ritual is not a matter of simply going through a set of prescribed bodily movements; it requires properly enlivening the relation-al grammar provided by a given ritual, infusing it with exemplary moral force or virtue (Ch: *de*; J: *toku*). This Confucian common sense is clearly evident in Prince Shōtoku's Seventeen Article Constitution and its declar-ation that the most effective way to achieve the benefits of good govern-ance—social harmony, prosperity, and state security—is to marry Confu-cian ritual propriety with the cultivation of Buddhist wisdom and com-passion. And it was central to Eisai's argument on behalf of Zen: promot-ing Zen would excel in fostering the ancestral Japanese ideal of harmony because life within Zen temples personified a fusion of disciplined sensi-tivity to ritual comportment with Buddhist conscience and compassion. For Eisai, the providence and productivity of this fusion were eminently apparent in China where Chan monasteries had eclipsed the ancestral traditions of Tendai and Shingon to become the most prestigious religious institutions in the empire.

This was not a perspective peculiar to Eisai. Although Dōgen did not require monks to take the full 253 *bhiksu* precepts—prescribing instead an expanded set of sixteen major bodhisattva precepts—he made a simi-lar argument in explaining the merits of sponsoring the establishment and growth of his own Zen community. Combining rigorous *zazen* with the strict observance of ritual propriety and monastic decorum, Dōgen argued that his monastic community constituted a true "field of merit" that would bear generous karmic fruit in reward for offerings made by sponsors and lay practitioners. And indeed, the reputation of Sōtō Zen monks for ener-getic *zazen* practice, moral clarity, and decorous conduct would later play an important role in the spread of Sōtō temples throughout Japan.

The presuppositions of the argument from moral virtuosity to ritual efficacy also seem to have informed Dōgen's and Eisai's vehement de-nunciations of the Darumashū. In their criticisms, these first-generation

Zen leaders did not focus on defects in the core teachings of the Darumashū, but rather on its reputation for allowing a morally lax attitude toward monastic discipline. For Eisai, Dōgen, and their prospective sponsors, this reputation would have shed a harshly critical light on the potential for Darumashū practitioners to generate real and sustained communal benefits. But more to the point, allowing a morally ambiguous Darumashū to portray itself as a legitimate Zen school would also have had the effect of casting doubts on the communal efficacy of the still fledging Rinzai and Sōtō communities. Especially for Dōgen—many of whose key disciples had once belonged to the Darumashū—guaranteeing the moral virtuosity of his own Zen community was crucial precisely because the moral rectitude of monks training under him was the primary warrant for the greater efficacy of rituals performed by his community on behalf of donors, the emperor, and the state.

THE MORAL EFFICACY OF COMMUNAL PRACTICE

The medieval common sense that ritual efficacy is linked to moral virtuosity played more than the rhetorical role of shaping arguments on behalf of Zen practice. It also shaped the organization and dynamics of early Zen communities in ways that distinguished them from other Buddhist communities, impacting virtually every aspect of monastic life, including even the core practice of *zazen*.

Although Zen was known as the "meditation" school—"*zen*" being a transliteration of the Sanskrit word for meditation, *dhyāna*—a very sophisticated repertoire of Buddhist and indigenous meditation practices existed in Japan by the time of Zen's emergence in the late twelfth and early thirteenth centuries. Zen training communities were unique in mandating daily *zazen* practice for all of their ordained members. But this alone was not enough to set Zen apart as a more ritually efficacious alternative to the Tendai, Shingon, and Nara schools, or to the native tradition of mountain asceticism. What warranted Zen's greater efficacy was its stress on the communal practice of meditation.

As previously noted, Buddhist meditation practices of various kinds had been transmitted to Japan from Korea and China beginning at least by the seventh century. These imported meditation traditions resonated with already existing practices of mountain asceticism and seem to have en-

couraged their further development. Like many premodern peoples, the
Japanese associated mountains with spirituality, and early Japanese history contains many accounts of mountain ascetics whose independent practice of meditation had brought them extraordinary powers. This association was reinforced by the arrival of esoteric Buddhist traditions and the
founding of the Tendai and Shingon traditions, both of which recognized
and valorized the attainment of extraordinary insights and powers through
extended periods of solo meditation in remote mountain areas. By the
time of Zen's emergence, indigenous traditions of mountain asceticism
had been amalgamated with elements of shamanism, Shintō, and esoteric
Buddhism to constitute a loosely institutionalized religious path known as
Shugendō, or "the path of cultivating extraordinary religious powers."
These powers enabled Shugendō practitioners to respond to local community needs by telling fortunes, praying for worldly benefits, performing
exorcisms, preparing charms and talismans, and addressing such natural
phenomena as droughts. More importantly, perhaps, these ascetic adepts
shared with their Tendai and Shingon counterparts an ability to serve as
intercessors with relevant *kami* and local spirits (*ryūten*)—an absolutely
central function in both popular and elite Japanese religious life.

These were Zen's meditation "competitors." And it was in sharp
contrast with these other approaches and their biases toward individually
attained powers and ritual efficacy that early Zen communities valorized
group meditation. Although leading Zen teachers did stress the importance of personal spiritual exertion, in keeping with Baizhang's then famous Chan monastic rules, the first Zen communities were organized
around the primacy of communal practice. In both Rinzai and Sōtō training centers, the normative ideal was for residents to live and practice
together, taking part in group *zazen* four times a day and engaging in
group sutra recitation and other ceremonial activities on strictly observed
daily, monthly, and annual schedules.

Indeed, the Zen norm was for every aspect of temple life to have a
strong, communal character. Whereas Shingon and Tendai monasteries
were often large complexes in which residents could live in relative independence, Zen temples were organically structured to reinforce commitments to communal living. A typical temple would be entered through a
so-called mountain gate—the only official entrance. To the left and right,
respectively, in a location closest to the secular world beyond the temple
compound, would be a latrine and bathhouse. Beyond them, on the left

would be a library or reading room, and on the right a tower featuring a large bell used to announce teaching, practice, and work periods. Further into the compound one would find on the left a Sangha Hall in which residents lived and practiced together, on the right a large kitchen, and directly ahead a Buddha Hall in which ritual offerings were made to images or statues representing the vows of past Buddhas (symbolized by Amida), the wisdom and compassion of the present Buddha (Shakyamuni), and the future Buddha (Maitreya). Behind the Buddha Hall, and thus higher in spiritual status, one would see directly ahead the Dharma Hall in which daily group instruction, public teachings, and ceremonies conducted by the abbot would take place. In the intervening space, one would often find on the left an Ancestral Hall dedicated to past abbots of the temple and other important lineage figures, and on the right an Earth Deity Hall dedicated to the spirits enlivening the local natural environment. Behind the Dharma Hall, in the highest position within the compound, one would find the abbot's living quarters, in which informal private interviews were also conducted.

This general temple layout was adapted from Song dynasty Chinese models, and most of the buildings in a typical Zen temple compound could be found at other, non-Zen temple complexes throughout East Asia. Zen temples were distinct, however, in two ways. First, although Zen temples were built according to generic Chinese Buddhist architectural norms, they were structurally adapted to reinforce a distinctive array of relationships, including those with the local environment and especially the local *kami*; with lineage ancestors; with the dynamic history of Buddhism; and among the abbot, the temple residents, and the lay community beyond the temple walls. The placement of the abbot's quarters at the "head" position atop the "body" of the Chan/Zen compound made clear that it was the abbot—residing "above" the Buddha Hall that represented Buddhism's past and future history—who was crucial to the temple's relational dynamics. The abbot's quarters in the temple housed the heart-mind of a living Buddha.

Second, there was no exact equivalent of the Chan/Zen Sangha Hall at other Buddhist complexes. In the Sangha Hall—a large space without interior walls—residents slept together, ate together, and meditated together. Visits to the bathhouse were scheduled and communal. Meals were taken in the Sangha Hall as a group, in silence, and in keeping with strict protocols about how both to consume one's meal and clean up afterward. Residents were required to participate in daily, scheduled communal work periods. And, aside from visits for personal interaction with the abbot, all teachings, sutra recitations, ceremonies, and rituals were conducted communally. Although officially scheduled periods for relaxation and reading did exist, the physical dimensions of the temple compound made it almost unavoidable that one would relax and read in the company of others.

In sum, although solitary practice in a hermitage or mountain retreat remained an option and an ideal of spiritual dedication, Zen temples were organized around the norm of communal living and practice. As symbolized by the architectural elevation of the Zen abbot to the position of a living Buddha, the Zen temple was understood as replicating in Japan the kind of community that had developed more than fifteen hundred years previously around the historical Buddha in India: an intentional community dedicated to creating the conditions for personally realizing liberation while serving as a "field of merit" for those supporting the community.

The Buddha himself had recognized, of course, that enlightenment could be realized outside of life in such a community. After all, he had done so himself. But he also recognized that those who realized enlightenment on their own often did not share his own commitment to teaching and relational enhancement. These he referred to as *pratyekabuddhas*, or "lone Buddhas"—beings who had realized enlightenment on their own and who were content to lead fully private lives, uninvolved in the travails of other sentient beings. From a Mahāyāna perspective, some members of the original Buddhist Sangha were also apparently content with achieving their own liberation and ending their presence in the cycle of birth and death. In spite of having realized awakening under the Buddha's personal guidance, these disciples were like *pratyekabuddhas* in that they lacked sufficient compassion to work for the enlightenment of all other beings. In many Mahāyāna texts, disciples like these were derisively labeled *śrāvakabuddhas*, or those who had "awakened [only] by hearing." They did not *act* like Buddhas.

In light of these Mahāyāna concerns about the compassion of those who were self-enlightened, the Zen emphasis on communal life and practice can be seen as insurance against the liabilities of individually achieved and privately construed liberation. The communal nature of virtually every facet of life in the temple aside from private interviews with the abbot communicated a thorough commitment to embodying the moral ideal of the bodhisattva, institutionally as well as personally.

THE PERSONAL NATURE OF COMMUNAL PRACTICE

This Zen ideal of communally embodying wisdom and compassion in response to the needs of others should not be construed as contrary to the ideal of personally demonstrating commitment to realizing enlightenment "in this very body." Communal practice does not eliminate the need for relentless personal striving. If anything, it intensifies that need.

There is a Zen saying that instead of washing potatoes one at a time, it's better to put a few dozen into a big pot of water and stir them up with a stout ladle so that the potatoes "wash themselves" as they bump into and roll over one another. It may still be necessary to scrub an individual potato here and there to fully clean it, but most of the dirt clinging to the potatoes is very efficiently knocked off by them jostling around together. This is precisely what happens in the Zen temple: the pot is the temple compound, the residents are the potatoes, the discipline is the water, and the ladle is in the hands of the abbot. Living in close quarters with others practically guarantees being confronted with ongoing—and often repeated and amplified—opportunities to evaluate one's own thoughts, feelings, speech, and actions. This is particularly true in a Zen context, where the training discipline includes large blocks of time devoted to sitting perfectly still and attending critically to the play of thoughts and feelings by means of which our sense of self is continuously being defined and reinforced.

In Buddhist terms, communal living is conducive to confronting our own karma. Although it is possible in any circumstance to attend to how our values, intentions, and actions shape our life experiences, communal living of the sort practiced in early Zen training centers makes it impossible to avoid doing so. In the temple, the particulars of time (when things occur), space (where things occur), and bodily comportment are all communally specified. As a result, personal habits, likes, and dislikes are raised into uncommonly acute prominence. Unable to persist in living "on automatic" and enjoined to refrain from being caught up in the pulsing stream of their thoughts and feelings, Zen practitioners are enlisted in tracing back the roots of their attachments, affinities, and aversions to discover for themselves the ever poised and virtuosic responsiveness revealed in the narratives of enlightening encounters between Zen masters and their disciples.

Confronting our karma is never a comfortable experience. It reveals how very little of what we think, feel, say, and do is truly natural and spontaneous, and how much of it is predetermined by our past experiences, by the processes of socialization and enculturation to which we have been subjected, and ultimately by our own patterns of ignorance—the maze of reactive triggers, concepts, and judgments that have been erected and reinforced in walled defense of who and what we take ourselves to be. Few people are capable of sustaining such discomfort sufficiently long on their own to burrow through or bring down those walls. Solitary retreats from social interaction can also be very revealing. Leading a hermit's life—even in the midst of a city—can present profound challenges to our sense of independent selfhood, including intense longings for communicative interaction and no less intense disappointments and boredom with the depth and quality of our own internal landscapes. This can result in erasures of the normal boundaries between self and others, dramatically accentuating awareness of the interdependence and interpenetration of all things. But sustained and severe solitariness can also result in a conflation of the subjective and objective—an inability to distinguish what is actually present from what is merely projected.

Another Zen saying is that the best teachings often come from mirrors—a saying that can be profitably associated with Huineng continually exhorting his students to "see your own nature." The now established fact that sensory deprivation often results in hallucinations sheds some important practical light on Chan and Zen emphases on group practice and their cautionary tales about "meditation sickness." In solitary meditation, one's own experience serves as a teacher/mirror. But it is not uncommon for this self-reflection to be directed in ways that result in an infinite regress—an endless and potentially entrancing reflection of reflections—and the dangers of this are legion. In communally disciplined practice, we find ourselves reflected as well in the ever-changing experiences and responses of others. If the quality of our fellow practitioners is high enough, we almost invariably find that it is in the eyes and expressions of others that we find ourselves most fully and significantly revealed.

Of course, traditional Chan/Zen narratives attest that the most revealing mirror is the presence of the abbot or Zen master. There is a wonderful story of Chan master Mazu when he was still a monk in training. Deep into a long solo meditation retreat, Mazu one day hears a grating sound coming from outside his hermitage. After remaining quietly focused for a time, his internal resistances break down. The sound gets under his skin like an army of ants and he finally explodes up off his sitting cushion and rushes outside to find his teacher, Huairang, seated in the grass outside the hut, methodically rubbing a broken roofing tile with a stone. Mazu demands to know what his teacher is doing making such an "irritating" noise outside his meditation quarters. Huairang looks up innocently and replies, "I'm making a mirror." Mazu is incredulous. "You can't make a mirror out of a roofing tile," he objects. "That's so," Huairang replies. "But if I can't make a mirror by polishing a roofing tile, what makes you think you can turn yourself into a Buddha by sitting all alone on a cush ion?" With this, Mazu awakened.[1]

What this story suggests—and the histories of Chan and Zen reveal— is that while the benefits of solitary meditation can be immense, solitary travel on the Middle Way cannot be relied upon to show us what we need in order to go beyond our own thinking and the horizons of our karma. As Dōgen put it in one of his Dharma Hall talks, "That which is not studying together is self; that which is studying together is all Buddhas" (see Leighton and Okumura, 2010:82).

The Liberating Nature of Discipline

That there is a relationship between a highly disciplined, communal way of life and moral rectitude is perhaps not very difficult to imagine. It is much harder to imagine the link between Zen discipline and Zen libera- tion. Especially if freedom is understood in terms of being individually able to exercise meaningful choices about what to do, when, how, and where, the highly regimented life of the Zen monastic can seem far from liberating. Every monk or nun living in a Zen training temple wears the same type of clothing, eats the same food, sleeps on the same kind of mat, washes at the same time, and exhibits almost the same patterns of bodily motion and comportment as every other. Indeed, residents in Zen training centers can seem to be living submerged in an almost "faceless" collec- tive, each interchangeable with every other.

This, however, is a way of seeing Zen monastic life that imports a view of persons as essentially individual and autonomous agents and then shears away from them every public vestige of selfhood—a vision of being forced into a life in which the Buddhist teaching of no-self (*anatman*) assumes an almost nightmarish quality. But in fact the populations in Zen training temples have never been uniform collectives. As the customary temple layout makes evident, abbots occupied a unique position in the Zen community. At a practical level, abbots were responsible for the character and quality of the teaching and practice taking place in the temple, as well as for the temple's primary interactions with the outside world, including sponsors. More importantly, they were also understood spiritually as embodiments of enlightened wisdom and compassion— living buddhas worthy of profound respect and loyalty.

Below the abbot was a personal hierarchy that blended considerations of ability and age (calculated from the time of ordination and/or entry into the Zen community). Closest to the abbot were senior disciples (ordained and lay), the most advanced of whom might already have attained significant awakening and earned the title of lineage holders or future successors to the abbacy. Typically, one senior student would serve as personal attendant for the abbot; one or perhaps more students would perform the function of "Dharma secretary," recording the abbot's informal talks and helping to edit and compile his written works. One monk would be in charge of daily practice; another would be responsible for organizing work periods; and another would oversee the kitchen, ensuring that the community was properly nourished. Still other students with particular aptitudes would be assigned duties, in the execution of which they would either excel or be challenged to develop new skills and sensibilities. Interacting with this monastic hierarchy was a parallel hierarchy of lay members of the temple, ranging from members of the imperial court and shoguns to wealthy sponsors, merchants, and—especially after the spread of Zen throughout the countryside—farmers and peasants.

The resolutely hierarchic structure of Zen relational dynamics might seem to be at odds with the Mahāyāna emphasis on realizing the nonduality of all things. But, again, this concern is somewhat misplaced. Here it is useful to recall the Chinese Huayan thinker Fazang and his response to a question about the persistence of apparent differences in a world that Buddhists characterize as nondual: all things are the same precisely insofar as they differ meaningfully from and for one another. Hierarchy establishes a ranking of differences, but also a clear set of possibilities—and in the Zen context, responsibilities—for contribution. In a situation in which every member of a community is equal in all respects to every other, there would be no need even for communication, much less contributory coordination. This would amount to realizing what might be called social entropy: the absence of sufficient differences of energy for any meaningful communication to occur. In actuality, everyone in the Zen training community has a role, not to play, but rather to inhabit fully in resolute and embodied commitment to realizing their Buddha-nature.

That, of course, is the ideal of Zen community as expressed in the writings of early seminal figures like Eisai and Dōgen. Some scholars recently have argued that the architectural structure of the Zen temple compound reveals a reality in which no one in the community was at liberty to question either the abbot's judgment and actions or the ethical merits of Zen institutions. With Zen's checkered twentieth-century wartime record in mind, other scholars have made comparisons between the dynamics of Zen training and the uncritical submission to superiors that is often valorized in military training as a necessary foundation for battlefield discipline. Some historical support for these criticisms can be found, for example, in the Muromachi period convergence among Zen communities, practices, and ideals and those of the samurai class, and in the explicit attempts made during the late Tokugawa and Meiji periods to ally the "spirit of Zen" with that of the "way of the warrior" (*bushidō*) in support of national strengthening.

Yet, while highly structured and built around a core of embodied discipline, Zen training has never valorized simply following orders; neither has it fostered belief in the infallibility of monastic authority. It is true that Zen teachers have been renowned for exhorting their students to disentangle themselves from the "vines and creepers" (*kattō*) of their karmically conditioned webs of thought and emotion. But the aim of doing so has not been to *induce* mindlessness or a robotic readiness to do as told, but rather to *educe* or bring forth the realization of what Baizhang referred to as "nonthinking" (*wu nian*). As he insisted, this is not the end of thought and critical engagement: "Nonthinking is the absence of errant thoughts; it is not an abeyance of corrective thinking" (*Xuzang Jing*, 119.421a). Indeed, as Huineng cautions in the *Platform Sutra* (no. 31), "If you do not think of the myriad things, but instead always cut off your thoughts, then you will be bound [and not liberated] by the Dharma." Finally, as Linji constantly reminded his students, the point of Chan/Zen training is not to seize upon the words of the abbot or past patriarchs or even the Buddha and then demonstrate slavish obeisance to them; those who do so go through life "trembling with fright like donkeys on an icy path" (*Zhen-zhou Linjihui-zhao-chan-shiyulu*, 1985:499b). Instead, the point is to become a "true person of no rank," responding freely to each changing situation.

The path to realizing this kind of responsive virtuosity has never been paved in advance. It is an always improvised path, and one that—as implied by the Zen norm of communal practice—is only rarely blazed alone. As Dōgen explains in the *Shōbōgenzō*, it is a path best opened collaboratively when master and student "practice together personally," slicing through *kattō* with *kattō*, using whatever karmic tools are ready to hand to craft an enlightening relationship. Although great emphasis is placed in Zen on the student's need for a fierce determination to rely on nothing and to take nothing for granted, that kind of determination is best realized in vigilant partnership with a "keen-eyed" master.

The Challenges of Zen Partnership

Embarking on Zen monastic training opens the possibility of realizing an enlightening relationship with a "living Buddha" in an environment publicly devoted to enhancing the security and flourishing of both surrounding communities and the state. Doing so in medieval Japan, of course, would also have been understood as benefiting one's family, in both karmic and social terms. By dedicating the merit made by becoming a monk or nun, a good son or daughter could positively affect not only his or her family's present welfare, but its future prospects as well. All in all, the potential fruits of Zen training would have been powerfully attractive.

But especially prior to the institution of the *gozan* system and the security of generous support from the government, members of the imperial family, and aristocratic and warrior elites, making the decision to embark on Zen training would still not have been easy. After Dōgen's move to Echizen, for example, there were many years when his community lived in conditions that were quite impoverished. Food was often scarce. There was generally no heat in the monks' draft-prone living quarters, even on nights of freezing rain and snow. And the monastic discipline observed by the community did not permit curling up under layers of quilts to sleep at least in relative comfort. For the first generations of Zen practitioners, daily life was austere, physically challenging, and designed to highlight and then undermine one's self-defining habits of thought, feeling, speech, and action.

For most of those who entered the first Zen training communities, the contrast with their previous life circumstances would have been dramatic. Promoted in Japan as based on direct transmissions of the preeminent form of Chinese Buddhism and as offering access to the leading edges of cultural developments in Song China, early Zen communities were relatively elite in nature. Although Zen presented itself as a "mind-to-mind transmission" occurring beyond the reach of "words and letters," Zen practice required fairly sophisticated language ability. The fact that both Rinzai and Sōtō communities stressed *kōan* study and a detailed familiarity with the recorded sayings and encounter dialogues of Chinese Chan masters made literacy—and more importantly, Chinese language and cultural competency—a practical necessity. Moreover, the Dharma talks delivered multiple times a day in Zen training temples often assumed knowledge of a wide range of Chan and other Buddhist texts, without which the talks would have been, if not unintelligible, then at least quite difficult to fathom at any useful depth.

There are varying estimates of literacy rates in thirteenth-century Japan, but it is almost certain that not more than a few percent of the population would have possessed the requisite linguistic qualifications to practice Zen, and virtually all of those so qualified would have come from aristocratic and high-ranking warrior families. That is, they would have been used to living in privileged conditions that—by comparison with those in Zen temples—would have been quite luxurious. Whereas a bright young man might easily have ordained in the Tendai tradition for social and political as well as religious reasons, leading a life that remained quite comfortable, this was not (at least initially) true for those attracted to Zen. And indeed a number of the earliest generations of lineage-holding Zen monks seem to have been spurred to enter Zen training by some sort of early life trauma or by a significant turn in their family's fortunes. Dōgen, for example, though born into a noble family, lost both of his parents while still a child. Many, like both Eisai and Dōgen, first ordained as Tendai monks, often as young children, and only later developed an interest in Zen.

But what seems to have motivated most of those who embraced the relative hardship and strict discipline of Zen monastic life was an intense desire to break through their own personal and religious limits to become a source of enlightening relationality. Becoming conversant with Song Chinese cultural trends and making merit did not require abandoning the pleasures of lay life. One could benefit one's family by commissioning the performance of rituals or by sponsoring temples. One could even practice *zazen* as a layperson—with any luck under the guidance of an eminent abbot—and leave others to endure the austerities and strict observance of Zen decorum. The fact that so many well-born and highly educated Japanese did commit to Zen training as monks and nuns reveals both the depth of their spiritual sincerity and the strength of their determination to embody the bodhisattva ideals of keen moral acuity, responsive virtuosity, and service to others.

ZEN BEYOND THE TEMPLE WALLS

Zen training was not restricted, however, to those willing to leave the home life and become a monk or nun. One of the most beloved Buddhist texts in East Asia—the *Vimalakīrti Sutra*—recounts a series of philosophically profound and yet touchingly humorous encounters between a number of the Buddha's key disciples and an enlightened layman, Vimalakīrti, who demonstrates his superior capacity for embodying Buddhist realization. In Chan and Zen, texts, the lay expression of enlightenment was perhaps most vibrantly exemplified in stories of Layman Pang (740–808) and his family. After becoming a successful businessman, Layman Pang began seriously practicing Chan along with his wife, son, and daughter. Eventually, they took up an itinerant lifestyle that enabled them to study with such famous Chan masters as Mazu, in dialogue with whom Pang realized enlightenment. Accounts of Layman Pang and his family members' exploits—especially his daughter, Ling Zhao, whose brilliance apparently equaled that of her father—were widely circulated, and some even came to be included in the most widely circulated collections of *kōans* and encounter dialogues.

With these textual and historical precedents, it is not surprising that the first generation of Zen teachers—Nōnin, Eisai, and Dōgen—all had serious lay students. In fact, Dōgen began his teaching career as a strenuous advocate of *zazen* as a universally beneficial practice open to all, including women, and had a large circle of lay practitioners while teaching on the outskirts of Kyōto. Although historical discussions of lay involvement often stress sponsorship activities—a form of lay involvement for which we have good documentary evidence—it is clear that lay commitments to Zen often went well beyond meritorious offerings of financial and other forms of material support and included engaging in both textual study and meditation. Dōgen's manual for the practice of sitting meditation, the *Fukanzazenji*, is conspicuous in not addressing an exclusively monastic audience, and extant written evidence indicates that significant numbers of imperial, warrior, and aristocratic families—the only strata of lay practitioners about whom such records exist—did go beyond engaging in Zen prayer ceremonies and other rituals to undertake regular meditation.

Lay practitioners of Zen would not have experienced the same kind of physical, emotional, and intellectual challenges as monks and nuns training twenty-four hours a day, seven days a week, within the temple's walls. But in some ways their challenges would have been both more extensive and more complex. In the diverse community of practitioners that surrounded the historical Buddha, ordination did not offer a *means* to sincere and committed practice; it offered a systematic *aid* for sustaining it. Especially in the context of Japanese Buddhism in which bodhisattva precepts were crucial, ordination signaled compassionate and horizonless dedication to leading an enlightening life. But even so, ordination also vastly simplified a practitioner's responsibilities and concerns. Those who formally renounced the "home life," especially in medieval Japan, did not cease interacting with or being deeply concerned about their family members and their material and spiritual well-being. But Zen monks and nuns did renounce—at least in principle—taking any direct role in securing the material circumstances for their families' welfare. While remaining intimately connected with their families and indirectly contributing to them through merit-transfer and ritual observances, monks and nuns were absolved of immediate participation in the complex webs of social, economic, and political relationships that shaped their families' fortunes. This was not true for lay Zen practitioners.

However humble or august their stations in life, the men and women who committed to Zen practice while remaining immersed in the social world were subject to the full range of that world's demands, distractions, dangers, and delights. Decisions to make such a commitment and the determination to sustain it would not have come easy. The practice of entering Buddhist reclusion as a means of gaining respite from the stresses of life in the imperial court or from the convoluted and often cutthroat struggles for political, social, and economic power that dominated the attentions of aristocratic and warrior elites was well established in medieval Japan. More generally, reclusion offered relief from the experiential turbulence of life during what many believed was an irreparably degenerate age—a relief that was poetically invoked by Kamo no Chōmei by way of explaining (in his *Hōjōki*, or "Account of My Hut") how he came to live as a Buddhist recluse in a humble dwelling modeled after Vimalakīrti's legendary sickroom. Yet Zen offered endorsement neither for the *mappō* thesis of inexorable social collapse and moral depravity, nor for the association of Buddhist practice with quietist retreat. Although those well progressed in Zen training were often characterized as maintaining equanimity in the midst of turmoil and even in the face of their own deaths, successful Zen training was itself often represented as an energetic and muscular activation of all one's resources, not a relaxing retreat into observational passivity. Indeed, many early Zen teachers, Dōgen among them, insisted that *zazen* should be practiced as if "one's head is on fire."

Dialogues in a Dream

We do not have extended subjective accounts of early Zen training written by lay men or women. We do, however, have an illuminating collection of the recorded conversations of Rinzai master Musō Soseki, one of the leading figures in the development of the *gozan* system, and Ashikaga Tadayoshi, one of the founders of the Ashikaga shogunate. After routing the forces of Emperor Go-Daigo in 1336 and bringing his short-lived restoration of direct imperial rule to an end, Tadayoshi and his older brother, Ashikaga Takauji, enthroned Emperor Kōmyō and assumed joint control of Japan, with Tadayoshi in charge of administrative affairs and Takauji in charge of the military. That same year, Tadauji asked to become a lay disciple of Musō. Tadayoshi preferred to study Buddhism formally with the expatriate Chinese Chan teacher Zhuxian Fanxian (1292–1348) and the Japanese Rinzai teacher Kosen Ingen (1295–1344), but he engaged in conversations with Musō over an extended period. A collection of Tadayoshi's questions and Musō's responses was edited in 1342 and has remained a favorite of the literate public interested in Zen since its publication in 1344 as *Dialogues in a Dream* (Muchū Mondō).[2]

Comprising ninety-three conversational exchanges organized into three main sections, *Dialogues in a Dream* chronicles the expansion and maturation of Tadayoshi's concerns and Zen training. But it also offers significant insight into the motivations and challenges of practicing Zen as a layperson. To be sure, as one of the two most powerful men in Japan—or four if one counts Emperor Kōmyō and the deposed Go-Daigo—Tadayoshi was far from being an ordinary lay practitioner of Zen. Yet, as is attested by the wide circulation and perennial popularity of the text, his concerns strike seemingly universal chords, and Musō's responses evidence both his rhetorical skills and sometimes scant regard for Tadayoshi's elevated status and his "realist" skepticism about the relevance of Zen training. At one point, Musō admonishes Tadayoshi for rationalizing his failures to practice Zen, referring to Tadayoshi's self-serving view as "the most deluded of all deluded thinking" and then capping his criticism by remarking that the worst fault of all is "the fault of allowing things to remain as they are."

The first several questions posed by Tadayoshi leave no doubt that he is still fully immersed in secular concerns, focusing on the relationship between Zen training and seeking prosperity—first and foremost for oneself, of course, but also for others. In a tone that seems to float between sincerity and the temerity of one accustomed to being treated with utmost deference, Tadayoshi seems most interested in determining if there are any "loopholes" in the law of karma that would enable him to reasonably indulge his desires for pleasure, power, and fame. Foiled by Musō's careful dissolution of his arguments and counterarguments, Tadayoshi shifts focus to the efficacy of rituals and prayers, and whether it is appropriate to seek influential supporters and sufficient fortune in this and future lives to have the leisure to practice Buddhism and show proper reverence for one's ancestors and the *kami*. Although Musō allows that ritual and prayer can work to attract material and social benefits, he again and again directs Tadayoshi's attention to the ultimate futility of the kinds of desires motivating his questions. If you are going to continue giving rise to desire, Musō insists, let it be the "great desire" of seeking to open the inexhaustible storehouse of our "original nature" and then making use of the treasures therein to bring limitless benefit to oneself and all other beings. Do not be satisfied "with arhatship or even the exalted status of a bodhisattva, let alone rewards in the human and heavenly realms," he flatly states; desire to become a Buddha!

As their interactions progress, Tadayoshi is repeatedly forced by Musō's deft use of Buddhist texts, Zen teachings, parables, and personal life lessons to grapple with the central matter of giving rise to *bodhicitta* or a mind committed to realizing Buddhahood. Eventually, Tadayoshi bluntly voices his doubts about whether it is possible to undertake Zen training, seek to do good works for others, and at the same time effectively engage in politics. Musō first responds by discussing the importance of the values and intentions that inform so-called good deeds and the importance of not falling into the habit of deluding oneself about one's true motivations. But then he minces no words and challenges Tadayoshi to measure the good and evil karma resulting from the rampant slaughter that had enabled him to establish himself and his brother as shoguns. How many shrines, temples, inns, and homes in the countryside and cities of Japan were put to the torch, with what loss of life, and with what wrenching collapses of community? What kind of "good government" can be spoken of under such circumstances?

One can almost see Tadayoshi bristling as in the next exchanges he reports having heard that those who practice Buddhism run risks of falling into the realms of demons, that devotion to Buddhist practice and the rejection of secular life is itself a form of dualism, and that Zen meditation often results in mental breakdowns.

To each of these challenges, Musō responds with quiet clarity, and Tadayoshi takes a less confrontational tack, asking a series of questions about the Zen rejection of scholarly understanding and intellectualism, about whether Zen training demands a rejection of traditional Confucian and Shintō practices, about what Zen means by "stopping deluded thinking," and about the utility of *kōan* practice. Gradually, he is guided to ask how one abandons the desire to *understand* the truth and instead to arouse commitment to embodying Buddha-nature. Musō offers a helpful distinction between "ordinary" and "true" *bodhicitta*: the former consists in realizing the impermanence of all things and on this basis gives rise to an unfaltering commitment to realizing enlightenment at some point in the future; the latter occurs when cultivation gives way to demonstration and one naturally realizes a harmonizing accord with all things by being utterly present and unreservedly open.

That sounds easy enough. But as Tadayoshi's subsequent questions intimate, the ever-changing circumstances of day-to-day life have a way of making equanimity and enlightened openness seem very distant and perhaps unattainable goals. Even if one attains a certain measure of equanimity on the meditation cushion, how does one sustain it in the face of intense worldly passions? How does one demonstrate responsive openness and clarity while enmeshed in densely tangled relationships and confronted by people who seem bent on acting in ways that practically provoke judgmental responses?

Musō's response is simple: by practicing *zazen*. Tadayoshi objects, arguing that even the ancient masters of Zen and Chan admitted that unless one can clearly apply one's mind, *zazen* is worthless. How are typical, ignorant laypeople ever to benefit from *zazen* when they lack the most basic control over their own thoughts and feelings? Wouldn't it be better to read sutras, chant *dhāranīs*, or recite the *nembutsu*? Musō admits that simply plopping onto a cushion and sitting there absentmindedly will produce nothing of value. But that is not practicing meditation; it is not *zazen*. More importantly, however, the very idea that *zazen* is too difficult for the average person is a mistake. Other Buddhist and non-Buddhist traditions all make use of meditation and focus on such hard-to-reach goals as achieving bodily stillness, cutting off thinking, engaging in specific forms of contemplation, or profoundly penetrating various doctrinal principles. In sharp contrast, the Zen practice of *zazen*

> is not about stilling the body and suppressing the mind, so one need not dismiss sitting facing the wall and letting go of thoughts as a difficult practice. *Zazen* does not involve contemplation of doctrinal principles, so one cannot claim to lack intelligence for it. *Zazen* requires no physical strength, so even the weak can do it. The Buddha-dharma does not conflict with human passions, so one cannot say one is too worldly to practice it. . . . Zen cultivation does not depend on the body, the mouth, or the intellect. How, then, can it be called difficult? (Kirchner, 2010:123)

This triggers a string of questions about whether Zen training involves striving or non-striving and, most crucially, about the difference between "practicing in the midst of worldly activities" and "performing worldly activities in the midst of practice." Musō allows that for many people, it may be necessary to schedule periods for *zazen* (ideally four times a day)—practicing "in the midst of worldly activities"—before being able to realize the freedom of performing all of one's daily activities "in the midst of practice." But upon realizing the non-duality of all things, he states, "no activities are outside of practice."

This might be taken by those still beset by mundane attachments as erasing the need to set aside worldly activities and relations in order to practice Zen. To undercut this interpretation of "no activities are outside of practice," Musō tells a story about one of the Buddha's disciples, Devasarva, who was born into a wealthy family and had grown up accustomed to fine clothes, luxurious living conditions, and only the most tasty and beautifully presented food. In spite of being intent on practicing with the Buddha, Devasarva could see neither a need nor purpose in giving up his accustomed lifestyle for the humble—and some might say humiliating—conditions of monastic life. Rather than insisting that Devasarva drop his attachments and accept the same living conditions as all of his other monks and nuns, the Buddha asked his attendant, Ānanda, to make up a beautifully adorned room in which Devasarva could spend the night. Ānanda reluctantly did so, and by sunrise Devasarva had realized awakening. Ānanda was deeply and visibly puzzled. In response, the Buddha noted that there are people whose aspiration for enlightenment grows through adorning their bodies and homes, and for them adornment is an aid to practice. Realizing enlightenment is a matter of the practitioner's mind, not one of his or her clothes or dwelling place. Concluding the story, Musō admits his own fondness for garden design and tea ceremony, and the passion that other Zen masters have for music and poetry. None of these, he informs Tadayoshi, are obstacles if one's enlightening intent is clear.

This is the climax of the second section. In the final group of exchanges, Tadayoshi seems most concerned with distinguishing between the Zen use of such terms as "original nature," "true mind," and "meditation" and the true meaning of Zen's claim to be a "separate transmission outside the teachings." The responses given by Musō are notable for their evenhandedness regarding the value of other forms of Buddhist thought and practice, as well as that of non-Buddhist teachings. But they are also notable for their masterful avoidance of forwarding any view as ultimate. Each of Musō's answers is at once a *saying* and an *unsaying*. At one point, pressed by Tadayoshi to express the meaning of realizing our "original nature" and "attaining Buddhahood," Musō rejects the standard canonical descriptions of radiating light and acquiring certain distinguishing physical characteristics and offers an earthy, experiential analogy. "It is more like someone who is drunk coming to his or her senses when the effect of the alcohol finally wears off," he says, adding that this statement is itself, of course, only a way of "explaining" and not "seeing" our original nature.

In their final substantive exchange, Tadayoshi asks pointedly if there is any truth to criticisms of Zen as neither following the Buddha's discourses nor investigating the doctrines of established schools of Buddhist thought. Musō first responds by dismissing such criticisms as rooted in failures to distinguish between the "letter" of Buddhist teachings and their "spirit." But he then goes on at considerable length quoting from sutras and teachers from all the major schools of Buddhism then extant in Japan to make the point that all acknowledge the reality of enlightening transmissions beyond words and letters. Finally, he presses for a nondualistic realization: "Followers of doctrine who criticize Zen have failed to understand not only Zen but the doctrine as well, and followers of Zen who criticize the doctrine have failed to understand not only the doctrine but Zen as well" (Kirchner, 2010:185). They are all engaged in lamentably and laughably useless efforts to "make rice by boiling sand."

ZEN TRAINING AS RELATIONAL OPENING

The conversational exchanges recorded in *Dialogues in a Dream* can on one level be read as revealing Tadayoshi's progression from relatively selfish to philosophically sophisticated concerns and questions—a narrative arc from clarifying the merits or virtues of individually achieving prosperity and influence to clarifying Zen's place in the religious landscape of medieval Japan. Written in a new hybrid script that combined Chinese characters and a Japanese syllabary, the text was clearly intended to reach a wide audience. Combined with the fact that the text was compiled at a time when Zen institutions had put down deep enough roots to ensure their long-term survival but were still in the beginning stages of expanding their reach and their dynamic integration into Japanese society, it is tempting to read the text as essentially polemical. But on another level, the text can be read as a unique collection of windows through which to glimpse the dynamics of teacher-student relations in early Zen and the scope of Zen's transformational aspirations.

Musō and Tadayoshi cannot reasonably be seen as a typical teacher-student pair. Each would have been recognized by any Japanese reader as an exemplar—Musō in the religious or spiritual sphere and Tadayoshi in the realm of military and political engagement. As such, they constituted an ideal teacher–student pair that in medieval Japan would have evoked associations with the legendary King Wen and his son, King Wu—founders of the Zhou dynasty praised by Confucius—and their intergenerational modeling of the marriage of moral/cultural (*wen*) and martial/political (*wu*) excellence. More immediately and powerfully perhaps, this pairing of moral/cultural and martial/political excellence would also have recalled the Japanese example—approvingly invoked by Musō in several exchanges—of Prince Shōtoku and his Seventeen Article Constitution. In both of these allusive contexts, the pairing of the moral/cultural and the martial/political is understood as essentially a partnership, albeit a hierarchic one in which moral/cultural excellence has primacy. Working through the vine-like tangle (*kattō*) of Tadayoshi's concerns is something that he and Musō undertake *together*.

The relationship they exemplify is one of mutual investigation and investment through which the horizons of Tadayoshi's concerns are repeatedly dissolved, resulting in the continuous expansion of the compass and depth of their shared attention. As Musō makes clear by insisting early on that the intentional ground of Zen practice consists in taking the Buddha as personal ideal and generating unwavering *bodhicitta*, this expansion is not something measured in increments of material gain or even spiritual powers, but rather in *qualities* of compassion and wisdom.

Musō does not set the agenda of their conversations and has no apparent "curriculum" according to which he shapes his conduct as teacher. His role is not prescriptive, but rather responsive. In part, this might be attributed to the unique circumstances of Tadayoshi not formally being a student of Musō's during their exchanges. Tadayoshi only takes the step of requesting a formal master–disciple relationship several years later, in 1349. Perhaps for this reason, we have no indication of Tadayoshi ever being given specific "homework" to do between their encounters—something that would have been natural in a formal master–disciple relationship. Nevertheless, the responsive character of Musō's engagement with Tadayoshi is perfectly consistent with Musō's explicit identification of Zen realization with becoming what Chan master Linji referred to as "a true person of no rank"—someone capable of according with any situation and responding as needed to orient its dynamics in an enlightening direction. Musō demonstrates a virtuosic capacity for working out from within the circumstances of his student's immediate concerns. Rather than imposing a structure on their encounters, he attends to enhancing the quality of their interactions by carefully and repeatedly breaching the conceptual walls within which Tadayoshi is able—or allows himself—to be present.

The general Buddhist view is that concepts are distillations of experiential regularities—a function of patterns in our interactions with the world around us. These patterns are not discovered, however; they emerge and evolve in parallel with the changing complexions of values and intentions that modulate the scale and scope of our attention, and that shape and orient our actions. Simply put, concepts are karmic abstracts. They do not reveal the world "as it is," but rather the world "as it has come to be" through the play of our past purposes and propensities. Life within our own conceptual walls is samsara: the experience of our present circumstances as other than enlightening. Breaching those walls is nirvana: opening up to the meaning of relating freely.

Given this, it is not surprising that a central connecting theme of Musō's and Tadayoshi's "dialogues in a dream" is the dramatic force of karma in shaping one's present and future relational circumstances and experiences. Again and again, Musō stresses the importance in Zen training of one's intentions and the values according to which they are formulated and sustained. In one crucial early exchange, Musō remarks that although enlightened beings or Buddhas have "perfect freedom of function in all things," they cannot guide those with whom they lack a karmic connection, and they cannot alter others' "fixed karma"—the pattern of outcomes and opportunities shaped by their own values, intentions, and actions. What an enlightened teacher can do is to draw attention to the ways in which present experiences and relational dynamics are being configured by one's past intentions and values so that one can turn those experiences and relationships to liberating account. The Zen training to which Musō introduces Tadayoshi is not fundamentally a matter of sitting in meditative silence or engaging in temple rituals; it is certainly not extinguishing thought or seeing all things as an illusion. It is training in karmic clarification: a "sobering" of awakening intent.

In keeping with this, Musō does not present Zen teachings and training as marking the culmination of Buddhist history—an evolutionary pinnacle below which all other forms of Buddhism stand as inferior. Instead, and much like Dōgen, he sees Zen as the revival of the primordial practice of the earliest Buddhist community—a community in which there were not yet any classifications of teachings as sudden or gradual, of practitioners as keen or dull, or of monks or nuns as either doctrinal, disciplinary, or meditative specialists. In this sense, Zen is not a school built around a particular set of doctrines or methods that might be contrasted and placed in competition with those of other schools, Buddhist or not. Zen training is not a means of transcending the mundane world and its entanglements, whether through rebirth in a Pure Land or through esoteric union with the cosmos as a whole. Zen training is reproducing or enacting, here and now, the transformative partnership realized by the Buddha and his disciples—realizing a world in which all things and all activities do the great work of enlightenment.

9

ZEN EXEMPLARS: DŌGEN, IKKYŪ, HAKUIN, AND RYŌKAN

Zen training is not an individual undertaking; it is a partnership, a shared relational journey "home" to spontaneous expression of one's original Buddha-nature. In Tang and Song China, it was customary for students to go "on the road" in search of teachers under whom they could train with confidence, traveling from monastery to monastery with what few possessions they could easily carry. Many of the first generations of Japanese monks who went to China in search of authentic Chan training adopted this practice and brought back with them an appreciation for the benefits of studying under different masters.

In spite of this, a consistent refrain in the teachings of Chan and Zen masters over the last fifteen hundred years has been to warn against interpreting the Buddhist path as a search for someone or something outside of oneself. One of the most basic rhythms in Zen training plays out as a teacher peppers his or her exhortations to hold nothing back in striving to realize Buddha-nature with a "backbeat" of admonitions to do so without expectations, without goals, and without thoughts of either freeing oneself from anything or arriving at any sort of completion. The most renowned teachers were masterful in their handling of this rhythm.

There is an illustrative tale in the *Blue Cliff Record* in which Chan master Huangbo uses one of his Dharma talks to raise the matter of students traveling about to taste and test various Chan teachings and teachers.[1] Looking out over the gathering of monks, nuns, and lay practitioners assembled for the talk, he disappointedly remarks that "all of you are just gorging yourselves on dregs." Shaking his head slowly from side to side as if somewhat mystified, he asks, "Don't you know that there are no Chan teachers in all of Tang China?" One of the monks steps forward to object: "If that's true, then who are those presently leading assemblies and correcting students?" Smiling mischievously, Huangbo clarifies that he didn't say anything about there being "no Chan," only that there are no "Chan teachers." Centuries later, when Dōgen rehearses this story for his own students, he insists that he, too, has never denied the existence of Zen, but only the existence of Zen teachers. In Zen training, he insists, there is just "self and self, standing shoulder to shoulder" (see Leighton, 2010:149).

This image of standing shoulder to shoulder wonderfully illustrates utter commitment to facing challenges together. Zen practice is not something that teachers and students have in common; it is a process in which each has a distinctive, contributory share. But this image should not be construed as indicating a leveling out of the differences between teachers and students. It is not as equals that teacher and student practice together. It remains a key responsibility of the teacher to help the student realize— as Dōgen puts in his essay, *Genjōkōan*—that "when one begins seeking the Dharma, one strays far from the Dharma's boundaries."[2] The teacher's role is to help students *emerge* from the self-defining attitude of searching for enlightenment to expressing it directly in action. There are no "Zen teachers" because awakening cannot be *taught*; it is not awarded like a degree earned by taking a certain number of university classes, or transferred like a skill that can be drilled into place through repeated physical or mental exercise. This is the point of Linji's cutting description of students who attempt to digest the wisdom of Chan ancestors by repeatedly mouthing their words: "That's like having taking a pile of shit into your mouth and then spitting it out to give to someone else!" (*Taishō shinshū daizōkyō*, 1985:47.501c). Likewise, students who aim at gaining entry to Zen by continually engaging in meditation and temple rituals have been compared to "mosquitoes biting an iron ox." The heart of Zen training is the live encounter of teacher and student.

Working effectively shoulder to shoulder, like dancing fluidly as a couple, involves trust born out of ongoing mutual attunement. It is an expression of intimate understanding, not something acquired from outside of the relationship. This kind of intensely personal and shared understanding is never a function of teacher and student merely *conforming* to each another, but rather of being wholly present for and *confirming* one another. This relational dynamic can take countless shapes. Speaking from the teacher's side, Dōgen characterized the spectrum of personal styles evident among Zen masters as stretching from those who engage students by means of "thunderous fists" to those who do so by means of "grandmotherly kindness." In each case, however, the intent is to alloy wisdom and compassion in the way needed for teacher and student to transform the dance of "self" and "other" into something more like a dancing of "oneself" with "oneself," realizing what Chan/Zen refers to as "a single heart-mind" (Ch: *yixin*).

It is this achievement of liberating intimacy that we are invited to witness in the encounter dialogues that are at the heart of the Chan and Zen narrative canons. In Zen training, every effort is made by both teacher and student to marshal the personal resources required to *inhabit* the achievement of liberating intimacy that can be glimpsed through these narratives. Of course, even getting to the point of glimpsing the personal heart of Zen in this way requires considerable familiarity with the characters peopling these narratives. Every encounter dialogue presents us with a dramatic turning point in a relationship—the equivalent of a film clip that enables us to view the "tipping point" from ordinary to enlightening relationality. But it is very hard to inhabit an episodic recording, no matter how wonderfully crafted. And this is perhaps a partial explanation for the astounding volume of Chan and Zen writings. For each encounter dialogue, there is an extensive backstage of carefully interwoven personal histories, both actual and imagined, that help to create a space capacious enough for practice-transforming habitation.

Fleshing out backstories for every recorded moment of transmission might be dismissed as part of the Chan/Zen obsession with lineage—an obsession, some might say, with crafting legitimizing discourses about Zen's own origins. But in the context of sincerely engaged practice, the interwoven narratives produced by Zen exercises of literary genius open onto a richly detailed landscape of intimate interpersonal encounters reaching all the way back to the historical Buddha and his offering of the "true Dharma eye treasury, the wondrous mind of liberation," to his disciple Mahākāśyapa. As many contemporary scholars have pointed out, when this seminal Chan/Zen tale began circulating in late Tang and early Song China, it can hardly be supposed to have been an accurate depiction of an event that purportedly took place over a thousand years previously.

Rather than history, it offers a myth of origins—an archetypal representation of the public authentication of interpersonally recognized enlightenment. But for those who are wholly immersed in practice, it brings into focus a "genetic" continuity among persons and communities spanning thousands of years and miles—an experience, ultimately, of becoming enfolded in enlightening interaction.

Born into a wealthy family, Mahākāśyapa had from early childhood aspired to a spiritual life. To please his parents, he had agreed to an arranged marriage with a beautiful woman from a good family, only to discover that his wife, Bhadda, shared his aspiration. They lived celibately together for a time and then decided to leave their home and go on the road as spiritual seekers. Though committed to one another and to their quest, they were harassed continually by people who could not credit the sincerity of a man and woman traveling together as celibate spiritual seekers. Eventually, they decided to separate, promising that whoever was first to meet a true teacher would let the other know. That good fortune fell to Mahākāśyapa, who met the Buddha and quickly became one of his foremost disciples. Bhadda soon followed and became a leading nun and one of the first women to realize enlightenment through training under the Buddha. With this backstory in mind, we are asked to envision the Buddha looking out over a sea of ten thousand monks, nuns, and laypeople assembled at Vulture's Peak and holding up a single white flower while sweeping his gaze silently over the assembly. From among the ten thousand faces turned toward him in the clear mountain air, a single subtle smile shines forth. Gazes lock in a measureless instant of mutual recognition, perhaps not unlike that shared by parents and their newborns in the almost psychedelic glow of a healthy delivery. The defining moment of teacher–student "encounter" and "transmission" is one of expansive and yet intimate communion.

Becoming familiar with the relational "landscape" of Zen has traditionally been an important part of entering the personal dimensions of Zen. Exploring that landscape with any degree of thoroughness, however, would be a lifetime endeavor. Here, we will have to be content with becoming modestly familiar with a small set of Zen "peaks" chosen to represent different eras in the evolution of Japanese Zen and different approaches to expressing the liberating intimacy of Zen awakening: the lives and teachings of Dōgen, Ikkyū, Hakuin, and Ryōkan.

DŌGEN KIGEN, 1200–1253: THE RELIGIOUS VIRTUOSO AND PHILOSOPHER

Dōgen is perhaps most widely renowned today as Japan's premier medieval philosopher. And to be sure, he stands out both as being one of the most prolific writers in Zen history and as demonstrating an almost postmodern sensitivity to language. But during his lifetime, Dōgen was less widely celebrated for his literary brilliance and intellectual prowess than for his religious charisma. So powerful and thorough was his demonstration of a virtuosic Buddhist monastic life that even the most ordinary circumstances in his presence were apparently imbued with a scent of the miraculous. Although he was fully convinced of the liberating potential of skillfully used language, the central focus of his Zen teaching and the community that coalesced around him was not intellectual understanding, but rather fierce confidence in "practice as verification" or the "equivalence of practice and realization" (*shushōittō*). Consistent with this, what comes through most clearly in his Dharma talks, letters to students, poetry, and *kōan* commentaries (collected as the *Eihei Kōroku*) is an almost palpable spiritual urgency—a forceful insistence on the *immediacy* of awakening.

Traditionally, Dōgen's urgency is traced back to the loss of his mother when he was just seven years old. There is some historical uncertainty about Dōgen's parentage, but in the narrative lore of Zen he is presented as a perhaps illegitimate offspring of Koga Michichiga and one of Fujiwara Motofusa's daughters. If true, Dōgen would have been well positioned to lead a life of considerable wealth and influence, with family connections both to the imperial court and to the foremost members of the literary elite of Kyōto. We do know, however, that Dōgen himself attributed his extraordinary sensitivity to issues of language and literary aesthetics to an early education that included reading widely from the classical canons of both China and Japan—clearly the mark of an elite upbringing. But whatever material comforts and exposure to great literary texts he might have enjoyed as a child, they would have offered neither solace nor satisfying explanations at the time of his mother's death.

The cause of his mother's passing is unknown. Given the conditions in Kyōto at the time, however, it's likely that she succumbed to one of the infectious diseases that swept through the city with both great regularity and virulence at the beginning of the thirteenth century. On her deathbed, she is said to have summoned Dōgen to her side and asked him to enter the monastic life in order to dedicate himself to learning how to dissolve the causal conditions that had made of her own life a sketchy tableau of tragically fleeting moments of understanding and happiness embroidered onto a darkly billowing tapestry of ignorance, trouble, and suffering. At her funeral, as the young Dōgen stood watching incense smoke swirl upward and disappear, he is said to have had his first deep insight into impermanence and to have consciously formulated his intent to realize enlightenment.

There is no way to establish the veracity of this account. But little imagination is needed to appreciate the life-altering trauma of a young boy yearning with all his might for his mother to get well, only to be forced to watch helplessly as her body progressively fails and she finally lets go, leaving him as gut-wrenchingly alone in the world as humanly possible. Surrounded later by members of his extended family, he would have been guided through rituals designed to ensure her spirit's safe departure: the cremating of her body as monks chanted Buddhist sutras, the sorting of bone fragments from her ashes, and then the placement of her ashes in an urn for burial. These funerary rituals offered the bereaved opportunities for taking cathartic leave of loved ones and ensuring their safe passage into the realm of ancestral spirits. But we can imagine that no matter how sincerely performed these rituals were, the young Dōgen would have been shot through with incomparable feelings of absence and would have held close his mother's dying wish.

Adopted by his mother's younger brother, Fujiwara Moroie, who had no heir of his own, Dōgen was groomed to enter the inner circles of Kyōto's aristocratic elite. But on the verge of ceremonial entry into manhood at age twelve, Dōgen decided that honoring his mother's final wish was more filial than accepting the course envisioned for him by his uncle. With another relative's help, he was admitted to one of the most respected Buddhist studies centers on Mount Hiei and was soon ordained as a Tendai monk. After a year of intensive study, he began looking beyond Mount Hiei for a teacher able to resolve what he experienced as a contradiction between the Tendai and Shingon teachings of "original enlightenment" (*hongaku*) and "enlightenment with this very body" (*shokushinjōbutsu*), and the turmoil and moral decay that were so evident both within the monastic walls on Mount Hiei and beyond them. In 1217, perhaps inspired by an earlier meeting with Eisai (who passed away in

1215), he began studying Zen at Kenninji under the direction of Eisai's disciple, Myōzen, and remained in residence there until 1223 when he accompanied Myōzen on a trip to China.

Dōgen received Dharma transmission in Eisai's Rinzai lineage from Myōzen in 1221 and regarded him as one of his two great teachers. Once in China, however, Myōzen and Dōgen were unable to remain together. Due to a bureaucratic mishap, Dōgen was forced to remain aboard their ship until his petition to enter China had been officially approved. Myōzen proceeded inland, leaving his student behind. But as the Zen saying goes, "a 'good' situation can be a bad situation, and a 'bad' situation can be a good one." This certainly proved to be true for Dōgen. During the three months that he was prohibited from disembarking, he had a turning-point encounter with an elderly monk looking for Japanese shiitake mushrooms.[3]

Nothing in Dōgen's training in Japan would have prepared him to regard meeting a monastic cook as a potentially momentous event. But he and the monk fell into lively conversation, and as dusk approached Dōgen was reluctant to end their discussion. "Why not share a pot of tea, spend the night on board, and return to the temple in the morning?" he asked. The monk explained that this wasn't possible. Being the temple cook (*tenzo*) was his training; how could he leave his duty for others to handle? Somewhat perplexed, Dōgen objected, "But in your old age, why not leave this duty to someone younger and devote yourself to meditation or studying the *kōans* of the ancient masters?" The old monk laughed for a while and then suggested that as a foreigner, Dōgen was perhaps ignorant of the true meaning of practice and the words of the ancients. Ashamed and taken aback, Dōgen asked, "So, what is practice? What are words?" The old cook replied that if Dōgen kept asking and fully penetrated these questions, then eventually he would be a person of understanding. As the cook departed, Dōgen felt as if he'd been offered a glimpse of something important.

Once permission to leave the ship had been granted, Dōgen went to study at the major Chan temple at Mount Tiantong. A few months later, he was happily surprised to see the old cook approaching across the courtyard. They greeted one another warmly, and the cook informed Dōgen that he had heard through the monastic grapevine that Dōgen was training at Mount Tiantong and had decided to pay a visit on his way into retirement in his home village. After serving tea, Dōgen recalled their discussion on the ship and again asked the *tenzo*, "What are words?" The old cook replied, "One, two, three, four, five." Dōgen then asked, "And what is practice?" Setting down his cup, the *tenzo* smiled and said, "Everywhere, nothing is hidden."

These encounters had a transformative effect on Dōgen. The Buddhism that he had studied in Japan affirmed that it was possible to realize "enlightenment with this very body," but even in Eisai's Zen community the meaning of this affirmation had been colored by the esoteric lenses of Tendai and Shingon, and by Japanese convictions about the efficacy of ritual. Through his encounters with the old Chinese *tenzo*, Dōgen came to realize that enlightenment with this very body is possible no matter what one's duties are or where one carries them out—in a kitchen, at a construction site, in an office, a library, or the Dharma Hall. As he would later put it in his essay, "Instructions to the Temple Cook" (*Tenzo Kyokun*), the true meaning of enlightenment with this very body is that "the mind that finds the Way actualizes itself through working with sleeves rolled up." The ingredients for enlightenment are always everywhere right at hand.

Dōgen had left Japan in search of an enlightening Buddhist community. While in China, he became convinced that if the ingredients for awakening were always present, what he had been missing was the right technique or practice and that the key to unlocking the gate of authentic practice was to fully embrace traditional Chan monastic rules and regulations. It shocked him to discover how deeply worldly concerns had come to be infused into the monastic life at the Chan temples he was visiting, and this convinced him further that properly "cooking" the ingredients for enlightenment depended on finding the right teacher with whom to work "shoulder to shoulder." Two years after arriving in China, much of it spent traveling from temple to temple, he despaired of finding such a teacher. Having heard that Myōzen was ill, he decided to pay a visit to his old master before returning to Japan. On the way, he chanced to hear that a new abbot was being installed at the temple on Mount Tiantong and that this new abbot, Rujing, was uniquely unconcerned with worldly affairs—a Caodong Chan lineage holder who emphasized the centrality of strictly observing monastic regimen and having a powerful commitment to "just sitting" (*shikantaza*). As it turned out, this was the teacher Dōgen had been seeking.

Tradition has it that not long after he had begun practicing under Rujing, Dōgen experienced his second great turning point during his sojourn in China. While sitting in meditation one day, he noticed that the monk next to him was falling asleep, swaying like a tree set in motion by regularly spaced gusts of wind. Just then, Rujing appeared in front of the monk and barked, "Our ancestral practice is dropping off body and mind. What do you hope to attain by drowsing?" Hearing this, Dōgen is said to have been overcome with profound joy. Whether this event actually occurred or is the invention of later generations is not clear. But after two years practicing with and eventually receiving Dharma transmission from Rujing, the teaching phrase "dropping off body and mind" was pivotal to Dōgen's understanding of Zen, and it became a crucial element in his own teaching style after returning to Japan in 1227.

The meaning of "dropping off body and mind" (J: *shinjindatsuraku*) and its inversion, "body and mind dropped off," have been the subject of considerable debate. But as is made clear in the conversations with Rujing that Dōgen recounts in the *Hōkyōki*—his own record of his years in China—Rujing did not use "dropping off body and mind" to refer to the achievement of some form of transcendental abstraction. Instead, Rujing identified "dropping off body and mind" with *zazen* and with parting from desires informed by greed, anger, drowsiness, distraction, doubt, and ignorance. Furthermore, he made clear that *zazen* should not be confused with the meditation activities of *arhats* and *pratyekabuddhas* who are content to realize liberation for themselves alone. In the *zazen* of Buddhas and Chan ancestors, Rujing insisted, it is compassion and vowing to save all sentient beings that have primacy; because of this they are able to practice *zazen* "within the world of desire" by "allowing their minds to be flexible."

In the *Fukanzazenji*, Dōgen's first effort to put the fruit of his time in China in writing, he presents *zazen* as the seminal expression of the Buddha Way.[4] Through *zazen*, he says, "your body and mind naturally fall away, and your original Buddha-nature manifests." *Zazen* is not a step-by-step method of meditation aimed at generating certain kinds of experience; it is the "easy and simple practice of a Buddha." To engage in this practice, he says, set aside both worldly concerns and thoughts of becoming a Buddha, find a quiet place to sit, and "think of not thinking." The essential art of *zazen*, he says, is just "nonthinking . . . realizing the

Dharma gate of great ease and joy" to manifest the simultaneous practice and verification of the Buddha Way.

This might be interpreted as an equation of "dropping off body and mind" with an inner realization that results from *zazen* or with the revelation of an abiding spiritual core as the elements of one's mundane and impermanent personal identity fall away. But Dōgen explicitly insisted that beliefs in body-mind dualism and in the existence of an abiding self or soul are not Buddhist and have no place in Zen. In one of his early Dharma Hall Discourses (no. 18), he caps his remarks about realizing an enlightening presence by urging his assembled students, "Without turning your backs on either a thousand or ten thousand people, drop off body and mind, go to the hall, and practice *zazen*."[5] Dropping off body and mind is not an act of spiritual transcendence or indifference toward the world; it is an intentional attitude—a *way* of being present while crossing the temple compound to engage in group practice, fully manifesting the compassionate purpose of the Buddha Way. As he writes in *Bendōwa*, his second work after returning from China, "Just drop off body and mind in the practice of *zazen*; if even once you sit up straight in attentive virtuosity (*samādhi*), imprinting the Buddha-seal in your bodily, verbal, and mental activities, each and every thing in the cosmos becomes the Buddha-seal and all space without exception is enlightenment."[6] Doing so, not only the person seated in *zazen* but everything in his or her environment—both natural and human—carries out "the Buddha-work of preaching and enlightening." Dropping off body and mind consists in intentionally manifesting nonduality.

Thus, in one of his later Dharma Hall Discourses (no. 449), Dōgen says, "What we refer to as *zazen* is sitting, cutting through smoke and clouds without seeking merit . . . becoming unified, never reaching the end." Elsewhere (no. 419), after drawing a circle in the air, he states, "Dropping off body and mind: function without effort." Drawing a second circle, he inverts the first phrase and states, "Body and mind dropped off: serenity without departure." As Mazu realized through Huairang's rubbing a roof tile to "make a mirror"—a story to which Dōgen turned on numerous teaching occasions—*zazen* is not sitting to *become* a Buddha. *Zazen* is sitting *as* a Buddha. For Dōgen, this was not something that was possible only for the religiously adept, the well educated, or the monastic within temple walls. Toward the end of *Bendōwa*, he poses a question about whether *zazen* is only for those who have "left the home life" or if lay men and women can undertake it successfully. His answer is unequiv-ocal: "When it comes to realizing the Buddha Dharma, no distinction obtains among men and women, whether high born or low."

Sitting as a Buddha is not, however, the same thing as simply settling onto a meditation cushion and imagining that one is an enlightened and enlightening being. Again, the essential art of *zazen* is nonthinking. This does not consist in an erasure or negation of thought—acts that imply the existence (the "standing apart") of someone to carry them out. Nonthink-ing is presence *without* thinking—sitting in the absence of even the cate-gories of thought and thinker. As Dōgen clarifies in *Genjōkōan*, the Bud-dha Way involves "leaping clear of both the richness and lack of catego-ries," including the category of enlightened beings. In perhaps the most quoted passage of this essay, he describes the dynamics of practice-real-ization: "To model yourself after the 'way' of the buddhas is to model yourself after yourself. To model yourself after yourself is to forget your-self. To forget yourself is to be authenticated by the totality of phenome-na. To be authenticated by the totality of phenomena is to completely drop away one's own body-mind as well as the body-mind of others." Having done so, "all traces of enlightenment disappear, and this traceless enlightenment continues on without end."[7]

Compassionately attuned presence without thinking is the heart of Zen practice: the authentication of one's original Buddha-nature. But the fact that sitting *thus*, as a Buddha, is possible for all should not be understood as indicating that it is a path without rigor. As Dōgen is keen to point out, it was not for nothing that Siddhartha Gautama trained six years prior to his awakening; it was not a matter of empty tradition that every Chan ancestor from Bodhidharma onward engaged in lifelong *zazen* after awakening. Not only is the Buddha Way actualized "with sleeves rolled up"; it is actualized continuously.

In recognition of this, it seems, Dōgen at times felt compelled to criticize those proponents of Linji Chan who advocated an intensive and exclusive focus on key phrases drawn from Chan encounter dialogues or "public cases" (*kōan*) for the purpose of triggering breakthrough experi-ences of awakening (*kenshō*). Explosive experiences of insight and ex-panded awareness do occur. But for Dōgen, these should not be seen as the culmination of Zen practice. In a passage written for a monk being placed in charge of the temple toilets for a year, Dōgen said by way of encouragement, "To be either a practice leader or follower, each time

raise it up; each time freshly. What is raising up is losing great enlightenment. What is fresh is to suddenly be greatly enlightened" (*Eihei Kōroku*,
8.7). To make sure there was no mistaking his point, he added, "When
you lose money in the river, you look in the river." If you lose your
Buddha-mind in the toilet, look for it there. Practice-realization is moment-by-moment remaining fresh.

As Dōgen points out in *Genjōkōan*, remaining fresh is not possible if
one is busy with "conveying one's self toward things to carry out practice-realization; that is delusion." Rather, practice-realization is "all
things conveying themselves toward and carrying out practice-realization
through one's self." The unity of practice and realization is not *made* to
happen. It is not a construct—the result of instrumental engagement with
one's own body and mind, or with others. But neither is it the result of
inaction—a "spontaneous" happening at which one is simply an observing bystander. We might say that if *zazen* is the expression of attentive
presence-without-thinking, practice-realization expresses the *relational
emergence* of responsive functioning-without-acting. Dōgen's Zen consists, in other words, in moving obliquely beyond the duality of thinking
and not thinking, acting and not acting, being and not being a Buddha.

As for many contemporary readers and practitioners, understanding
these teaching phrases and actualizing them proved elusive for many of
Dōgen's students. Explanations only go so far. Acknowledging this,
Dōgen recommended, "Where explanatory documents are of no use, en-
act in detail the ancient ones' intentions" (*Eihei Kōroku*, 1.87). In other
words, emulate their *relational direction*—the values being enacted in
their lived commitments. On another occasion, he recounts a *kōan* in
which the fourth Chan ancestor, Daoxin, asks his master, Sengcan, to
present him with the Dharma-gate of liberation. Sengcan responds by
asking, "Who has bound you?" Daoxin innocently admits, "Nobody has
bound me," and Sengcan deftly shoots back, "Then why are you seeking
liberation?" Hearing this, Daoxin had a great realization and spent the
next nine years refining it under Sengcan's guidance. After reciting this
story, Dōgen caps it with a poem of his own that practically twinkles with
both candor and humor: "If you want to know the meaning of a wheel
freely spinning, only someone turning somersaults can show you."

While in Kyōto, Dōgen expressed the meaning of the Buddha Way for
a wide range of people, including monks, nuns, laymen, and laywomen,
from both elite and humble backgrounds, "turning somersaults" in per-

sonal and written demonstration of the meaning of practice-realization. For reasons that are unclear, after leaving Kyōto for the remote mountains of Echizen, Dōgen became much more intensely focused on his core monastic followers and the realization of an ideal institutional environment within which to practice Zen. Although he continued working with lay students, including women, the emphasis of his writings shifted in the direction of clearly articulating the behavioral and attitudinal dimensions of living an exemplary life in a Zen temple. In part, this may have been the result of the fact that most of his close disciples had first trained as Tendai monks or in the Darumashū community in Echizen. Dōgen's vision of the ideal Buddhist monastic community was at considerable variance with the actual communities in which these disciples had previously lived and practiced, and the disparity between his institutional ideal and the reality assumed by many of his students may partially account for the markedly new slant of his teachings from 1243 until his death in 1253.

Yet this emphasis on monastic rules and comportment can also be seen as part of Dōgen's convictions about the generative power of serious and sustained communal Buddhist practice. As already noted, Dōgen openly endorsed the possibility of successfully undertaking practice-realization in the midst of the world of desires. But he was also well aware of the principle expressed by the Chan adage that "the more mud, the bigger the Buddha." His monastic community at Eiheiji was his attempt to bring together enough dedicated monks capable of sitting continuously *as* Buddhas to respond to the enormity of the "mud" in which Japanese society was mired at the time. The community at Eiheiji was, perhaps, his attempt to realize in manageable microcosm the conditions needed for authenticating the nonduality of personal practice-realization and communal practice-realization, setting in motion an epochal, Buddhist transformation of Japan and the world beyond its shores.

IKKYŪ SŌJUN, 1394–1481: THE SOCIAL CRITIC AND ICONOCLAST

In the century and a half after Dōgen's passing, Zen flourished. The *gozan* system of elite-sponsored temples evolved into a lavishly supported and culturally sophisticated network. The stricter lifestyle of intensive *zazen* and *kōan* study practiced in the *rinka* temples of the Ōtōkan

Rinzai line attracted ever greater numbers of advocates. Sōtō Zen spread throughout the country and played increasingly important roles in ministering to the religious needs of the common people, merchants, and rural samurai. But a golden age was not forthcoming. Alongside great advances being made in culture and the arts, tensions persisted among warrior elites and between the Northern and Southern courts of the divided imperial family. Weakness at the center of the shogunate in Kyōto enabled enough of a centrifugal transfer of power to the geographical and social peripheries of provincial *daimyo* to finally result in the eruption of a devastating civil war. Largely fought in and around the capital for over a decade, from 1467 to 1477, the streets of Kyōto were often blocked with piles of the dead. By the end of the war, the city had been almost completely burned to the ground, and Japan sank into a half century of low-grade but persistent armed conflict. This *sengoku-jidai*, or "warring states period," would not end until the Tokugawa overthrow of the Ashikaga shogunate.

Ikkyū was both literally and figuratively a progeny of central forces at work in this conflict-laden era. Two years prior to his birth, the shogun, Ashikaga Yoshimitsu, had brokered a peace treaty that specified a generation-by-generation alternation of the right to the throne between the Northern and Southern lines of the imperial family. Ikkyū's mother was a lady-in-waiting at the Southern Court and seems to have been the daughter of an eminent general; his father was the lineage holder of the Northern line, the sixteen-year-old Emperor Go-Komatsu. This alliance did not meet with the approval of powers at the Northern Court. Ikkyū's pregnant mother was sent away to live with family members in Kyōto, and Ikkyū was born as an illegitimate commoner on New Year's Day of 1394.

In response to what he perceived as the misguided emphases of Japanese Buddhism at the beginning of the thirteenth century, Dōgen had attempted a revitalization based on the primacy of sitting *as* a Buddha. This was an approach to practice-realization that he deemed universally applicable, but one that he also understood as most powerfully exemplified by leading a simple and strictly disciplined monastic life. For Dōgen, absolute dedication to monastic discipline was the root expression of the ancient masters' enlightening intention. Ikkyū also dedicated himself to the revitalization of Buddhism. But rather than turning to the historical Buddha as a model, he took the route of personally exemplifying the at times shocking capacity for relating freely that featured so prominently in the recorded encounter dialogues and *kōans* attributed to such Tang dynasty Chan masters as Mazu, Huangbo, and Linji. In turn dismayed and angered by what he saw as the decadent aestheticism and almost fetishistic desire for power that shaped life in both *gozan* and *rinka* temples, Ikkyū came to feel a special kinship with Linji and his iconoclastic disdain for convention. But whereas Linji seems to have maintained a relatively uncontroversial monastic lifestyle, Ikkyū went well beyond rhetorical iconoclasm, making a shambles of both monastic and social convention. If Dōgen's greatest legacy lay in his philosophical writings and his personification of freedom in the medium of language, Ikkyu's lay in his poetry and calligraphy and his personification of relating freely in the medium of human passions.

Like Dōgen, Ikkyū was introduced to formal Buddhist training at a very early age, also at his mother's wishes. In Ikkyū's case, however, it was for his own protection that his mother sent him to live and study at a nearby Rinzai temple at age five, two years before Emperor Go-Komatsu's second son was born. There, and later at one of the top *gozan* temples, Ikkyū was treated to an excellent education in the Chinese and Japanese classics, but also in the complacency of most Rinzai monks. In 1410, "filled with shame" at the lackadaisical practice and manifestly skewed commitments he had witnessed, Ikkyū deserted the *gozan* system and began training under a Zen recluse by the name of Ken'o (d. 1414), living in a ramshackle hut in the hills outside of Kyōto. When Ken'o died, Ikkyū fell into a deep despair and is said to have contemplated throwing himself into the waters of Lake Biwa and placing himself at the mercy of the Bodhisattva Kannon to either be saved or become food for lake fishes. The timely arrival of a messenger from his mother and her assurances that he would find a new teacher and realize the meaning of enlightenment led him to reconsider.

After living for a time with his mother and becoming even more firmly convinced of the need for hard training, he earned a place in a small practicing community located on the shores of Lake Biwa. This small group was headed by Kasō (1352–1428), a notoriously strict Zen master in the Ōtōkan Rinzai line founded by Daitō. There, Ikkyū practiced for over twelve years and had two major experiences of awakening. The first occurred while he was listening to a wandering minstrel sing a tragic Heian-era love story that chronicles the lives of two ladies-in-waiting and their eventual abandonment of the sexual and political intrigues of court life to ordain as Buddhist nuns. The second and more powerful experience occurred in 1420 as he meditated in a small fishing boat adrift on the starlit summer waters of Lake Biwa. After offering a convincing response when Kasō later challenged the validity of his awakening, Ikkyū went on to admit that he had practiced for a decade "seething with anger" only to find that as the raucous cawing of a crow shattered the evening's silence "an enlightened disciple of the Buddha suddenly surfaced" from within the mud of his emotional torment.

Ikkyū continued practicing under Kasō for another four years, earning the deep respect of his master as well as a reputation for eccentricity. According to a biography compiled by Ikkyū's disciples not long after his death, when Kasō offered Ikkyū a "seal" of his enlightenment (*inka*)—a document essential for anyone seeking advancement in the Rinzai hierarchy—Ikkyū refused to accept it. Later discovering that Kasō had given the document to a laywoman for safekeeping, Ikkyū took possession of the *inka*, tore it to shreds, and asked his disciples to burn it. On another occasion, when Kasō was hosting a memorial service for his own master, Ikkyū spurned the custom of wearing ceremonial raiment and showed up in patched robes and grass sandals, drawing the considerable ire of the rest of the community. Questioned by Kasō about his behavior, Ikkyū said that he was dressed simply, as a monk should be, while everyone else was prancing about in sumptuous "shit covers." At the end of the service, when Kasō was asked who would be his Dharma successor, he reportedly surveyed the gathering and said, perhaps with some reluctance, "the crazy one."

But that was not to be. Ikkyū moved out of Kasō's community in 1426 and embarked on an itinerant lifestyle that he maintained almost continuously for the next five decades. It is not clear whether his eccentricity—which may have extended to fathering a son with the daughter of an art store owner—had eventually outweighed the respect he had earned from Kasō, or if Ikkyū himself had wearied of the spiritual pretensions and material preoccupations prevalent among those seemingly destined to rise in the ranks of institutional Zen. A contributing factor, to be sure, was the acute mutual disdain (and, at times, animosity) that characterized his relationship with Kasō's most senior disciple, Yōsō (1376–1458)—a conservative and institutionally adept monk who eventually inherited Kasō's community and lavishly renovated the ancestral temple of the Daitō lineage. Ikkyū had devoted himself to Kasō precisely because he carried the torch of Daitō's personification of a "true person of no rank"—a rigorously ascetic approach to Zen exemplified by Daitō having tempered his own enlightenment by living under a bridge with beggars and other outcasts for five years. That Yōsō would inherit the mantle of Daitō's and Kasō's unfettered Zen and become abbot of Daitokuji was apparently too much for Ikkyū.

Although Ikkyū was at one point granted a small residence in Kyōto and late in life maintained a retreat named Shūon'an in the hills between Nara and Kyōto, from his early thirties until his sixties he was for the most part "on the road," traveling in the environs of Kyōto, Nara, and the port city of Sakai (near modern Osaka). During these middle decades of the fifteenth century, Japan was undergoing major political upheaval. The central government of the Ashikaga shoguns was steadily weakening. Provincial *daimyō* were becoming ever more militarily and politically assertive. And as both central and provincial powers repeatedly failed to respond effectively to an uncommon string of natural disasters, the resulting waves of famine and disease triggered a series of peasant rebellions, many of which were organized around pleas for debt amnesties in times of severe hardship. It was a period that would later be known as an era of *gekokujō*—an era when "those below overturn those above."

At the same time, however, trade with Ming China was booming, much of it brokered by leading *gozan* temple monks whose Chinese-language skills enabled them (quite profitably) to serve as "foreign relations" officers. As the monetary economy expanded and technological efficiencies improved agricultural production, spaces opened for considerable social mobility. Market towns like Sakai became what amounted to realms of the "unbound," or those living "without ties" (*muen*)—places where hereditary elites mixed with the newly wealthy and with artists, performers, actors, artisans, and other "marginals" or *kawaramono* (literally "riverbed riffraff"), celebrating and giving ever more expansive expression to the new cultural ideal of the *basara* or "extravagant" and "eccentric."

It was in this unbound world that Ikkyū nurtured his awakening. A vivid portrait of his life during this period is presented in his poems, nearly a thousand of which were compiled by his disciples within a year of his death. Making use of Ikkyū's penname, they titled the collection the *Kyōunshū*, or "Crazy Cloud Anthology."[8] The term *kyō* can be translated as "mad," "wild," or "violent," and a figurative rendering of *kyōun* might be "roiling cloud." It is a fitting image for Zen's most iconoclastic and countercultural master. In Japan, monks on pilgrimage were often characterized as *unsui* or "cloud-water" floating high above the turmoil of daily life. For agricultural peoples, like the medieval Japanese, clouds were both sources of life-replenishing rain and a primal manifestation of the vital energy (*ki*) that was at once comprised in and coursing through all things, taking on ever different shapes and colors. By referring to himself as a "crazy cloud," Ikkyū certainly would have had these associations in mind.

But he was also drawing on a complex array of allusions to Chan, Zen, and classical Chinese literary works. In the prose preface to one of his poems (*Kyōunshū*, no. 45), he cites a *kōan* in which Chan master Yunmen, or "Cloud-gate" (d. 949), poses a question to his students, pauses, and then answers himself by saying, "On the south mountain, clouds rising; on the north mountain, falling rain." Ikkyū takes this spatial juxtaposition—one that calls attention to the way apparently different places and events can be intimately connected—and adds a parallel, but also provocative, image: "How did Little Bride consort with Master Peng? In a dream tonight: clouds and rain." In the folk geography of China, Little Bride refers to a small island in the Yangzi River and Master Peng to an imposing boulder on the bank nearby. "Clouds and rain" is a euphemism for sexual intercourse that derives from a pre-imperial Chinese tale in which a sorceress appears as a local woman in the dreams of a king staying overnight in a country inn and offers to serve as his "pillow," revealing her identity to him afterward, remarking that, "in the morning, I am clouds; in the evening, I am rain." Ikkyū continues with the theme of juxtaposition and intrinsic relatedness in his final two lines: "At dawn, I'm at Tiantai; at dusk, at Nanyue. Not knowing, where to meet Shaoyang." Tiantai and Nanyue are the names of two important Buddhist mountains in China, while Shaoyang was one of Yunmen's nicknames. These final lines thus overlay the languid sexual associations of the first two lines with august associations of the sacred. They also reference the polarized nature of Ikkyū's own practice of Zen—a practice that he described as merging "mornings in the mountains" (ascetic Zen) with "nights on the town" (unbound Zen).

As a poet, Ikkyū was a master of weaving rich ecologies of allusion, composing and layering images and anticipations in such a way that skilled readers are suspended in an apparently horizonless associative space that nevertheless manages to bring into poignant focus a refined sense of relational appreciation.[9] At his best, Ikkyū accomplishes with words what Mazu described as the hallmark of enlightened action: "Having realized understanding kindness and the excellent nature of opportunities and dangers, one ably breaks through the net of doubts snaring all sentient beings. Departing from 'is' and 'is not,' and other such bondages . . . leaping over quantity and calculation, one is without obstruction in whatever one does. With penetrating understanding of the present situation and its informing patterns, [one's actions] are like the sky giving rise to clouds: suddenly they exist, and then they don't. Not leaving behind any obstructing traces, they are like phrases written on water" (*Ta Tsang Ching*, 45.406b).

As a self-described "crazy cloud," however, Ikkyū was also prone to being blown about by the "winds" of passion. This propensity endeared him to those who appreciated the freedom of a life "without ties" and drew considerable criticism from those committed to a more traditionally structured social order. In a prose introduction to a quartet of poems dedicated to his study, "The Dream Chamber," Ikkyū observes that while "those who are thirsty dream of water [and] those who are cold dream of fur robes, dreaming of the bed chamber is *my* nature." Not surprisingly, when after years of traveling freely he accepted an invitation to serve as the abbot of a Daitokuji subtemple, he lasted only just over a week and on his departure wrote, "Ten days as abbot and my mind is reeling, beneath my feet a 'red thread' stretching interminably. If you come looking for me another day, try a fish shop, tavern, or a brothel" (*Kyōunshū*, no. 85).

Although Ikkyū accepted that there might be people for whom sensual— and, in particular, sexual—pursuits were not an attraction, he refused to masquerade as one of them. He wholeheartedly and openly embraced his own physicality, writing at times in ribald terms about his arousal at the sight of an attractive woman or about the dexterity with which his lover was able to bring him to climax, and on other occasions expressing tenderly amazed appreciation for the bittersweet longings and releases of physical intimacy. "At times, the sorrows of sensual love are so profound that prose and poetry are entirely forgotten. Never before having known such spontaneous joy, I'm delighting still in the sound of the winds (passions) that soothed my thoughts" (*Kyōunshū*, no. 383).

Ikkyū's investment in sensual love was not, however, just a matter of being true to his own nature—an investment that some of his contemporaries denounced as mere self-indulgence. He adopted the image of the "red thread"—a metaphor for the ties of blood and passion that bind a man and woman as they consummate their marriage—from a practice-sharpening question used by Chan master Songyuan (d. 1202): Why is it that under the feet of even bright-eyed monks the red thread is not yet severed?[10] For Ikkyū, answering this question was possible only through grappling with the fact that even the Buddha had been tied to his mother and father by the "red thread" woven through their conjugal intimacies. Without the "red thread," there can be no birth and death, no immersion in samsara. But there also can be no release from birth and death (nirvana), no awakening of wisdom and compassion, no bodhisattva action, no Buddha. This is crucial to Ikkyū's commitment to demonstrating the nonduality of monastic and unbound Zen. "Without beginning and without end: our one-mind. Incomplete is Buddha-nature's original mind. 'Fundamentally complete' is just the Buddha's foolish talk. The way of living beings' original mind: infatuation" (*Kyōunshū*, no. 385). Although the yearning that informs physical intimacy and the compassion that expresses the intimacy of enlightenment are easily distinguishable, they are also ultimately inseparable, each establishing the conditions of possibility for the other. Understanding why the "red thread" stretches out beneath our feet is to understand why we are here, together, and why it is that among all the birth realms, including that of the gods, it is only in the human realm that enlightenment is realized.

Affirming the nonduality of the sensual and the sacred raises questions about the structures of institutional Buddhism and, especially, about the purposes of monastic discipline. Moral customs may serve to domesticate our passions, but they cannot—and from Ikkyū's perspective, should not—eradicate them. "Following the precepts (*śīla*) is being a donkey; breaking the precepts is human. The ways of rousing our vital spirits are as numerous as the sands of the Ganges River, and a red thread binds brides, grooms and their newborn children. Over countless seasons . . . scarlet blossoms (intimate passions) opening and fading" (*Kyōunshū*, no. 128). Following monastic precepts can be an effective element in training to take full ownership of one's intentions and actions. But in Ikkyū's experience, "rising above the 'dust' of sensual passions as an *arhat* leaves you still far from the Buddha-land; just once enter the pleasure quarters and great wisdom issues forth" (*Kyōunshū*, no. 255).

At one level, Ikkyū insists that consummating the marriage of wisdom and compassion is possible only *within* the world of human experience, in the midst of and along with other beings caught up in suffering, trouble, and conflict. The work of enlightenment, in other words, is ultimately a work that is shared. But at another level, he directs us toward seeing that if nonduality is realizing that all things *are* what they *mean* for one another, then practice-realization can occur in any medium of communication—any medium in which we can share in making real the bodhisattva ideal of appreciative and contributory virtuosity. As Ikkyū notes, "What you can do depends on your situation, and your situation depends on what you can do" (*Kyounshū*, no. 73). Living within the walls of the monastery enables doing some things. Living in the pleasure quarters or a merchant neighborhood or a village enables doing others. But the teaching of nonduality enjoins realizing that whatever our situation is, it offers opportunities for practice-realization—circumstances in which we can make enlightening use of the karma informing our presence within it.

For Ikkyū, it was crucial that nonduality not be misunderstood as offering an excuse for selfish indulgence in one's base desires. In a poem written in 1460 as the area around the capital was being wracked by an unprecedented series of natural calamities, he bitterly protested the way some people in the upper echelons of society continued playing music and throwing parties while the lives of the common people were being reduced to ruin (*Kyōunshū*, no. 203). In another poem, he decried the failure of these same elites to show even a modicum of compassion when they were asked for debt amnesties by the poor and displaced (*Kyōunshū*, no. 287). Opening to one's nature is not an excuse to ignore others.

Contrary to the expectations of those dismayed by his refusal to live within the confines of conventional morality, Ikkyū took karma quite seriously. "Students who ignore karma are sunk. This single sentence of an old Chan master is worth a thousand pieces of gold: 'As for evil, don't do it; as for the good, practice sharing it.' Must have been something sung by a drunken gentleman!" Importantly, in the prose introduction to this poem (*Kyōunshū*, no. 250), Ikkyū rehearses an encounter between the famous Tang poet, Bo Juyi (772–846), and Chan master Niaokou (741–824). When the poet asked for the true meaning of Buddhism, Niaokou replied, "As for evil, don't do it; as for the good, practice sharing it." This offended Bo Juyi who objected that any three-year-old could understand such a simple teaching. Niaokou agreed, but added that though three-year-olds can easily mouth the words, lots of eighty-year-olds are incapable of putting them into action. To this exchange, Ikkyū then appends a comment by the Japanese Zen master Ryōzen (1295–1369), who expresses his gratitude for Niaokou's one-sentence summary of Buddhism. Without it, Ryōzen says, we'd all be depleted by mulling over such pivot phrases about nondualism as "from the beginning, not one single thing," "good and evil are not two" and "the false and true are one and the same." This would lead to ignoring karma and to a proliferation of people passing themselves off as teachers while justifying their personal depravity.

In one of his own "self-appraisals," Ikkyū describes himself as "a crazy madman" raising gales (bouts of passion) coming and going among the brothels and liquor shops. But he follows these lines with a challenge to skeptics about his real motives and the integrity of his Zen path. "So which one of you astute patched-cloth monks will give me a shove as I paint the town to the south, north, east, and west?" (*Kyōunshū*, no. 156). An unrelenting critic of institutionalized Zen, Ikkyū found little to praise in what he characterized as engaging in *kōan* study that emphasized memorization and literary word-mincing, doing nap-taking *zazen*, sucking up to important officials, and indulging in the travesty of buying and selling Dharma succession documents—a "business" that he compared unfavorably to the transactions conducted in houses of prostitution.

Ikkyū's own self-appraisal notwithstanding, he spent a significant amount of time both alone and with students in small, out-of-the-way hermitages and temples. There were times when the hunger, the cold, and the dampness hit him like hammers and he wrote with longing about the warmth, savory aromas, and feminine charms of the city. But he also advised those who lived in comfortable temples studying the Dharma, having scholarly discussions, and chanting sutras to first read the "romantic verses sung by the wind and rain, the snow and the moon." And in fact Ikkyū often expressed an almost Daoist appreciation of nature and the homely rituals of daily life. "Study the Way, practice Zen, and lose your Original Mind. A single fisherman's tune is worth ten thousand in gold. Rain dappling the twilight river, the moon gliding among clouds: limitless *fūryū* in an evening of song" (*Kyōunshū*, no. 216).

The term *fūryū* was a favorite of Ikkyū's. It combines the characters for "wind" and "current" or "flow," and given that "wind" is a common metaphor for passions in classical Chinese and Buddhist literature, *fūryū* suggests freely flowing emotion. Ikkyū often used it to convey a sense of aesthetic and erotic communion—a commingling of naturalness and romance through which the utterly ordinary gives birth to the relationally enchanted. But he also used it to give voice to a spontaneous and otherwise inexpressible feeling of affirmation, not unlike jazz audience members erupting in hoots and shouts of approval when they and the performers are swept up together into completely uncharted and yet emotionally consummate musical spaces by the interactive intensity of their joint improvisations.

Ikkyū's keen aesthetic sense came to personal fruition in his poetry, calligraphy, and drawings, but also in his friendships with and influence on many of the leading writers, artists, and performers of the day. His retreat at Shūon'an served as a kind of literary and artistic salon, and among those who visited frequently as friends and students were such creative pioneers as the *rengu* poet Sōcho, the tea master Murata Shukō, the renowned *nō* actor Komparu Zenchiku, and the painter Bokusai. Although part of the initial secular appeal of Rinzai Zen had been the access it provided to the latest artistic trends in China, the wider infusion of Zen sensibilities into Japanese society and culture can in large part be attributed to Ikkyū and his personification of Zen practice-realization in the midst of daily life, both in the countryside among farmers and woodcutters, and in the city among entertainers, artists, and merchants.

In his last years of life, Ikkyū was in many ways at his controversial best. To the consternation of many, in the midst of the chaos of the Ōnin War, he fell deeply in love with a blind singer, Mori—a beautiful woman almost half a century his junior. Over the next decade, they shared an intimacy that was by turns delicately thoughtful (see, for example, *Kyōunshū*, nos. 539 and 544), lusty (*Kyōunshū*, nos. 535, 536), and spiritually elevated, while at the same time enduring the hardships of hunger and being forced from one makeshift accommodation to another as bands of warriors crisscrossed the country. It was in the midst of this same period that Ikkyū was invited to assume the abbacy of Daitokuji, which had been reduced to rubble in the first years of the civil war. Feeling that this was not a task he could refuse, he took charge of the temple's restoration when hostilities waned. In this work, his wide-ranging contacts among merchants and artisans proved to be a great advantage. The resources of the warrior and imperial elites who normally would have been the major sponsors in a temple restoration project were severely depleted after a decade of clan-funded war. But even as he was raising funds and overseeing the restoration of Daitokuji and its practice community, Ikkyū remained in residence with Mori at Shūon'an and insisted that she be included in his official portrait as abbot.

Given Ikkyū's flaunting of convention, it is tempting to see him as an iconoclastic exemplar of Zen individualism. But his lifelong, almost tidal alternation between urban excess and rural retreat, his continual efforts to anneal the aesthetic and ascetic, his keen sensitivity to the workings of karma, and his unwavering effort to bridge the secular and sacred suggest that his conduct might better be interpreted as an expression of his unwavering commitment to personifying as fully as possible the meaning of relating freely. If Dōgen can be characterized as distilling the spirit of Zen through the practice-realization of sitting *as* a Buddha, especially in monastic retreat, Ikkyū can be characterized as doing so through standing, walking, and lying down with others, wherever and whenever possible.

HAKUIN EKAKU, 1686–1768: THE RELIGIOUS FIREBRAND AND REFORMER

Not long before passing away, Hakuin requested a brush, ink, and paper. Drawing a long and heavy vertical stroke down almost the entire length of the paper, he then used three weighty strokes to add a box near the top of the paper, creating the Chinese character for "centering" or "the middle." On either side, he added much smaller characters to complete a sentence that he had long used to summarize his "poisonous" approach to Zen: "Meditation in the midst of action is a million times better than meditation in stillness."[11]

Like Dōgen, Hakuin was an advocate of a no-holds-barred approach to Zen that centered on rigorous *zazen* and a fiercely cultivated commitment to realizing enlightenment in this life. And like Ikkyū, he was convinced that while Zen might be most effectively practiced in the disciplined context of temple life, it was also possible to undertake in both town and country, regardless of one's circumstances. Among his students—more than eighty of whom received Dharma transmission (*inka*)—were monks and nuns, and both laymen and laywomen from practically all walks of life, including a young woman who attained enlightenment while working in the pleasure quarters to support her family.

Some of Hakuin's ability to connect with and teach a remarkably wide range of people—both educated and illiterate, from both powerful families and poor ones—can perhaps be attributed to being raised by parents who operated a village inn and post office. Located at a convenient stopping place on the main highway between Kyōto and Edo (modern day Tōkyō) in the shadow of the towering volcanic presence of Mount Fuji, the family inn did a brisk business. Due to the Tokugawa government's policy of *sankin-kotai*, or "alternating presence," that required provincial lords to spend the equivalent of one out of every two years residing in the capital, Edo, the inn enjoyed a steady stream of well-to-do government patrons, as well as merchants, farmers, migrant laborers, and itinerant monks. Whereas most Japanese children in the late seventeenth century would have interacted regularly with a small number of people, most of them relatives or neighbors, Hakuin grew up in a "home" organized around hospitably attending to the needs of ever-changing, happenstance groups of travelers. At an inn, no one is greeted or treated as a stranger; everyone who enters is judged solely by their actions, not their family connections or the polish of their words. This openness to others seems to have become one of Hakuin's lifelong traits.

Apparently a bright and intellectual child, Hakuin's first encounters with Buddhism came while he was still quite young, when his mother took him along with her to lectures at local temples. Many of these lectures were built around stories that used fear to instill moral awareness, and Hakuin claims that they made a deep and lasting impression on him. One set of lectures that he attended when he was ten years old had a particularly powerful effect. Focused on karmic retribution, these lectures featured painstakingly detailed descriptions of hellish rebirths. Hearing these descriptions plunged Hakuin into profound worries about whether such a fate would befall him and what he could do to avoid it. He began meditating, reading Buddhist texts, and even conducting protection rituals. After almost three years of pleading, he finally succeeded in convincing his parents to allow him to enter the monkhood.

Hakuin began studying with the abbot at the local temple, Shōinji, and after a few years undertook a study of the *Lotus Sutra*, which was then widely regarded as the consummate expression of the Buddha's teachings. But to Hakuin, it seemed to contain nothing more than simple parables and vague references to the ultimate teaching of the "one vehicle." Discouraged, he set Buddhism aside for a time to immerse himself wholly in Chinese and Japanese literature. But this ultimately proved to be unful-filling. In 1703, at the age of seventeen, he decided to become an *unsui*—a "floating cloud" monk traveling about Japan in search of able teachers, effective teachings, and circumstances in which he would be able to attain liberation.

Over the next fourteen years, Hakuin tasted many different kinds of Buddhist teaching and practice and enjoyed a number of experiences of awakening (*satori*). But he also became convinced that, far from signal-ing arrival at the end of the need to practice, these experiences only expanded the horizons of his responsibility to engage in deeper and more intense practice. For a two-year period in his early twenties, the cumula-tive impacts of his intense practice regimen, poor diet, and lack of sleep caught up with him both physically and mentally. He was beset by contin-ually aching joints, chaotically alternating fevers and chills, stomach-aches, poor digestion, and moods that fluctuated wildly among elation, anxiety, and depression. Eventually, with the help of a Daoist recluse, he was able to practice his way through this "Zen sickness" and would likely have continued his quest with only modestly reduced intensity if his father had not fallen ill.

At his father's request, Hakuin returned to his home village in 1716 and found that the resident monk at the local temple had passed away. The temple buildings were in a decrepit state, and it seemed natural for Hakuin to assume responsibility for restoring them. For several months, conditions remained so bad that he slept and meditated in a palanquin because there wasn't a square yard of space inside the temple that wasn't open to the rain and snow. A year after moving back home, he was invited to serve as head monk for the three-month winter retreat at Myōshinji, one of the two or three most important Rinzai temples in Japan. Such an honor speaks volumes about the esteem he had earned within the Rinzai community during his years on the road. For almost anyone else, this invitation would have become a springboard for migra-tion into the upper echelons of Rinzai leadership. For Hakuin, it was a one-off event. After the retreat, he returned to Shōinji and continued his restoration efforts with the aim of turning it into a Zen training center.

Within a few years, just as his reputation as a Zen teacher was begin-ning to grow, an unmarried young woman in the village became pregnant. Under considerable pressure to reveal the identity of the baby's father, she finally broke down and tearfully named Hakuin. Even though Hakuin had briefly led a somewhat rakish life, visiting local brothels and flirting with village girls before he decided to become a monk, the villagers were astonished by this revelation. They were even more astonished when Hakuin said nothing in his defense. The girl's father angrily demanded that Hakuin take responsibility for the child. When the baby was born and brought to him, Hakuin arranged for a local woman to serve as a wet nurse and established a routine of taking the infant along with him during his daily alms rounds through the village, quietly enduring the villagers' indignant curses and embarrassed silences. It was not long, however, before the girl's conscience got the better of her and she confessed that a neighbor her age had fathered her child. When the girl's father went to the temple to retrieve his grandson, he found Hakuin working in the courtyard. Throwing himself to the ground, he begged Hakuin's forgiveness. Hakuin gestured for the man to get up off his knees, said "don't worry about it," and turned back to his chores. Word of the affair spread like wildfire, greatly enhancing Hakuin's reputation.

A decisive turning point in Hakuin's career occurred one evening in 1726 as he was reading a chapter of the *Lotus Sutra* devoted to describing the unsurpassed personal ideal of the bodhisattva. As he pored over the text, completely immersed in his effort to read through the words on the page before him to penetrate the Buddha's full meaning, a cricket— unexpectedly nearby—burst into songlike chirring. Hakuin's sense of "being present" was torn asunder. Just like that, it was as if a thousand-pound burden of worries and doubts lifted from his shoulders and dissolved in midair. From that moment, he later wrote, he lived in great emancipation, without any doubts whatsoever, one with the enlightening conduct of Buddhas and Zen ancestors.

Forty years old and no longer concerned about his own enlightenment, Hakuin turned his attention wholeheartedly to teaching. He took as his ancestral guides the Chan luminaries, Dahui and Xutang, and their Japanese Rinzai heirs—especially Daiō Kokushi (1235–1309), his student Daitō, Kanzan Egen, Ikkyū, and a little-known Ōtōkan lineage holder, Shōju Rōjin (1642–1721), with whom Hakuin had studied for some eight months in his midtwenties. Like them, Hakuin advocated rigorous *zazen*, uninterrupted *kōan* practice, and regular *sanzen* (private interviews with a master). There was nothing particularly remarkable about this combination. At Rinzai temples throughout Japan, monks and laypeople could be found engaging in sitting meditation and *kōan* study; and abbots at train-

ing centers regularly conducted public lectures and held private interviews with students. But Hakuin vehemently denied that what went on in
most temples had anything at all to do with authentic Zen. More often
than not, he insisted, so-called Zen training amounted to nothing more
than a self-promoting charade. Real Zen means engaging in unrelenting
inquiry, holding nothing back, fearlessly swallowing the "poisonous"
words and *kōans* of enlightened ancestors and holding them like a red-hot
ball of iron deep in the pit of one's belly until experiencing the "great
death" of the ego-self. Having seen one's own enlightening nature
(*kenshō*), one then had to just as intently and continuously hone one's
insights and responsive capabilities in order one day to be able to help
others cut through their own thickets of attachments and resistance.

In a work that he composed in 1740 as introductory remarks for a set
of lectures on Xutang that ended up being attended by almost four hundred people—the *Sokkō-rokukaien-fusetsu* [12] —Hakuin goes through case
after case of enlightening encounters between Chan/Zen masters and their
students. Each case is used to drive home the same crucial point: Zen
training requires extraordinary perseverance on the part of the student,
and a capacity for delivering perfectly aimed and timely verbal blows on
that of the teacher. Not surprisingly, he devotes considerable energy to
criticizing his "do nothing" Zen contemporaries who proclaimed the ease
with which enlightenment can be realized, justifying their claims with
quotes about "innate enlightenment," the "unborn" Buddha in each of us,
and the pervasiveness of Buddha-nature. If enlightenment was so easy,
Hakuin objected, why did Bodhidharma meditate for nine years in a
cave? Why did the Buddha, the world-honored one, spend six hard years
in ascetic training?

Never one to pull his punches, Hakuin described most Rinzai teachers
as weaving complicated webs of words and letters around themselves.
Then, "after sucking and gnawing on this mess of literary sewage until
their mouths suppurate, they proceed to spew out an endless tissue of
irresponsible nonsense" (Waddell, 2010:52). Shackled with students who
are "generally ignorant, stubborn, unmotivated types who aren't even up
to sitting through a single stick of incense . . . they might as well take a
load of dead cow-heads, line them up, and try to get them to eat grass" (p.
93). Even worse in Hakuin's estimation were teachers and students who
entirely misunderstood the meaning of Zen being a transmission "beyond
words and letters." These Zen pretenders gave up on *kōan* practice and

the study of ancestral encounter dialogues and devoted themselves full time to "silent illumination," sitting contentedly "submerged at the bottom of their 'ponds of tranquil water'" (p. 24). In Zen circles like this, he lamented, all you find is an "incorrigible pack of skin-headed mules" gathered together to sit in "rows of inanimate lumps" (p. 25). Worst of all, though, were monks who gave up completely on both *zazen* and *kōan* practice and turned to reciting the *nembutsu*, aiming for rebirth in the Pure Land. Instead of realizing that the Pure Land is in their very own minds, they engaged in slobber-mouthed recitation until they resembled "listless old grannies, dropping their heads and closing their eyes in broad daylight" (p. 57).

These harsh criticisms should not be taken as evidence that Hakuin disdained tailoring Buddhist teachings and practices to people's specific needs and abilities. In fact, that was part of the bodhisattva work that every Mahāyāna practitioner vowed to undertake. "Seen by the light of the true Dharma eye, all people—the old and the young, the high and the low, priests and laypeople, wise and otherwise—are endowed with the wonderful virtue of Buddha-wisdom. It is present without any lack in all of them" (p. 56). The only thing that was required for them to express this virtue was a method well matched to their natures and circumstances. Rather, Hakuin's point was that Zen should not be sold short by reducing it to a matter of pasting standardized Chinese verses onto a few *kōans*, sitting immobilized with an empty head, or numbly intoning pleas for help from some celestial Buddha or bodhisattva. Zen is realizing—in the midst of any activity whatsoever—the apt and liberating functioning of a Buddha. It is realizing a limitless "vitality pertinent to all situations," so that no matter what situation or emergency arises, one is ready to respond as needed to bring about an enlightening shift in relational dynamics.

For Hakuin, Zen training is doing whatever is necessary to cause a breakthrough to "seeing your own nature" (*kenshō*) and then afterward continuously cultivating your capacity for responsive and communicative improvisation. "If you want to catch a fish," he observes, "you start by looking in the water, because fish live in water and are not found apart from it. If a person wants to find buddha, he must look into his own mind, because it is there, and nowhere else, that buddha exists" (p. 61). Writing to one of his lay students, the governor of Settsu Province, Hakuin asserts that, "for penetrating to the depths of one's own true self-nature, and for attaining a vitality valid on all occasions, nothing can surpass meditation in the midst of activity" (Yampolsky, 1971:34). He is not talking about sitting meditation, of course. The term translated here as "meditation," *kufū* (Ch: *gongfu*), refers to a practical ability developed through sustained effort. Today the term is most often used in connection with martial arts (often spelled *kung fu*), but during Hakuin's lifetime it had a much wider application and he used it to stress the *practical* or *functional* nature of Zen training.

Although Hakuin's approach to Zen training included sitting meditation done in a quiet setting, he placed greatest stress on "uninterrupted mediation" that can be carried out in any situation whatsoever. Quoting his teacher, Shōju, he says that whoever "practices meditation without interruption, even though he may be in a street teeming with violence and murder, even though he may enter a room filled with wailing and mourning, even though he attends wrestling matches and the theatre, even though he may be present at musical and dance performances, is not distracted or troubled by minutiae, but conscientiously fixes his mind on his *kōan*, proceeds single-mindedly, and does not lose ground" (Yampolsky, 1971:50).

For carrying out uninterrupted meditation in the midst of action, Hakuin says, nothing is more effective than engaging in *naikan*: placing one's *kōan* in the two vital energy (*ki*) centers located an inch and a half and two inches below the navel—the *tanden* and *kikai*—and focusing it inwardly, no matter what occurs outwardly. Although *naikan* is often translated as "introspection," a more effective rendering might be being present "within observing." In practicing *naikan*, it is not that one takes the position of an outsider observer and "looks at" a *kōan* placed "in" one's belly. *Naikan* is being wholly present *with* or *as* the *kōan*—realizing an unconquerable interrogative presence.

Engaging in *naikan*, Hakuin claimed, will result without fail in enlightenment experiences. But it will also result in a vast amplification of one's vitality. "Even though I am past seventy now my vitality is ten times as great as it was when I was thirty or forty. My mind and body are strong and I never have the feeling that I absolutely must lie down to rest. Should I want to I find no difficulty in refraining from sleep for two, three, or even seven days, without suffering any decline in my mental powers. I am surrounded by three- to five-hundred demanding students, and . . . it does not exhaust me" (Yampolsky, 1971:32). Hakuin traces the origins of *naikan* back to the Buddha himself and describes a line of transmission that includes the Chinese founder of Tiantai Buddhism, Zhiyi. He had learned the practice himself from a Daoist recluse named Hakuyū and credited it with saving him from the "Zen sickness" that had nearly been his undoing in his early twenties.

In a letter to a sick monk, Hakuin admits that he had been so ill and out of balance, both mentally and physically, that he had initially been unable to undertake *naikan* continuously. Fortunately, Hakuyū had been kind enough to instruct him in a complementary technique that Hakuin heartily recommends to the monk and anyone else who wants to progress smoothly on the Zen path: the "soft butter" (*nanso*) practice. In the letter, he then provides the monk with a humorously detailed "recipe" for making soft butter by combining various amounts of different Buddhist teachings, steeping them in patience, and seasoning them with a dash of wisdom (see Yampolsky, 1971:83–84). The practice is remarkably simple. Imagine that a delicately scented and buttery soft object about the size of a duck egg is resting on the top of your head. After a time, you will feel "a strange sensation" as your head becomes moist and as this feeling of moistness flows downward through you neck and torso, through your hips and legs, all the way to the soles of your feet. Repeating this process, Hakuin attests, will sharpen one's senses, bringing about a feeling of inner harmonization and radiance, and the waning of any diseases present in the body. Then, with true determination, nothing will be able to stand in the way of practicing "uninterrupted meditation."

For his own students, Hakuin recommended that they initially engage in *naikan* using either the so-called "mu" *kōan* or his own (even more effective) pivot question, "What is the sound of one hand clapping?"[13] But he readily admitted that it is not necessary to use a *kōan*. For example, in a letter to a Nichiren Buddhist nun, he goes to considerable lengths to support the possibility of using the phrase that Nichiren Buddhists recite as their core practice: "*Namu Myōhōrengekyō*" or "Reverence to the Lotus of the Wondrous Dharma." The same is true for the words and images used in Tendai, Shingon, or Pure Land practices. What is essential is that practitioners, at all times and in all places, without interruption, strenuously and bravely refuse to leave undone what they have determined to achieve or to leave unfinished what they have resolved to accomplish (Yampolsky, 1971:105).

Hakuin accepted that not everyone had the personal karma to meet and practice under a Zen teacher, and that some people needed first to prepare

themselves for Zen training by engaging in other kinds of Buddhist practice. For all of them, enlightenment was possible. What he could not
abide was those who had the good fortune of encountering Zen and then
failed to commit fully to it. He could be quite scathing in denouncing
what went on in most Zen temples, and almost caustic in urging his
students to resist both the temptations of "do nothing Zen" and the travesty of adding Pure Land "legs" to the true Rinzai Zen "snake." He described his role as Zen master as one of "pulling out nails" and "knocking
out joinery wedges" in the elaborate constructions by means of which
people box themselves into believing either that they do not have what it
takes to really practice Zen—whether the intelligence, temperament,
time, or circumstances—or that they have already attained all there is to
attain. Prior to the realization of enlightening breakthrough, the primary
work of Zen is deconstruction.

But, for Hakuin, attaining an experience of enlightenment is *not* the
ultimate aim of Zen training, and all of Zen training is not deconstructive.
As Hakuin was reading over his response to the Nichiren nun, a monk
sitting nearby took the opportunity to also read through the letter. When
the monk finished, he accused Hakuin of "handing a yellow leaf" to the
woman—giving her something that might look like gold, but isn't.[14] The
monk explained further that thirty years previously he had attained enlightenment and had it certified by his teacher, but after hearing Hakuin
lecture he had realized just how shallow his own understanding had been:
the "Zen of a corpse in a coffin." Hakuin first encourages the monk to
continue with his practice and then tells the story of two brothers, Lu and
Wu, who had set off on a long journey. While resting one day, they
discovered two gold bars in the deep grass bordering the road. Jumping
for joy at their good fortune, they each hid a gold bar in their clothes and
continued happily on their way. Time passed, and one day they parted
ways and completely lost track of one another.

Many years later, Lu decided to track down his sibling and after following one lead after another finally arrived at his long lost brother's
home. It was a stunningly opulent estate, and Lu was afraid even to enter
the gate. What could explain such wealth other than having pledged life
and limb to some powerful lord or having fallen in with the cutthroat
denizens of organized crime? Just as he was about to leave, two servants
arrived to invite him in, and he soon found himself standing before his
brother. Wu was seated amid a group of splendidly dressed women, and

all around them were tables with flowers, succulent treats, and jeweled drinking vessels. As it happened, Wu had not fallen into league with either politicians or criminals. While Lu had kept his bar of gold safely wrapped in cloth and tied around his belly for thirty years, Wu had "lost" his gold. First he had used it to buy a large quantity of salt. Then, with the profits from selling the salt, he had bought silk floss, then hemp, then grain and fish, and all manner of other goods until he had several stores and three hundred men and women in his employ. Further profits enabled him to buy rich farmland, timber forests, and finally the estate in which he now lived.

Studying Zen, Hakuin tells the monk, is just like this story. Our original decision to embark on the path of practice and our initial experience of seeing into our own nature is like the two brothers leaving home and discovering gold bars. What differentiated the two brothers is that one brother put this treasure into circulation, using it to offer others what they needed and desired, while the other brother held it close, polishing it reverently away from others' eyes. After rehearsing his own long and convoluted spiritual journey, Hakuin exhorts the monk to push ever onward because the further you venture into the ocean, the deeper it gets; the further you climb up a mountain, the higher the mountain becomes and the more elevated your perspective. The point of Zen is not to attain and retain one's own enlightenment; it is to know with uninterrupted intimacy the "dignity of the bodhisattva": tireless responsive virtuosity in the midst of any activity.

RYŌKAN TAIGU, 1758–1831: THE GENTLE AND POETIC COUNTRY "FOOL"

It would be hard to imagine a sharper personal contrast than that between Hakuin and the Sōtō monk, Ryōkan. Hakuin was renowned for reviving serious *kōan* study and for being such an effective and tireless teacher that virtually all Rinzai monks by the middle of the nineteenth century traced their lineage back through him. Wholly committed to returning Zen to its elemental roots, Hakuin was a fierce critic of those who were content with literary or artistic Zen, and especially those who had no stomach for serving up "poisonous" words and who failed to forge their experiences of enlightenment into effective instruments for knocking out ignorance-securing "nails" and "wedges." Ryōkan spent most of his life beyond the borders of institutional Zen. He had few actual students and no Dharma heirs. He became widely known through his poetry, his calligraphy, and his personification of a gentle and quiet Zen that was as free as Ikkyū's, but without even a trace of iconoclasm.

Ryōkan was in fact a great admirer of Hakuin, Ikkyū, and Dōgen. But he derived his greatest personal inspiration from Jōfukyō (Skt: Sadāparibhūta), or "Never-Disparaging," a bodhisattva-monk to whom the twentieth chapter of the *Lotus Sutra* is devoted. An itinerant monk living during an era of the decline of the Dharma in a prior world age, Jōfukyō is said to have read no sacred scriptures, chanted no mantras, and engaged in no esoteric rituals. His lifelong practice was simply greeting everyone he met—whether monk or nun, layman or laywoman, elderly person or child—by bowing to them and then saying, "I have utmost reverence for you and will never treat you disparagingly or with arrogance. Why? Because you are already practicing the Bodhisattva Way and are certain one day to attain Buddhahood." Over the course of his life, Jōfukyō was cursed, beaten, and reviled by those who could not accept his reverent affirmation of their Buddha-nature. Eventually, though, he was able to receive and retain the One Vehicle teaching and became an eloquent teacher who led countless sentient beings to enlightenment. Modeling himself on Jōfukyō, during most of his life Ryōkan maintained a daily routine of "bowing to all in the morning" and then again "bowing to all" before retiring in the evening. He humbly claimed that, between dawn and dusk every day, "respecting others is my only duty."[15]

Like Dōgen, Ikkyū, and Hakuin, Ryōkan was a well-educated and gifted writer, a master calligrapher, and a daily practitioner of *zazen*. But unlike them and most premodern Japanese monks, until the very last years of his life he never resided in a temple that was supported by either the government or a private donor. For monks living in a sponsored temple or monastery, it was not necessary to engage in Buddhism's most basic ritual: the daily practice of *takuhatsu* (Pali: *pindacara*), or walking silently through the local community holding an empty bowl into which offerings might be placed, opening a relational space for the karma-transforming practice of generosity (*dāna*). Once Ryōkan embarked on the path of an *unsui*, or "cloud-water" monk, he never entirely abandoned it until he was too old to continue. Relying completely on daily "begging" to meet his needs for food, clothing, and shelter, he seldom owned much more than a single bowl, a single robe, and the most humble bedding. Even though he was a passionate calligrapher and poet, he usually lacked even the basic writing supplies of paper, brush, and ink.

We have no account of Ryōkan's motivations in becoming a monk and no explanation for why he chose the life of a Buddhist "recluse" living entirely on the kindness and generosity of others. His father was the hereditary village headman of Izumozaki, a seaside village in northern Honshū across from the small island of Sadō which was renowned both for its population of political exiles and its gold mines. As the eldest son, Ryōkan was expected to take over the role of headman from his father. In preparation for his future duties, Ryōkan was placed in a Confucian academy where he proved to be an avid and thoughtful student. And although he drew his greatest pleasure from reading Chinese classics and taking long, solitary walks in nature, he was a dutiful son and seems to have been reconciled to his destiny as a minor government official in a small but relatively prosperous village. His father—whose greatest interest lay in enjoying the finer things in life, including poetry and sake—was keen to turn over his responsibilities as quickly as possible, and when Ryōkan was seventeen, his father had him adjudicate a local dispute. Ryōkan had very little worldly experience and was profoundly depressed by the readiness with which the contesting parties seemed willing to lie and disparage their opponents in hope of a favorable ruling. On another occasion, he was taken to witness the beheading of a convicted criminal—an experience that resulted in a short but intense period of acting out the life of a dissolute youth, spending his evenings drinking and visiting geishas.

One morning, with no apparent warning, he shaved his head, dressed himself in a white kimono, and announced that he intended to seek admission to the local Sōtō temple. Five years into his training as a Zen monk, the temple was visited by a Sōtō master, Kokusen (d. 1791), who was intent on reviving Dōgen's monastic discipline and teachings. Ryōkan sensed a strong connection with Kokusen and asked permission to return with him to his training center, Entsūji, in a small harbor town west of Kyōto. For Kokusen, Zen was mostly about "moving boulders and hauling dirt," and Ryōkan spent the next ten years happily immersed in manual labor, meditation, and textual study, including the works of Dōgen. At thirty-two, he received Dharma transmission from Kokusen and was made head monk of the temple. A year later, however, Kokusen passed away, and rather than staying on at Entsūji, Ryōkan decided to become a "cloud-water" monk.

Training at Entsūji had encouraged appreciation of life's simple pleasures—a particularly ripe piece of fruit, a warm and sunny day in midwinter, a flask of sake to share in the shade of tall trees, cooling off with a few friends before the bell for evening practice. During his years on the road, Ryōkan was well served by his early training, sleeping on beds of leaves and in field sheds, drinking from streams, and eating only what was offered or what he could forage. His travels ended in 1795 when he heard that his father had committed suicide in Kyōto. Ryōkan traveled there immediately to conduct his father's memorial service, and then he went to Mount Kōya to perform a ceremony for both his father and his mother, who had died while Ryōkan was still living at Entsūji. Afterward, he went home for the first time in nearly twenty years.

We do not know what he anticipated, but he later wrote of returning with just a begging bowl and the robe on his back to find that almost all of his childhood friends had become "names on tombstones." He seems to have drifted around for a time, refusing any help from his family, before settling into a one-room hut behind a Shingon temple on Mount Kūgami, the tallest peak in the province. This was his home for twenty years, until he moved downslope a short distance to live in a two-room hermitage. At sixty-nine, he admitted that he was too old to continue supporting himself by begging and reluctantly accepted the offer of a lay student to share his family home. But true to his lifelong embrace of material simplicity, Ryōkan refused to live in the main house and moved into an old woodshed in the garden. There he spent the final five years of his life.

Having lived the second half of his life as a recluse, it is not surprising that Ryōkan left behind no formal Dharma heirs, no collection of teachings, and no institutional legacies. He compared himself once to a stream, "making its way through mossy crevices, quietly turning clear," and described his likely personal legacy as just "flowers in spring, cuckoos in summer, and maple leaves in fall." Instead, what is surprising is the number of friends, poems, and calligraphic works he left behind, and how quickly anecdotes about him spread across Japan.

A collection of stories about Ryōkan (the *Ryokan Zenji Kiwa Shu*) was compiled by an admirer, Yoshishige Kera, who had known Ryōkan during his days as an itinerant monk. Kera described Ryōkan as tall and slender, blessed with a lofty and yet relaxed spirit, but so slow in moving and speaking as to seem like a village idiot.[16] In one anecdote, Kera recounts how Ryōkan was once invited by his sister-in-law to visit and hopefully set his nephew on a more productive life path than the one of sensual indulgence he had adopted. Ryōkan agreed and stayed with the family for three days, but during the entire time he never said a single word. Only as he was getting ready to return to his hermitage did he speak, asking his nephew to tie the straps of his grass sandals. Somewhat surprised by this request, his nephew knelt before Ryōkan, and as he was tying the straps he felt something wet fall on his neck. Looking up, he saw his uncle's eyes brimming with tears and felt an immediate upwelling of remorse for his recent behavior and its effects on his family. Without another word, Ryokan stood and departed (Tanahashi, 2012:5). Another anecdote recounts how the typically barefoot and disheveled Ryōkan was once mistaken for a thief and was being tied up by angry villagers to be buried alive when an acquaintance luckily happened by and gave his word that Ryōkan was no thief but in fact a pure-spirited itinerant monk. Later, when Ryōkan was asked why he had said nothing in his own defense, he pointed out that everyone in the village was already convinced he was a thief and they would have expected him to deny it. So what good would that have done? In such cases, he laconically observed, "there's nothing better than saying nothing."

Ryōkan's practice of speaking little was part of his commitment to listening well. He once advised that, "before listening to the [Buddhist] way, do not fail to wash your ears. Otherwise it will be impossible to listen clearly. What is washing your ears? Do not hold on to your view. If you cling to it even a little bit, you will lose your way. What is similar to you but wrong, you regard as right. What is different from you but right, you regard as wrong. You begin with ideas of right and wrong. But the Way is not so. Seeking answers with closed ears is like trying to touch the ocean bottom with a pole" (Tanahashi, 2012:137). Here, Ryōkan makes clear that his reluctance to speak was not just a matter of being silent. It is possible, after all, to be speechless with anger or disdain, biting our tongues while calculating how to exact revenge or make a quick escape. Traveling the path of Zen requires "washing our ears" to remove the conceptual and emotional filters through which we normally view the world and establish our separateness from it. Listening in Ryōkan's sense is being wholly attentive, free from all efforts to gauge what is happening or measure others against some standard of our own manufacture.

This capacity for "listening" to others undoubtedly contributed to Ryōkan's ability to make friends with village children. Many of the anecdotes that circulated about him focused on how he often happily played with children, and not just for a few minutes before moving on to more "important" activities, but all day long and with apparently total involvement. In one story, he was playing hide-and-seek in the late afternoon and hid himself in a toolshed. One of the children saw him go into the shed but mischievously suggested that they play a joke on Ryōkan, slipping away to their homes without letting him know they'd stopped playing. The next morning, when a villager opened the door, Ryōkan shushed her, saying, "I don't want the children to find me!" In one of his many poems about children, he describes himself putting off his begging round to play catch. "Playing like this, here and there, I have forgotten the time. Passersby point and laugh at me, asking, 'What is the reason for such foolishness?' No answer I give, only a deep bow; even if I replied, they would not understand. Look around, there is nothing besides this!" (Stevens, 1993:124).

For Ryōkan, playing with children was not just a pleasant diversion; it was part of his embrace of the nonduality of all things. In a poem about playing *temari*—a game of kicking, tossing and catching skills using a woven wicker or straw-filled leather ball—he writes that when we see clearly, we realize there is no difference in the various Buddhist teachings. "If we gain something, it was there from the beginning; if we lose anything, it is hidden nearby. Look at the cloth ball in my sleeve—surely it is the precious jewel of enlightenment!" (p. 125). Relating freely with children and participating in their unbridled joy while playing games or coming across a meadow of sun-drenched violets was part of his practice-realization of compassion—not as a sympathetic feeling *for* others, but rather an intimately shared feeling *with* them.

The lives of children are not spent in continual joy, of course. Ryōkan describes being left alone at twilight, when the last of his young playmates had returned to home and hearth, and "only the bright moon helps me endure the loneliness." He also writes at length about sharing the feeling of being utterly bereft, standing alongside the parents of children who had fallen to one of the smallpox epidemics that seemed to sweep with tragic regularity through the countryside. To a man and woman who had lost both their children, he sent a poem: "Smoke disappears / into the heavenly sky. / A child's image / is all that remains" (Tanahashi, 2012:159–160). Later, imagining that he is someone who has lost a child, he writes two other poems. "Seeing other people's / children play, / I stand in the garden, / shedding / bottomless tears." And then, "If I die / of this unbearable grief, / I may run into my child / on the way / to another world" (p. 163).

Ryōkan's ability to feel with others made him a popular guest and an always willing host who often offered a parting calligraphy for those heading homeward. "Dew-covered, the mountain trail will be chill. Before you leave how about one last cup of warm sake?" (Stevens, 1993:134). On evenings when he found himself alone, he often reminisced about past visitors. "All night long in my grass hut warmed by brushwood we talked and talked. How can I forget that wonderful evening?" (p. 135). At times, he also seems to have dreamed of friends coming to visit: "How did you wriggle / your way / into my dream path / through such deep snow / on the night mountain?" (Tanahashi, 2012:190).

Later in life, when he had less energy for walking the mountain trails from village to village, Ryōkan once wryly remarked that, "in reality, as in dreams, I expect no visitor—but old age keeps calling" (Tanahashi, 2012:151). Yet as it turned out, old age was not destined to be his only steady visitor. Not long after he had moved into the garden shed of his lay student, Ryōkan was visited by a young nun, Teishin—a twenty-nine-year-old widow without children who had heard of Ryōkan and shared his passion for writing occasional poetry. Over the last five years of Ryōkan's life, they met regularly and developed a deep mutual appreciation. As he wrote once to her, "Chanting old poems, making our own verses, playing *temari* together in the fields—two people, one heart." On another occasion, he delightedly suggests that they send off his most constant "visitor" together: "The breeze is fresh, the moon so bright— together let's dance until dawn as a farewell to my old age" (Stevens, 1993:157). In one of his last poems, composed on her arrival as his final illness was taking a turn for the worse, he wrote, "The one I longed for has finally come; with her now, I have all that I need" (p. 158).

In Tokugawa Japan, there apparently were many Zen monks who adopted an air of unapproachable sanctimony. Others dressed Zen in samurai garb and maintained a militantly stern and implacable expression. Ryōkan embodied an unassuming and welcoming Zen, situating his practice-realization in the most elemental human exchanges. Speaking directly about Zen training, he counseled simply to "stop chasing new knowledge" and "leave old views behind." But like Dōgen and Hakuin, he also cautioned against confusing this with doing nothing or waiting for enlightenment to come all on its own. Instead of recommending exertions as intense as if brushing fire off one's head, however, Ryōkan softly invokes an early Buddhist metaphor for impermanence and follows it with a poignantly simple observation. "Human life resembles a dewdrop. Time for practice easily evaporates" (Tanahashi, 2012:77). True to his Sōtō roots, he was a lifelong advocate of simply "sitting as a Buddha." As a focus of meditation, nothing more was needed than the always present process of breathing. "Breathing out and breathing in," he exulted, are our "proof that the world is inexhaustible."

CHARACTERIZING ZEN: THE ABSENCE OF AN "IDEAL TYPE"

The preceding narrative sketches have been presented to exemplify the personification of Zen practice and enlightenment. Coming from different families and historical periods, Dōgen, Ikkyū, Hakuin, and Ryōkan had distinct physical, emotional, social, and intellectual endowments. Their ways of engaging Zen were remarkably wide ranging, and their lives eventually became the stuff of very different kinds of legend. Given this, it is natural to wonder exactly what they personify. Why are they held up by Zen tradition, not just as having led interesting and perhaps inspiring lives, but as exemplars of "living Zen"?

The "insider" Zen response might be that these questions are akin to those that Dōgen asked the old temple cook in China or those found in the *kōans* of the ancient masters: questions that can only be answered truly through practice. Even so, it's possible to make a few useful observations. First, none of these four teachers is a "true-to-type" Zen master. They do not exemplify a "norm"—a predefined ideal of Zen mastery. In fact, each one of them "stands out" from the others in his utterly unique way of working through his familial and relational karma to be unforgettably present with and present for others. In other words, each of these Zen masters was "one of a kind," impossible to confuse with anyone else.

Some of the personal uniqueness attributed to each of these Zen figures may be an artifact of the careful crafting that their life narratives underwent over time. But even so, the insight embedded in each of their life stories remains. Enlightenment does not entail jettisoning personality and self; it is the transformation of personality and self into a source of illumination. Sitting as Buddha is not sitting as "someone else"—an act of impersonation. Sitting as Buddha is sitting as a realization-expression of nonduality that does not erase differences but instead restores the normally excluded "middle ground" between self and other—a manifestation of *presence without remainder.*

It is also striking how profoundly Dōgen, Ikkyū, Hakuin, and Ryōkan opened themselves to the experience and expression of both joy and sadness. There is a common image—rooted historically, perhaps, in the parallel rise of Zen and samurai culture—of Zen masters exuding an air of inner motionlessness even in the midst of action and remaining nearly expressionless even in the most tumultuous circumstances. But while displaying an almost supernatural poise might be seen as resonating with Zen's advocacy of nonthinking as the key to responsive virtuosity, this image also suggests a kind of affective distance for which we find little evidence in the lives of Dōgen, Ikkyū, Hakuin, and Ryōkan. Instead, their writings and the stories that circulate about them are embroidered with passages that evince extraordinary capacities for aesthetically and emotionally keen attunement to others and the world around them. We witness them appreciating spring blossoms spinning asymmetrically to the ground, an autumn-burnished leaf pasted by recent showers to a garden stone, a breathtakingly green sprout pushing up out of winter-shocked soil, or the laughter spilling from children playing shoeless in summer grass. We encounter them standing at the door to a friend's home, listening to the last of their fruitless knocks echoing through the emptiness within, scanning an evening-cocooned path in hope of the glimmer of a friend's approaching lantern, or reveling in the afterglow of merging understandings with a fellow traveler on the Buddhist Way. And then there are primal belly shouts of dismay and release, heart-rending laments and passion-winged exhortations that give voice to a kind of Japanese "blues" welling up out of fathomless depths of compassion or being "with feeling," coursing through whatever life and karma present in expression of indomitable *bodhicitta,* an unshakably resolute "mind of awakening."

The analogy between "living Zen" and "singing the blues" may be somewhat far-fetched. But it points toward an importantly shared aspect of the otherwise quite different communicative practices favored by each of these seminal Zen masters. The characterization of Zen as a path "beyond words and letters" has nothing to do with valorizing either a stubborn rejection of language or being struck mystically dumb. Each in his own unique way, Dōgen, Ikkyū, Hakuin, and Ryōkan show how Zen is "beyond" words and letters in a way reminiscent of how music, without representation or reference, nevertheless can evoke profoundly personal insights into what it means to be human. They reveal how Zen communication, at its best, is not about *telling* anyone anything; it is about *eliciting*. They show how writing and speaking can be ways of crafting and holding out immaterial "alms bowls" into which understanding might be generously poured and circulated—opening ever vaster spaces of mutual offering and appreciation.

Generation after generation of Zen practitioners have not held up Dōgen, Ikkyū, Hakuin, and Ryōkan as exemplars of "living Zen" because they led pure or perfect lives, or even because they dedicated themselves to doing so. They have been elevated and revered for the virtuosity with which they cut through and along their own imperfections, like jewelers working with the "flaws" in rough diamonds, crafting presences suited to catching light, concentrating it, and transmitting it superlatively to others. Because of this, they cannot be held up as figures on whom we might model our own behavior—a fact that has been positively used by some modern commentators as a springboard for identifying Zen with expressions of spirited individualism and at times fierce independence. But a more modest and traditional understanding is simply that their lives compel recognition that no one ever becomes a Buddha by imitating others. The only viable path of Zen is the one we realize *as* our very own.

10

ZEN HERE AND NOW

Challenging conventions has been crucial to the emergence and evolution of Zen. Although many of the most eminent, tradition-shaping Zen teachers portrayed themselves as returning to the roots of Buddhist emancipatory and communicative practice, this appears to have been more of an aspiration or strategy of legitimization than a historical fact. A more accurate characterization might be that they were improvising Buddhist countercultures, bringing into practical and articulate focus a critical counterpoint to accepted Buddhist tradition. Seen from this perspective, Zen claims about transmitting the perennial essence of Buddhist practice and liberation are perhaps best seen as a kind of "Dharma candy" offered to help motivate those remaining wrongly convinced (from a Zen perspective) that the authentic path of Buddhist practice originates somewhere other than in one's own determination to be present *as* Buddha.

In our contemporary context, Zen's combination of a willingness to challenge convention and an insistence on the necessity of personally embodying specific values and ideals can easily be seen as suggesting a familiar kind of rugged individualism. The colorful iconoclasm of Chan masters like Mazu and Linji and the independent spirit and lifestyles of Zen luminaries like Ikkyū and Ryōkan imply an extraordinary and appealing freedom from both internal and external constraints. This liberal vision of Zen has played an important role in the globalization of Zen over the course of the twentieth century. It resonated well with the tenor of Western societies that had broken free of old traditions and were still actively engaged in the invention of new ones, but also with Japan's

embrace of the modern "cosmopolitan agenda" (Toulmin, 1990) of crafting a world ordered and unified by commitments to universality, autonomy, equality, sovereignty, and independence.

The precedents for such a liberal view of Zen are not insubstantial.
The development of the Buddhist Sangha as an intentional community
organized around shared ideals and a practical retreat from prevailing
social conventions suggests common ground with the modern conception
of the human "individual" as a being primarily responsible for his or her
own salvation and ultimately unbound by the constraints of the natal
family and all forms of inherited community. Mahāyāna emphases on the
universality of prospects for enlightenment and Buddhism's more general
rejection of class- and caste-based determinism also strike a modern
chord, as does the existence—in early Buddhism and especially in certain
forms of Chan and Zen—of both practical and theoretical support for
gender equality. Finally, the Chan/Zen valorization of "depending on
nothing" resonates with modern ideals of personal autonomy, while its
use of apparent paradox and its celebration of humor suggest an almost
postmodern embrace of irony and play.

As many scholars have been keen to point out over especially the last
several decades, however, this liberal, universalist view of Zen maps
relatively poorly onto the institutional history, popular practice, and cultural import of Zen in Japan. And in fact it has not been uncommon for
those introduced to "liberal Zen" in the West to experience some disillu-
sionment upon arriving in Japan to taste Zen at its source and encountering Zen communalism and conformism, and a practical resistance to
Western-style individualism both within Zen temples and beyond their
gates. But this should not be surprising. The story of Zen is one replete
with instances of ideas, ideals, practices, and institutions crossing cultural
boundaries and being made locally relevant through greatly varying acts
of appropriation and adaptation—a complex interplay of what we would
now call globalization and localization processes. The consternation of
the Japanese Rinzai community on the arrival of Chinese Ōbaku monks
in the mid-seventeenth century is a classic example of how much developmental drift can occur when different local conditions shape "the
same" tradition. In fact, Zen claims of *originality* might best be understood as imperatives to reclaim the origins of Buddhist practice and
teaching, but also as assertions of the inventiveness needed to do so. In
the Song dynasty catchphrase, what defines Chan/Zen is "according with

the situation, responding as needed." Since situations are always changing, an unchanging Zen would be "Zen" in name only.

COMING TO THE WEST: CHANGING ZEN

The origins of the most recent phase in the globalization/localization of Zen can plausibly be traced to the 1893 World Parliament of Religions—the first opportunity Zen teachers had to present and personify Zen for a large, international audience at a high-profile public event. This gathering, with its emphasis on revealing the underlying universality of religious experience, opened a new global field for Zen originality. As we have seen, toward the end of the nineteenth century, Japan was intentionally and aggressively geared up for modernization, industrialization, and national strengthening. Like their counterparts in China—where similar, if less systematically orchestrated, processes were under way—Buddhist reformers in Japan were generally inclined to take either conservative approaches that stressed the inseparability of Buddhist traditions and Japanese national-cultural identity, or modernist approaches that presented Buddhism as a force for progressive social change. The representatives of Zen at the World Parliament of Religions—Shaku Sōen and his lay student D. T. Suzuki—were decidedly in the latter camp.

In the West, however, many of those who were most attracted to Buddhism in general and to Zen in particular were intellectuals and artists disenchanted with the materialist "progress" brought about by modernization and industrialization, and profoundly disturbed by the horrific destructiveness of modern militaries inflamed by ideological fevers and competing nationalisms. What they found most attractive about the Zen they encountered was a combination of emphases on simple yet refined aesthetics, humor, comfort with the limitations of rationality, and the promise of experientially breaking through the confines of self and society to realize a freedom beyond the reach of conventional categories. These emphases did not constitute any sort of norm for Zen in Japan over the first half of the twentieth century. But they were easily read into the distinctive stream of Zen originality running from Imakita Kōsen through Shaku Sōen, D. T. Suzuki, and Sōen's less publicly visible monastic student, Senzaki Nyogen (1876–1958). Kōsen was a powerful advocate for deepening lay Zen practice. Among the most important of his legacies was a lay meditation group that he established in Tōkyō in the 1870s—the *Ryōmō Kyōkai* or Association for Abandoning Concepts of Subjectivity and Objectivity. Although it was short-lived, this group can be seen as setting an institutional precedent for the predominantly lay "Zen centers" that began mushrooming across the United States and Europe over the second half of the twentieth century.

The leading lights of this spread of Zen to the West were all connected with either Kōsen's Rinzai lineage or that of the equally innovative Sōtō master Harada Sogaku (1871–1961). These included Shaku Sōen's student Sōkatsu Tetsuo (1870–1954), who formally carried on Kōsen's efforts to promote modern, lay Zen practice and set up the first American Rinzai temple in San Francisco in 1906; Yasutani Hakuun (1885–1973), who had trained under Harada; Suzuki Shunryū (1904–1971), who founded the San Francisco Zen Center in 1962; Maezumi Taizan (1931–1995), a lineage holder in the Yasutani-Harada line who opened the Los Angeles Zen Center in 1967; and the Rinzai monk Sōen Nakagawa (1907–1984), who first came to the United States at Senzaki's invitation and went on to open the New York Zen Center in 1968.

Seen at a glance, the dynamics of the spread of Zen to the United States and Europe had relatively little in common with the dynamics of Chan's transmission to Japan in the twelfth to fourteenth centuries. The first generations of Zen teachers coming to the West did not enter societies already familiar with and shaped by Buddhist traditions. They did not find themselves welcomed into or by elite society, and they did not have the luxury of teaching in their own native language or engaging students hungry for what they had to offer both culturally and religiously. Instead, they faced considerable and often quite humbling material, linguistic, and cultural challenges. There was, however, one important way in which the Westerners who were most interested in Zen resembled the medieval Japanese who had embraced Chan teachings and teachers. Like their premodern Japanese counterparts, those most receptive to Zen in the West were convinced of the need for social and political change guided by more authentic spiritual engagement and a moral revitalization of the public sphere. This was especially true after the global conflagration of the Second World War and the onset of Cold War arms races, proxy wars, and intensifying nuclear brinkmanship.

The 1960s was a decade of globally mounting challenges to dominant societal, political, and cultural norms. These included the civil rights, women's, and peace movements; antiestablishment student activism; postmodern criticisms of received intellectual traditions; and a youth counterculture that celebrated naturalism, indigenous and Asian spiritualities, the exploration of altered states of consciousness, and experimentation with both body-mind integration and communal living. In this context of social and cultural upheaval, Zen presented—or, perhaps more accurately stated, represented—possibilities for arriving at a "still point" of calmly focused and kindly disposed attentiveness. In no small part because of the limited material means of their teachers, most of those introduced to Zen during this period encountered elemental simplicity: a bare wooden floor; a few rows of homemade cushions; and a framed work of brushed ink calligraphy hanging above a makeshift altar adorned with just a sand-filled bowl for burning incense, another bowl filled with water, and a pair of candles. And given the language thresholds being crossed and the absence of an already shared vocabulary of Buddhist experience and ritual, the Zen teachings they received were typically delivered in spare, straightforward, and often highly concrete terms. For many, the minimalism of "just sitting" epitomized the post-psychedelic ethos of personal authenticity announced in the popular call to just "be here now." At the same time, struggling to pass through apparently reason-mocking *kōans* seemed an entirely apt preparation for living in a world gone mad with "rationally" justified nuclear proliferation, political assassinations, race riots, and escalating war in Southeast Asia.

Since that tumultuous period, the context and extent of Zen's presence in the West have changed dramatically.[1] Virtual communities have replaced "back to the earth" communes as places of refuge for those seeking freedom from social conventions; college and university campuses are increasingly outposts of corporate rather than countercultural values and practices; and sushi, karaoke, karate, manga, and anime are all globally familiar parts of contemporary life. Zen is now regularly studied in college and university courses on religion, philosophy, psychology, and humanities. Hundreds of books are available in English and other Western languages on the history and practice of Zen. And the word "zen" itself has entered the popular-culture lexicon as an adjective connoting coolheadedness, serenity, extraordinary focus or concentration, and almost magically effective spontaneity. In the United States today, instead of there being just a handful of Zen practice communities in California and along the metropolitan corridor from New York to Boston, enduring communities of both lay and ordained practitioners can be found in nearly all major urban areas and in close proximity to colleges and universities from the Deep South to the Pacific Northwest.

In the process of taking root in the West, Zen has changed. Compared to their Japanese counterparts, Zen centers and temples in the West remain comparatively simple in both ritual and iconographic terms. At breakfast, fresh-baked bread and oatmeal are as common as rice porridge. *Kōan* practice is conducted in English, not Chinese or Japanese. And whereas funerary services are almost unheard of in Zen centers and temples in the West, marriages are not. But perhaps the most notable changes have been in terms of the readiness of Zen communities in the West to make liberal institutional commitments to gender equality. Men and women meditate, chant, eat, and sleep together in Western Zen communities as a matter of course. Women who have received Dharma transmission serve as teachers for both men and women. A second notable difference has been the degree to which many Western Zen communities have blended personal practice with social responsibility, undertaking a range of social services including, for example, feeding the homeless, assisting with elder care, and offering meditation instruction in prisons.

Throughout this most recent phase of globalization and localization, however, Zen has maintained an important line of continuity threaded through questions about its own identity, provenance, and purpose. In the early days of Chan, these concerns were given summary expression in the stock question about why Bodhidharma came from the West (India)—a question that was often used to invite a demonstration of Chan communicative virtuosity. But however expressed, questions about Zen's origins, nature, and purposes have been asked and provisionally answered by every Zen generation, not as a matter of principle, but because this is integral to being able to "accord with the present situation" and "respond as needed." Fittingly, the meanings of Zen practice and realization and the purposes of Zen coming *to* the West remain very much open to negotiation.

A significant amount of this negotiation about what Zen *is* and what Zen *ought* to be is presently taking place at the intersection of what we have been referring to as the "public" and "personal" dimensions of Zen. One way of characterizing this point of intersection is as a node of tensions between "external/objective" and "internal/subjective" perspectives on Zen, around each of which there have developed highly polarized bodies of literature. On one side are scholarly works using documentary and other kinds of empirical evidence to contextualize and critique traditional Zen histories and self-understandings; on the other are "Dharma" books written by/for practitioners that aim to transmit the tradition and render it personally relevant in a contemporary setting.[2] Of central concern to the former is generating an increasingly high-resolution picture of Zen's historical development and how this has both been shaped by and in turn helped shape political, economic, social, and cultural realities. Of central concern to the latter is presenting Zen as immediately relevant to the process of revising our life stories from within, generating the depth of personal resolve needed to commit to the Buddhist ideal of compassionate and wise liberation.

These bodies of literature are necessarily specific to our contemporary moment. But the coexistence of disparate approaches to writing about Zen and tensions among them are not contemporary inventions or accidents. Disparities and tensions regarding what Zen is and ought to be have continuously animated the emergence and evolution of Chinese Chan, Korean Sŏn, and Japanese Zen as explicitly "revolutionary" forms of Buddhist thought and practice that—from at least the eleventh century—claimed for themselves the distinction of being a special "transmission from heart-mind to heart-mind, apart from words and scriptures." Indeed, the tension between *documenting* and *demonstrating* Zen can be seen as having been a perennial factor in Zen's vitality and sustained relevance. The astonishing volume of Zen writings and the superb command of Buddhist and other bodies of literature that has typified leading Zen masters across the centuries are not ironically related to Zen's self-understanding; they are intimate to it. Seen in this way, the presence in the contemporary West of tensions in how Zen is understood can be seen as a sign of maturation—a sign that Zen is being aptly localized.

Of course, current scholarly approaches to documenting Zen are quite different from those that historically were the norm in China, Korea, and Japan. Prior to the modernization of East Asian education systems over the last hundred years, Japanese scholarship was conducted in accord with predominantly Confucian and Buddhist hermeneutics and assumptions about knowledge. Today, the predominant global standards of scholarship reflect broad commitment to a scientific method of inquiry, and hermeneutics is itself a field of intense contestation. More importantly, perhaps, contemporary scholarship on Zen is being conducted in socioeconomic and political circumstances wherein Zen's institutional footprint is quite small and Zen's influence on public life very limited.

These differences may have a positive effect on Zen's localization. In medieval Japan, the first generations of Zen proponents were compelled to devote considerable energy to distinguishing Zen from other Buddhist traditions, resulting at times in acrimonious and apparently self-promoting polemics. Later, once Zen was well established, elite commitments to maintaining existing power structures combined with their sponsorship of Zen in ways that resulted in at least rhetorically troubled relationships among Zen communities, considerable institutional inertia, and an erosion of Zen readiness to challenge convention. Contemporary exponents of Zen in the West are unencumbered by these kinds of historical and institutional conditions.

This does not mean, of course, that there are no significant difficulties in localizing Zen in the West and heightening both its personal and public significance. One of the peculiarities of Zen's localization in the West is that it has generated a great deal of critical energy devoted—in both scholarly and practicing circles—to laying bare the often painfully wide gap between Zen idealities and Zen realities. The stakes in closing this gap are extraordinarily high. As it has been so many times in its past, Zen is at an important turning point.

Contemporary Zen Prospects

Zen has always been concerned about documenting itself. Or put somewhat differently, Zen has always been committed to the crafting of tradition. Cynically viewed, the history of Zen has been littered with apologists and advocates who have "cooked" the historical books to legitimize their own lineages and authenticate their own inventions.[3] But Zen appeals to tradition and lineage have never had a solely *retrospective* orientation. In fact, a great deal of the energy invested in the elaboration of tradition and lineage has been *prospective*, aimed less at setting the Zen record straight than at correcting Zen's current trajectory with an eye to ensuring the viability of present and future Zen generations. In facing the challenges associated with its contemporary globalization and localization, Zen will likely continue looking to its past to orient its negotiations of a skillful and sustainable way forward.

One certainty is that the density of documentation now accessible about Zen's past will have major impacts on this process. Promoting a particular agenda for shaping Zen's future by claiming continuity with past lineages and traditions is now highly problematic because it has been made evident that the purported "integrity" of these lineages and traditions has owed as much to what was being forgotten by Zen tradition as to what was being remembered. Zen's past is incredibly more complex than Zen has been accustomed to admitting. This suggests that as Zen puts down deeper global roots and anticipates its own evolutionary arc, comparatively greater significance will attach to the immediate and exemplary personal demonstration of Zen virtuosity.

This should not be taken to mean that Zen's past is destined to become less relevant. What we now know about the lives and teachings of the seminal Zen masters offers persuasive evidence that Zen virtuosity is situation-specific and rooted in readiness for responsive differentiation Put somewhat differently, the historic viability of Zen as a distinctive "ecology of enlightenment" has had much to do with its diversity, and there is much to be learned from that. Dōgen, Ikkyū, Hakuin, and Ryōkan all struggled personally to close the gap between the ideal and the real. Yet at the heart of each of their very different approaches to doing so are powerful affirmations of the focal point of Imakita Kōsen's vision of realizing a modern and socially responsive approach to Zen: the abandonment of dichotomous concepts, especially those of subjectivity and objectivity. As the exemplary lives of Dōgen, Ikkyū, Hakuin, and Ryōkan show, the gap between the ideal and real is ultimately filled by authenticating the *nonduality of aspiration and realization*: the nonduality of enlightening intent and enlightening conduct.

One implication of this is that the challenges facing contemporary global Zen are at root karmic. The gap between Zen idealities and Zen realities is neither a necessity nor an accident; it is a function of failures to align enlightening intent with a complexion of values—or modalities of relational appreciation—suited to activating emancipatory resources already present in a given set of circumstances. Closing that gap can never be a matter of avoiding, rejecting, or even instrumentally adjusting our karma. Instead, it entails dissolving the conditions that are presently keeping the pattern of outcomes and opportunities generated by our karma from being realized *as* enlightening.

An important factor in Zen's transmission to and localization in the West is that it coincided with the global triumph of scientific inquiry and its biases toward objectivity, duplicability, and linear causality as the ultimate arbiters of public truth and knowledge. Especially through the middle of the twentieth century, although moral truths and knowledge remained important concerns, they came increasingly to be seen as matters of subjective conscience with limited explanatory value in relation to larger-scale objective events. In the scientific cosmos, conscience is a minor force at best. At roughly the same time, the new discipline of psychology was busily "mapping" an inner world shaped by biologically generated drives that dynamically mirrored the outer world of material forces, casting considerable doubt on the productive roles of conscience and intention even in relation to subjective experience. In the context of this epistemic shift, those seeking the acceptance of Zen (or other forms of Buddhism) in the West found it expedient to downplay the critical centrality of the Buddhist teaching of karma and its proclamation of the emancipatory potential of appreciating the interdependence of the material and moral spheres.

With this in mind, it is useful to reflect on Zen's high regard for what has come to be known as Baizhang's "fox *kōan*"—the second *kōan* presented in the most widely read *kōan* collection in Japan, the *Mumonkan* (Ch: *Wumen-guan*). Following the *kōan* known as "Zhaozhou's *mu!*" which invites engagement with the nonduality of Buddha-nature, the fox *kōan* recounts how Chan master Baizhang came to notice an old man attending his lectures, standing at the back of the Dharma Hall until the talk was finished and then disappearing. One day, the old man stayed behind after everyone else had left. When Baizhang asked who he was, the old man replied that prior to the birth of Shakyamuni Buddha he had been abbot at a temple on the very same spot as Baizhang's temple. At that time, he had told a student that those greatly accomplished in Buddhist practice are not subject to karma, and because of this he had suffered five hundred lifetimes being born as a wild fox spirit. He then asked Baizhang, "So, what do you say? Are people like this subject to karma?" Baizhang's response freed the old man from being born again and again as a wild fox spirit: "They don't obscure karma."[4]

This seems a curious response. Conventional Buddhist wisdom is that sentient beings under the influence of ignorance, craving forms of desire, and physical, emotional, and cognitive habits invariably find themselves embroiled in troubling patterns of cause and effect that are ultimately of their own making—the results of their own karma. Buddhist practice enables us to realize this and break the causal chains binding us to the wheel of birth and death. The fox *kōan* makes clear, however, that it was precisely belief in this conventional understanding of karma that had plunged the former abbot into a series of five hundred lives as a fox spirit—a being known in East Asian folklore as a trickster and shape-shifting tempter into moral mishap. Baizhang counters conventional wisdom about karma and its relationship to freedom by saying that superlative practitioners do not obscure (or suppress) cause and effect (Ch: *pu-mei yin-guo*; J: *fumaiinga*), where "cause and effect" renders an early Buddhist term, *hetu-phala*, that refers to the interdependence of situation-informing "conditions" and experiential "fruits." In other words, Bai-zhang characterizes superlative practitioners as having gone beyond either concealing or resisting their karma. Zen freedom is not freedom *from* intention-inflected patterns of relational dynamics, but rather *within* them.

This should not be construed as the equivalent of simply accepting our present karma. Eliding the gap between enlightening intent and enlightening conduct is ultimately a function of realizing that our karma is *not* an impediment. That is, closing this gap involves personally authenticating—practicing and realizing—the nonduality of intentional activity and experiential outcomes. In other words, it involves dissolving the standpoint of *acting on* things or being *acted upon* by them—dissolving the habit of dividing the world into "subjects" and "objects" defined and constrained by their mutual resistance. Granted that in East Asian Buddhism "nonduality" invokes the *dynamic interpenetration* and *mutual nonobstruction* of all things, realizing that our karma is not an impediment is not a capitulation to circumstance; it is making manifest our original nature—our potentially superlative capacities for involvement in the *relational* activation of appreciative and contributory virtuosity.

A second implication of seeing the authentication of nonduality as crucial to reconciling Zen idealities and realities is that superlative practice cannot be instrumental. Driving this point home was, of course, a special concern for Dōgen, who wrote extensively about the need to refrain from seeing practice as a means to some separate and still only imagined emancipatory end. But all of the Zen teachers we have looked at insisted on the need to cut through the subjective presupposition that sitting as Buddha or realizing the nonobstructiveness of karma is something that we have to work our way up to or that circumstances could necessitate deferring until some future date. Once enlightenment is projected into the future as a goal, as an object of our desire, we have committed ourselves to regarding practice as something *other* than the immediate expression of our Buddha-nature. Authenticating the nonduality of enlightening intent and enlightening conduct only occurs *in* practice, not as a result achieved *through* it.

An Achievement of Practice

Seeing enlightenment as an achievement *of* practice and not something attained *through* it confounds many of our most basic convictions about how the world "works." Infants learn first to roll over, then sit, and then crawl. With time, they haltingly learn to stand and stumble forward and become "toddlers." Only after lots of trial and error do they finally master walking and running, fully entering the child's world of play. A dry stone wall is built by digging a foundation trench and then fitting rock atop rock until a functional structure of the desired height has been constructed. A business is built by first identifying an abiding pattern of needs and then crafting a plan for being able to assemble the material and human resources needed to address those needs in a profitable manner. Those who do nothing accomplish nothing. And if anything results from doing something once or twice, it is almost guaranteed to be negligible. To combine adages: "practice makes perfect," but only for those who "try, try again."

This is all common sense. We set our sights on some desired attainment, figure out a method for moving toward it, and then get going. With perseverance and perhaps a bit of good luck, we incrementally make headway and one day "arrive." The fact that a primary occupation of many Buddhist scholastics in Tang China was sorting out "sudden" teachings from "gradual" ones is proof that this is not a common sense peculiar to the present moment. Even in premodern China, Korea, and Japan, major tensions historically centered on how properly to conceive the relationship between practice and enlightenment, with some advocating for "sudden realization followed by gradual cultivation" and others for "gradual cultivation culminating in sudden realization." The currents of Zen represented by Dōgen, Ikkyū, Hakuin, and Ryōkan seem to carry us obliquely to these tensions.

All of these teachers were lifelong advocates of *zazen* and other basic Buddhist practices and rituals. For them, practice clearly was not irrelevant; neither was it something to abandon like a raft once we have arrived at the "other shore" of enlightenment. All of these Zen masters insisted in one way or another on the lifelong fusion of enlightening intent (*bodhicitta*) and vigorous practice. For them, authentic practice consists in enacting enlightenment—not as an exercise of imagination, but as a distinctive modality of embodiment, here and now, as irreducibly relational persons in liberating community-with-others.

This way of understanding practice-realization was clearly difficult for their students to demonstrate. It is perhaps harder still for those who have grown up socialized into highly valorized convictions that the individual is the basic and proper unit of political, economic, social, and ethical analysis; that freedom is synonymous with autonomy and independence; and that mind and body are related somewhat like driver and car or rider and horse. Yet even in medieval Japan, where there was little if any metaphysical investment in mind/body dualism, the Tendai, Shingon, and Zen claims that we can attain enlightenment "in this very body" (*sokushin-jōbutsu*) were most readily accepted as claims about the swiftness with which enlightenment might be attained, not as claims about the bodily manifestation of enlightened/enlightening relationality. More difficult still to countenance was Kūkai's clarifying claim that "this very body" is itself Indra's net—the relational manifold of horizonless interdependence, interpenetration, and mutual nonobstruction.[5]

The conception of mind and body as a non-dual "single presence" (*shinjinichinyo*), however, is crucial to Zen convictions about the possibility of sitting as Buddha and dissolving—not bridging—the conventionally experienced gap between practice and realization or the "interiority" of intention and "exteriority" of manifest outcomes. Here it's perhaps useful to draw an analogy to the relatively familiar process of learning to hit a tennis ball. Having made the decision to play tennis, we step out onto the court for the first time, perhaps with a friend or family member who shows us how to hold the racket, demonstrates a forehand swing (saving the more difficult backhand and overhead swings for later), and indicates how to adjust our stance as the ball approaches. Armed with this "theory" about how to hit the ball, we take a few "practice swings" just to see how the motion feels and then ready ourselves to receive the gently hit ball coming over the net toward us. What happens next? In most cases, our timing and aim are off and our awkwardly swung racket either misses the ball entirely or delivers an oddly glancing blow that sends the ball flying off the court or into the net. Then we try again. Eventually we gain some facility with the racket, our eyes become attuned to the task of anticipating the ball's trajectory, and our timing improves. With any luck and with sufficient dedication, we one day find ourselves swinging smoothly through the ball and experiencing an indescribably satisfying "thwack" as the ball leaps off the sweet spot of the racket and streaks exactly where it should.

What has happened? According to conventional thinking, we have learned how to move our bodies in the way needed to accomplish the intended task of accurately and effectively hitting the tennis ball. We've traversed the developmental arc from intention to action to result. But in fact our almost magically satisfying shot is not a goal that we arrived at through practicing how to swing—something like the cake we get as a result of faithfully following a recipe. The cake is an objective and instrumental result of our actions. The satisfying tennis shot is neither a purely "objective" occurrence nor a "result" in anything like the senses in which these words are used in relation to a cake. Practicing hitting tennis balls involves hitting tennis balls. The successful tennis shot is not a *product of our efforts*; it is the situation-conditioned *perfection of effort*.

Similar descriptions could be given of practicing other sports like surfing, or arts like calligraphy, acting, and writing poetry, where practicing is performing, not producing. In all such endeavors, as effort is perfected, agency dissolves into activity. Self is sublimated in success. When the thinking, calculating, anticipating self reappears, the shot goes wide, the bottom turn spins out, the brushstroke turns graceless, the delivery falls flat, the image truncates. As practice deepens, as effort perfects, we more and more come across self as an interruption, an intrusion, realizing that being without self is not being without responsiveness and resolve. Sitting *zazen* is not about producing enlightenment; it is performing enlightenment. It is not sitting to become or create a Buddha, making instrumental use of our bodies to conjure an experience of our Buddha-nature. *Zazen* is sitting as a Buddha in quintessential expression of the meaning of embodying our original, enlightened, and enlightening nature.

This analogically supported characterization of *zazen* might be taken as warrant for seeing *zazen* as ritual activity. And if ritual is understood as a choreographic score for attaining and expressing relational virtuosity on behalf of one's community, there is some merit in doing so.[6] Yet while Zen primers have typically presented *zazen* as best undertaken in a quiet place after observing some basic preliminary preparations regarding one's dress and physical comportment, exemplary Zen teachers have regularly insisted that we not identify or confuse *zazen* with the act of sitting in a certain setting and posture. Again and again, we are reminded that practice can and should be conducted in all circumstances, whether we are standing, sitting, walking, or lying down; whether in a temple, our home, a market, or a concert hall. The perfection of effort realized *in* Zen practice—and not *through* it—is ultimately a process of improvisation.

This seems to fit well with Western and more globally modern propensities to valorize freedoms of choice—an assumed validation of our right to do things our own way. In fact, however, the individualism implicit in this assumption runs counter to Zen's stress on disciplined communal practice and its association of freedom with responsive rather than elective conduct. One way of understanding the relationship between the formal structures actually observed in Zen temples and the Zen ideal of responsive virtuosity is to draw a more general sports analogy. The rules of a sport constrain what can legitimately occur on the playing field or court. Likewise, monastic discipline specifies what can and should be taking place in a temple or training center. Rules concentrate attention. In sports, they frame the scope of allowable actions in accord with a predetermined set of rubrics for assessing competitive quality and success. On a playing field or court where "anything goes," there is no way of determining which actions matter or who is winning. There is also no way of telling whether anything is being done well. Similarly, the rules observed in Zen training ensure that everyone involved shares a framework within which to intensify their efforts and begin discerning what personally deepening practice—the perfecting of effort—might actually mean.

A major difference between the Zen temple and the tennis court or soccer field, however, is that sports are played to win. That is, they are played as explicitly finite games that culminate in a sorting out of winners and losers. In contrast, monastic rules specify patterns of conduct that are better described as the playing of an infinite game—a game that is not entered into so that we can see who wins (or loses), but rather to enhance the overall quality of play.[7] As many Zen exemplars lamented, this ideal has not always been realized. The custom of "buying" Dharma transmission certificates and prestigious abbacies is evidence that at least some

Zen monks have played advancement through the monastic system as a finite game. And the Tokugawa era construction of a Rinzai curriculum in which students are in effect graded based on how many *kōans* they study and "pass" also suggests a kind of finite play.

But however common playing Zen as a finite game might have been at various points in time, it has never been a norm. This is made practically evident in Zen temples and training centers by the daily group recitation of four all-encompassing bodhisattva vows: sentient beings are infinite in number, and yet we vow to save them all; anxiety, hatred, and craving desires are inexhaustible, and yet we vow to break through them all; Dharma gates (teachings) are numberless, and yet we vow to learn them all; and the Buddhist path is endless, and yet we vow to traverse it all. There is, of course, no way to "accomplish" these vows. They are not vows of omission: promises that we will not engage in or allow ourselves to become embroiled in certain kinds of activities or situations. They are vows of commission: affirmations that we are and will continue moving in a certain direction. To save an infinite number of beings or learn an infinite number of teachings would require an infinite amount of time and an infinite amount of effort. We have neither and cannot in good conscience make promises contingent on them. Keeping these four all-encompassing bodhisattva vows is a *way of being present*.

A sense of what this means can be gained by considering a bit more deeply the contrast between embarking on finite and infinite endeavors. In finite endeavors, success is a function of one's *power* or ability to determine how things turn out. In competitive sports and games like chess, winning involves working within the rules to limit others' attempts to control the course of play. In finite games of the sort played in the political arena and the market, winning not only requires power; it often results in power, including the power to change the rules of the game. In infinite endeavors, success is a function of *strength* or one's ability to sustain the interest of all those playing while enhancing the overall quality of play. Infinite games, like marriages or parenting or musical improvisation, are not played to finish (and hopefully win). They are played to expand our shared horizons of anticipation and to elicit from our differences ever more robust patterns of mutual contribution. The bodhisattva way is a path without culmination—a path of continuous appreciative attunement and relational enrichment.

Seen in this way, Zen rules and regulations apparently serve two purposes. As we have already noted, one is to create a shared framework for intensifying practitioners' efforts and clarifying their intent—a simple set of rubrics for comporting oneself *as* Buddha. The other is to institutionally structure opportunities for practitioners to observe directly the arising of habitual reactions and patterns of resistance. During an intensive training period, especially for those who are new to practice, it is a matter of course to experience physical hardships: too little sleep, not enough food, being too cold or too hot, and various degrees and types of pain from sitting cross-legged for hours on end. Unexpectedly, most people find that while the body adapts relatively quickly to these rigors, the same is not true of the psyche. The detailed management of virtually every moment of the day places personal likes and dislikes in uncommonly high relief, offering nearly continuous opportunity to see what we might call the infrastructure of the "self" -the habitually reinforced patterns of objection, attraction, worry, fear, and longing through which the "self" ensures its own identity and continuity. When undertaken well, conforming to temple rules and regulations functions as a primary lesson in opening to the meaning of "no self" and the origins of responsive freedom.

In considering aesthetic endeavors like playing classical music or composing haiku, it is not hard accepting that the experience of constraint can be a crucible for creativity. Just as a current of water forced through a sufficiently narrow nozzle can be strong enough to cut stone, channeling imaginative energies can make it possible to plumb the human experience to extraordinary depths Behavioral constraints like those found in Zen temples, monasteries, and training centers can serve a similar purpose. They can, of course, also become instruments of coercion if enforced as tests of loyalty and if unquestioningly following orders is held up as a norm. In traditional Zen temples and monasteries, the authority of abbots was not absolute. But it was certainly great enough to open wide-ranging possibilities for its abuse, and the transmission of Zen to the West has not forestalled the replication of such possibilities.[8]

Since Zen teachings and practices began being globally circulated from roughly the turn of the twentieth century, it has only been infrequently that attempts have been made to transport Zen institutions and traditions in their entirety. The process has instead been one of at times critically and at other times only conveniently editing or tailoring Zen to fit its new cultural circumstances. This has opened opportunities for asking pointed questions about what is crucial to Zen and what is best regarded as an expendable overlay of Japanese culture and East Asian historical legacies. As already suggested, this can be viewed as a healthy (and in fact quite traditional) process of discovering what Zen is and should be, here and now. Importantly, this is a process that also involves questioning why one would be interested in Zen or commit to practicing it. In other words, it is ultimately a recursive process that involves simultaneously questioning the meaning of Zen conduct and assessing the quality of one's own intentions.

GLOBAL ZEN: THE EVOLVING INTERDEPENDENCE OF PUBLIC AND PERSONAL ZEN

This is necessarily a context-specific process. One of the apparently unsettling revelations of recent historical studies of Zen is that during Zen's initial period of flourishing it was given elite support for what would seem to be quite instrumental purposes—that is, for explicitly material benefit and not spiritual advance. This might be seen as evidence of an "inauthentic" engagement with Zen. But that is perhaps too hasty a judgment. The medieval Japanese conception of religion did not create a hard dividing line between the material and spiritual realms or between publicly manifest benefits of practice and privately experienced ones. Granted this, although the initial elite embrace of Zen often might have been partial, this need not have been an indication of its inauthenticity.

Similarly, many of those initially attracted to Zen in the West seem to have had very partial and often plainly romantic interests that revolved around their individual quests for personal meaning. Especially in the period of rapid growth that occurred in the 1960s and 1970s, getting a taste of Zen practice was often part of broader adventures in "finding oneself." This kind of adventure has apparent resonances with Zen injunctions to "see one's own nature," but it also runs hard against the grain of traditional Japanese Zen training. Nevertheless, as in the premodern Japanese case, the possibility must be granted that the partiality of Western engagements with Zen has not necessarily been a shortcoming or an indication of failures to authentically engage in Zen practice.

Consider, for example, that among the promising effects—both in Asia and the West—of modern liberal constructions of Zen has been a tendency to direct heightening attention to squaring personal liberation with social justice.[9] Whatever its liabilities, the traditional Japanese religious goal of engaging in personal practice for public benefit had the positive effect of limiting justification for any divergence of enlightening intent and conduct. Mahāyāna Buddhist theory and practice, with their focus on realizing the personal ideal of the bodhisattva, can be seen as casting this linkage between personal practice and public benefit onto a wider screen, broadening its relational scope to extend beyond the family or clan to include (however generically) all sentient beings. This widening qualification of the benefits of religious practice evolved further with Chan's more pointed emphasis on the sociality of liberation—an identification of the quintessential locus of enlightenment with improvised interpersonal encounters. In traditional Japanese Zen histories, it is possible to discern a further and variously dense blending and articulation of these emphases.

Movement toward conceiving of enlightenment as social virtuosity may have been largely rhetorical over much of Zen's history—a movement taking place primarily in the documentary dimension of Zen and not in actual demonstrations of Zen conduct and community. Nevertheless, it describes an evolutionary arc toward a Zen ideal that accords particularly well with contemporary global realities, speaking to the needs of those who would work toward the dissolution of global conditions for both human and planetary trouble and suffering. If histories are not understood as records of things past but rather as rehearsals of meanings still in the process of being composed, it is a current of Zen tradition and transformation that could be affirmed as authentic and worthy of further valorization.[10]

Demonstrating movement in this direction would inevitably lead to new kinds of Zen institutions and practices. Granted the approach we have taken in envisioning a reconciliation of enlightening intent and conduct, these would likely include institutions and practices attuned to the task of extending the critical ambit of karma to encompass the complex dynamics of global interdependence that are now resulting in deepening social, political, and economic inequality.[11] If sustained, movement in this direction—manifest already in broader Buddhist commitments to expand the horizons of social engagement—might carry Zen out of a "phase of accommodation" in which primary concerns center on negotiating the terms of permanent residency within Western societies. Zen might then enter a contemporary "phase of advocacy" in which concern shifts to evaluating the constellations of values informing personal conduct and public policy, and to practically challenging conventions implicated in the local, national, regional, and global persistence and intensification of trouble, conflict, and suffering.

This would not be a "Zen" that could be found in Zen's documented past. It might be, however, a "Zen" true to the origins of Zen in practiced originality. In one of the texts attributed to Bodhidharma and his circle of students, it is said that those aiming to course along the bodhisattva way and make it robust should "project the heart-mind beyond the boundaries of the norms."[12] That is, they should position themselves to offer an effective counterpoint to prevailing values and norms, engaging in what Linji referred to as "facing the world and going crosswise" (*Taishō shinshū daizōkyō*, 1985:497c), moving obliquely to existing tensions and oppositions in ways that find expression in enlightening relationality.

Whatever path contemporary Zen takes in realizing the liberating nonduality of intent and conduct, however, it could never be a path cut off from Zen's past. Hakuin expressed well the terms of Zen's appropriate engagement with its current circumstances. In a poetic ending to a work intended to inspire his students by rehearsing the struggles of great masters of the past, Hakuin ends on a poetic note by encouraging his readers to "expend every effort to make the true, penetrating wind blow once again through the ancestral gardens, and breathe vigorous and enduring strength into the original principles of our school" (Waddell, 2010:103). In East Asian Buddhism, wind is used as a metaphor for the passions, but also for anything—like the Buddha Dharma—that has the nature of endlessly circulating and permeating everywhere. As Dōgen noted in writing to a lay student on the necessity of practice (the *Genjōkōan*), the point of expending every effort to stir up the Dharma wind is never just to revitalize connections with the past. Like a breath blowing continuously through a flute, opening a way for the "wind" that has coursed through Shakyamuni Buddha and all the lineages of Zen, it is a practice the perfecting of which would "enable us to make manifest the gold of this Earth of ours and transform its long rivers into sweet cream."

NOTES

1. BUDDHA, DHARMA, AND SANGHA FROM INDIA TO CHINA

1. See, for example, the *Atthakavagga* section of the *Sutta Nipāta*.

2. The "critical Buddhism" movement that emerged out of Sōtō Zen scholarly circles in the late twentieth century is in part a response to the disturbing fact that many Zen teachers had supported Japan's colonization of Korea and its war efforts—effectively sanctioning state violence. Identifying Buddhist practice with criticism, exponents of critical Buddhism regard this degree of Sangha support for the state to be damning evidence of a failure to retain the true spirit of Buddhism in Japan. (A fuller discussion of critical Buddhism is undertaken in chapter 7.)

3. Early Chinese commentators calculated that the age of the Degenerate Dharma would commence in roughly 550 CE and last some ten thousand years—a calculation of the onset of *mappō* or the "end of the Dharma" that would be hugely important in the evolution of Japanese Buddhism and Zen. A scholarly discussion of this anticipation of decline can be found in Nattier (1991).

4. For a detailed study of the role of Buddhism in trade relations, see Sen (2003).

5. In Japan, the Buddha-nature concept would be logically extended to the claim that all beings are "originally enlightened" (*hongaku*), including even crickets, bamboo, mountains, and rivers—a claim that would not be seriously contested on Buddhist grounds until the late twentieth century and the "critical Buddhism" (*hihanbukkyō*) movement.

6. Somewhat ironically, by the time Zen begins to develop in Japan—the late twelfth and early thirteenth centuries—this identification of individual experience with social expression was itself firmly "canonized" in collections of

gongan (J: *kōan*), or "public cases," recording the enlightening interactions of Chan masters and their students—collections that have since then been part of the core "curriculum" of most Chan, Sŏn, and Zen practitioners, especially those who trace their lineage back through the famed ninth-century Chinese master Linji (J: Rinzai).

2. THE JAPANESE TRANSFORMATION OF BUDDHISM

1. A fine translation of the Constitution can be found in Heisig et al. (2011:36–39).

2. For a fascinating discussion of the roots of this conception of Japanese identity in interethnic conflicts and competitions, see Como (2008).

3. For an extended investigation of this perspective on Kūkai's presentation of Shingon, see Abé (1999).

4. For an extended discussion of the development of original enlightenment thought, see Stone (1999).

5. Original enlightenment teachings came under highly critical regard in the late twentieth century with the critical Buddhism movement. See, for example, Shields (2011b).

6. There is a great deal of lore about Buddhist "warrior monks" in Japan and in global martial arts circles. A responsible academic study of the history of the *sōhei* phenomenon is Adolphson (2007).

7. Commonly rendered as *The Awakening of Faith*, this seminal East Asian Buddhist text is available in English translation with commentary by Hakeda (1967).

8. Adapted from a passage quoted and translated in Abé (1999:288).

3. FROM CHINESE CHAN TO JAPANESE ZEN

1. Linji's intent, of course, was not to condone irreverence or murder, but rather to call critical attention to the tendency of many Buddhist practitioners to objectify enlightenment as a goal to reach—something distant and exemplified, if at all, only by others. For him, as natural as this is, it creates conditions under which it is very easy—and tempting—to say that before realizing enlightenment, one must first go halfway, and then halfway again and again and again. Setting up enlightenment as a distant achievement is to live in the spiritual equivalent of Zeno's paradox. Killing "Buddha," then, is killing one's concept of enlighten-

ment: removing the conceptual barrier between oneself and one's own Buddha-nature.

2. For a discussion of the critique of Hongzhou Chan made by more "conservative" and conceptually grounded approaches to Chan, see Broughton (2009). For a detailed historical reading of the development of the Hongzhou School, see Jia (2006).

3. An extended discussion of the Darumashū in relation to Sōtō Zen can be found in Faure (1987).

4. RINZAI ZEN

1. For a thorough and now classic history of the Rinzai tradition, see Collcutt (1981).

2. For insight into Musō's teaching and character, see Kirchner (2010) and the collection of poems and teachings presented in Merwin (1989).

3. An accessible introduction to medieval Japanese aesthetics and the impact of Zen can be found in Varley (1984), chapter 5.

4. Several of Takuan's essays on Zen and the sword are translated and placed in historical context in Haskel (2013).

5. For a translation of many of Bankei's essays and an introduction to his life and teaching, see Waddell (2000).

6. A fine scholarly introduction to and translation of a collection of Hakuin's work is Philip Yampolsky (1973); a colorful translation of selected works by Hakuin can be found in Waddell (2010).

5. SŌTŌ ZEN

1. Two classic historical studies of Sōtō Zen are Bodiford (1993) and Williams (2006).

2. A translation and introduction to one of Keizan's major works outlining his approach to Zen and his crafting of a Sōtō Zen history stretching back to the historical Buddha is Cook (1991).

3. A taste of Menzan's thought can be found in his lively account of the life of Sōtō Zen master Tosui Unkei (d. 1683), translated in Haskel (2001).

4. An introduction to Suzuki Shōsan and a translation of some of his works can be found in Braveman (1994).

5. Two works that introduce Ryōkan and his teachings are Haskel (1996) and Tanahashi (2012).

6. ŌBAKU ZEN

1. Baroni (2000) offers a comprehensive history of the arrival and development of Ōbaku Zen.

2. A comprehensive discussion of these controversies and of Ming dynasty Chinese Buddhism is Wu (2008).

7. ZEN IN A MODERNIZING JAPAN

1. An introduction to Tominaga's thought with a translation of key works can be found in Pye (1990).

2. Three excellent introductions to Tokugawa thought are Nosco (1990), Nosco (1997), and Harootunian (1988).

3. For a discussion of Zen and nationalism, see Heisig and Maraldo (1995).

4. A wide-ranging discussion of Buddhist encounters with modernity is McMahon (2008), and a more detailed discussion of Buddhist modernism in Japan is Shields (2011a). For a very interesting comparison of two Zen monks and their responses to modernization in Japan, see Ishikawa (1998).

5. Works by Hisamatsu in English are Hisamatsu (1983; 2002).

6. A fine introduction to critical Buddhism is Shields (2011b). An edited collection of scholarly responses to critical Buddhism is Hubbard (1997).

8. PRACTICING ZEN

1. This and other references to the life and teachings of Mazu are based on my own translation of the materials traditionally ascribed to him. A detailed scholarly discussion of Mazu that downplays his iconoclastic approach is Poceski (2007); a translation of Mazu's discourse records can be found in Chien (1992).

2. A careful translation and introduction to this classic is Kirchner (2010).

9. ZEN EXEMPLARS: DŌGEN, IKKYŪ, HAKUIN, AND RYŌKAN

1. A full and accessible translation of the Blue Cliff Record (*Hekiganroku*) and the Gateless Barrier (*Mumonkan*), an earlier collection of Chan/Zen *kōans*, can be found in Sekida (1995).

2. For a translation and commentary of this brief but influential text, see Okumura (2010).

3. This story is related in Dōgen's essay, *Tenzo Kyokun*, or "Instructions to the Temple Cook," which is widely available as an independent translation online or as part of the full text of the *Shōbōgenzō*.

4. An excellent discussion of this text, including a full translation, is undertaken in Bielefeldt (1988).

5. This and other Dharma Hall Discourses are collected in the *Eihei Kōroku*, which has been translated as *Dōgen's Extensive Record* by Taigen Dan Leighton and Shohaku Okumura (2010).

6. Several alternatives to my rendering of this passage can be found at the Zensite website: http://www.thezensite.com/ZenTeachings/Dogen_Teachings/Shobogenzo_Complete.html (accessed August 2, 2013).

7. The first part of this passage is from the translation of *Genjōkōan* in Heisig et al. (2011); the final line is from Waddell and Abe (2002). Dōgen is extraordinarily difficult to translate, and it is instructive to compare these two renderings with the translation and commentary in Okumura (2010).

8. No complete translation is available in English. A very accessible and lively translation of selections from the *Kyōunshū* can be found in Stevens (2003). Covell (1980) offers an extended and appreciative biography of Ikkyū that makes use of selections from the *Kyōunshū* and other works. Arntzen (1986) provides a scholarly discussion of Ikkyū's poetic genius and carefully informed translations of 144 of the 880 poems collected in the Japanese original.

9. For a detailed discussion of this poem, see Arntzen (1986:53–57).

10. For a scholarly investigation of the sacred and the sexual in Buddhism, see Faure (1998).

11. A reproduction of this calligraphy can be found in Waddell (2010).

12. A full and lively translation is available in Waddell (2010).

13. In the "mu" *kōan*, Chan master Zhaozhou is asked by a student whether a dog has Buddha-nature and answers "mu" (Ch: *wu*)—which might be translated as either "no" or "without"—in effect contracting the standard Mahāyāna teaching that all sentient beings have Buddha-nature. Why did he do so? In Hakuin's method, it is Zhaozhou's "mu" that is placed into the *tanden* and *kikai*.

14. For this exchange, see Yampolsky (1971:106–123).

15. A number of these anecdotes and a selection of Ryōkan's poetry in translation can be found in Tanahashi (2012) and Stevens (1993).

16. There are many good translations of the *Lotus Sutra*. A very literary rendering is Watson (1993).

10. ZEN HERE AND NOW

1. Those interested in more detail about the history of Zen in the West, especially the United States, might want to begin by looking at Tworkov (1989), Fields (1992), and Prebish (1999); for a somewhat more global history of Buddhism's transmission to the West, see Batchelor (1994).

2. An academic and yet both balanced and accessible introduction to the history and major currents of this tension can be found in Heine (2008).

3. An incisive expression of something akin to this view of Zen historical consciousness, focused primarily on Chinese Chan, can be found in McRae (2003).

4. A book-length textual history of the fox *kōan* and its philosophical and folkloric underpinnings can be found in Heine (1999).

5. A useful comparative study of mind-body issues, with chapters on both Kūkai and Dōgen, is Yuasa (1987).

6. Such an understanding of ritual (*li*) is lucidly developed along Confucian lines by Roger Ames (2011).

7. I owe this very helpful distinction between finite and infinite games to James Carse (1986).

8. There is a growing body of literature aimed at exposing the less than savory uses of Zen authority. Victoria (2006) offers a look at the complex—and often troubling—interplay among authority, nationalism, and militarism in Japanese Zen. Downing (2001) presents an account of authority-focused difficulties at an American Zen center.

9. One of the first efforts to document the rise of activist Buddhism in Asia is Queen and King (1996). For a more recent and topical treatment of so-called engaged Buddhism, see King (2009).

10. In a thoughtful piece that makes use of Buddhist conceptual resources to challenge the perpetuation of violence in and through history, Timothy Brook (2008) describes the primary work of the historian as articulating both the contexts in which experienced events took place and those through which experiences come to be indexed to certain meanings. This is a promising approach for contemporary historians of Zen who would seek a reconciliation of the documentary and demonstrative dimensions of Zen.

11. My own approach to envisioning the precedents and prospects for such a move can be found in Hershock (2012).

12. See Broughton (1999) for translations and critical commentaries on a body of texts attributed to Bodhidharma and his circle. This passage is from Record 1, no. 20.

WORKS CITED

Abé, Ryūichi. *The Weaving of Mantra: Kūkai and the Construction of Esoteric Buddhist Discourse*. New York: Columbia University Press, 1999.

Adolphson, Mikael S. *The Gates of Power: Monks, Courtiers, and Warriors in Pre-Modern Japan*. Honolulu: University of Hawaii Press, 2000.

———. *The Teeth and Claws of the Buddha: Monastic Warriors and Sōhei in Japanese History*. Honolulu: University of Hawaii Press, 2007.

Ames, Roger T. *Confucian Role Ethics: A Vocabulary*. Honolulu: University of Hawaii Press, 2011.

Arntzen, Sonja. *Ikkyū and the Crazy Cloud Anthology*. Tokyo: University of Tokyo Press, 1986.

The Awakening of Faith, Attributed to Aśvaghosha. Translated with commentary by Yoshito S. Hakeda. New York: Columbia University Press, 1967.

Bailey, Greg, and Ian Mabbett. *The Sociology of Early Buddhism*. London: Cambridge University Press, 2003.

Baroni, Helen Josephine. *Obaku Zen: The Emergence of the Third Sect of Zen in Tokugawa, Japan*. Honolulu: University of Hawaii Press, 2000.

Batchelor, Stephen. *The Awakening of the West: The Encounter of Buddhism and Western Culture*. Berkeley, CA: Parallax Press, 1994.

Bielefeldt, Carl. *Dōgen's Manuals of Zen Meditation*. Berkeley: University of California Press, 1988.

Bodiford, William. *Sōtō Zen in Medieval Japan*. Honolulu: University of Hawaii Press, 1993.

Braveman, Arthur. *Warrior of Zen: The Diamond-Hard Wisdom Mind of Suzuki Shosan*. New York: Kodansha USA, 1994.

Brook, Timothy. "Violence as Historical Time." Globalization and Autonomy Online Compendium, http://anscombe.mcmaster.ca/global1/article.jsp?index=RA_Brook_violence.xml.

Broughton, Jeffrey Lyle. *The Bodhidharma Anthology: The Earliest Records of Zen*. Berkeley: University of California Press, 1999.

———. *Zongmi on Chan*. New York: Columbia University Press, 2009.

Carse, James. *Finite and Infinite Games*. New York: Free Press, 1986.

Chien, Cheng Bhikku. *Sun-Face Buddha: The Teachings of Ma-tsu and the Hung-Chou School of Ch'an*. Berkeley, CA: Asian Humanities Press, 1992.

Clifford, James. *The Predicament of Culture: Twentieth-Century Ethnography, Literature, and Art*. Cambridge, MA: Harvard University Press, 1988.

Collcut, Martin. *Five Mountains: The Rinzai Zen Monastic Institution in Medieval Japan*. Cambridge, MA: Harvard University Asia Center, 1981.

Como, Michael. *Shōtoku: Ethnicity, Ritual, and Violence in the Japanese Buddhist Tradition.* New York: Oxford University Press, 2008.

Cook, Francis. *The Record of Transmitting the Light: Zen Master Keizan's Denkoroku.* Los Angeles: Center Publications, 1991.

Covell, Jon Carter. *Unraveling Zen's Red Thread: Ikkyū's Controversial Way.* Elizabeth, NJ: Hollym International, 1980.

Digha Nikāya. Translated by Maurice Walsh as *The Long Discourses of the Buddha.* Boston: Wisdom Publications, 1995.

Downing, Michael. *Shoes Outside the Door: Desire, Devotion, and Excess at San Francisco Zen Center.* Washington, DC: Counterpoint, 2001.

Eihei Kōroku. Translated by Taigen Dan Leighton and Shohaku Okumura as *Dōgen's Extensive Record.* Boston: Wisdom Publications, 2010.

Faure, Bernard. "The Daruma-shu, Dogen and Soto Zen." *Monumenta Nipponica* 42, no. 1 (Spring 1987): 25–55.

———. *The Red Thread: Buddhist Approaches to Sexuality.* Princeton, NJ: Princeton University Press, 1998.

Fields, Rick. *How the Swans Came to the Lake: A Narrative History of Buddhism in America.* Boston: Shambhala, 1992.

Harootunian, Harry. *Things Seen and Unseen: Discourse and Ideology in Tokugawa Nativism.* Chicago: University of Chicago Press, 1988.

Haskel, Peter. *Great Fool: Zen Master Ryokan; Poems, Letters, and Other Writings.* Honolulu: University of Hawaii Press, 1996.

———. *Letting Go: The Story of Zen Master Tōsui; Tōsui Oshō Densan.* Honolulu: University of Hawaii Press, 2001.

———. *Sword of Zen: Master Takuan and His Writings on Immovable Wisdom and the Sword Taie.* Honolulu: University of Hawaii Press, 2013.

Heine, Steven. *Shifting Shape, Shaping Text: Philosophy and Folklore in the Fox Kōan.* Honolulu: University of Hawaii Press, 1999.

———. *Zen Skin, Zen Marrow: Will the Real Zen Buddhism Please Stand Up?* New York: Oxford University Press, 2008.

Heisig, James W., and John C. Maraldo, eds. *Rude Awakenings: Zen, the Kyoto School, and the Question of Nationalism.* Honolulu: University of Hawaii Press, 1995.

Heisig, James W., with Thomas P. Kasulis and John C. Maraldo, eds. *Japanese Philosophy: A Sourcebook.* Honolulu: University of Hawaii Press, 2011.

Hershock, Peter D. *Valuing Diversity: Buddhist Reflection on a More Equitable Global Future.* Albany: State University of New York Press, 2012.

Hisamatsu, Shin'ichi. *Zen and the Fine Arts.* New York: Kodansha International, 1982.

———. *Critical Sermons of the Zen Tradition: Hisamatsu's Talks on Linji.* Honolulu: University of Hawaii Press, 2002.

Hubbard, Jamie, ed. *Pruning the Bodhi Tree: The Storm over Critical Buddhism.* Honolulu: University of Hawaii Press, 1997.

Ishikawa, Rizikan. "The Social Response of Buddhists to the Modernization of Japan: The Contrasting Lives of Two Soto Zen Monks." *Japanese Journal of Religious Studies* 25, nos. 1–2 (1998): 87–115.

Jia, Jinhua. *The Hongzhou School of Chan Buddhism in Eighth- through Tenth-Century China.* Albany: State University of New York Press, 2006.

King, Sallie B. *Socially Engaged Buddhism.* Honolulu: University of Hawaii Press, 2009.

Kirchner, Thomas Yūhō, with Fukazawa Yukio, translated with annotation. *Dialogues in a Dream* [*Muchū Mondō*]. Kyoto: Tenryū-ji Institute for Philosophy and Religion Press, 2010.

Leighton, Taigen Dan, and Shohaku Okumura, trans. *Dōgen's Extensive Record.* Boston: Wisdom Press, 2010.

Majjhima Nikāya. Translated by Bhikku Nanamoli and Bikkhu Bodhi as *The Middle Length Discourses of the Buddha.* Boston: Wisdom Publications, 1995.

McMahon, David L. *The Making of Buddhist Modernism.* New York: Oxford University Press, 2008.

McRae, John R. *Seeing through Zen: Encounters, Transformation, and Genealogy in Chinese Chan Buddhism*. Berkeley: University of California Press, 2003.

Merwin, W. S., and Sōiku Shigematsu, trans. *Sun at Midnight: Poems and Sermons by Musō Soseki*. San Francisco: North Point Press, 1989.

Nattier, Jan. *Once Upon a Future Time: Studies in a Buddhist Prophecy of Decline*. Berkeley, CA: Asian Humanities Press, 1991.

Nosco, Peter. *Remembering Paradise: Nativism and Nostalgia in Eighteenth-Century Japan*. Cambridge: Harvard University Press, 1990.

———, ed. *Confucianism and Tokugawa Culture*. Honolulu: University of Hawaii Press, 1997.

Okumura, Shohaku. *Realizing Genjokoan: The Key to Dogen's Shobogenzo*. Boston: Wisdom Publications, 2010.

Poceski, Mario. *Ordinary Mind as the Way: The Hongzhou School and the Growth of Chan Buddhism*. New York: Oxford University Press, 2007.

Prebish, Charles S. *Luminous Passage: The Practice and Study of Buddhism in America*. Berkeley: University of California Press, 1999.

Pye, Michael. *Emerging from Meditation: Tominaga Nakamoto*. Honolulu: University of Hawaii Press, 1990.

Queen, Christopher S., and Sallie B. King, ed. *Engaged Buddhism: Buddhist Liberation Movements in Asia*. Albany: State University of New York Press, 1996.

Reischauer, Edwin O. *Ennin's Travels in T'ang China*. New York: Ronald Press, 1955.

Samyutta Nikāya. Translated by Bhikkhu Bodhi as *The Connected Discourses of the Buddha*. Boston: Wisdom Publications, 2003.

Sekida, Katsuki. *Two Zen Classics: Mumonkan and Hekiganroku*. New York: Weatherhill, 1995.

Sen, Tansen. *Buddhism, Diplomacy and Trade: The Realignment of Sino-Indian Relations, 600–1400*. Honolulu: University of Hawaii Press, 2003.

Shields, James Mark. "Awakening between Science, Art & Ethics: Variations on Japanese Buddhist Modernism, 1890–1945." In *Rethinking Japanese Modernism*, edited by Roy Starrs. Leiden: Global Oriental Press (Brill), 2011a.

———. *Critical Buddhism: Engaging with Modern Japanese Buddhist Thought*. Burlington, VT: Ashgate, 2011b.

Stevens, John. *Three Zen Masters: Ikkyū, Hakuin, Ryōkan*. New York: Kodansha International Press, 1993.

———, trans. *Wild Ways: Zen Poems of Ikkyū*. Buffalo, NY: White Pine Press, 2003.

Stone, Jacqueline Ilyse. *Original Enlightenment and the Transformation of Medieval Japanese Buddhism*. Honolulu: University of Hawaii Press, 1999.

Sutta Nipāta. Translated by H. Saddhatissa. London: Curzon Press, 1985.

Tanahashi, Kazuaki. *Sky Above, Great Wind: The Life and Poetry of Zen Master Ryokan*. Boston: Shambhala, 2012.

Toulmin, Stephen. *Cosmopolis: The Hidden Agenda of Modernity*. Chicago: University of Chicago Press, 1990.

Tworkov, Helen. *Zen in America: Profiles of Five Teachers*. San Francisco: North Point Press, 1989.

Varley, H. Paul. *Japanese Culture*. Honolulu: University of Hawaii Press, 1984.

Victoria. Brian Daizen. *Zen at War*. Lanham, MD: Rowman and Littlefield, 2006.

Waddell, Norman, trans. *The Unborn: The Life and Teachings of Zen Master Bankei, 1622–1693*. New York: North Point Press, 2000.

Waddell, Norman, trans. *The Essential Teachings of Zen Master Hakuin*. Boston: Shambhala, 2010.

Waddell, Norman, and Masao Abe. *The Heart of Dōgen's Shōbōgenzō*. Albany: State University of New York Press, 2002.

Watson, Burton, trans. *The Lotus Sutra*. New York: Columbia University Press, 1993.

Williams, Duncan. *The Other Side of Zen: A Social History of Sōtō Zen in Tokugawa Japan*. Princeton, NJ: Princeton University Press, 2006.

Wu, Jiang. *Enlightenment in Dispute: The Reinvention of Chan Buddhism in 17th Century China*. New York: Oxford University Press, 2008.

Yampolsky, Philip. *Zen Master Hakuin: Selected Writings*. New York: Columbia, 1973.

Yuasa, Yasuo. *The Body: Toward an Eastern Mind-Body Theory*. Edited by T. P. Kasulis and translated by Nagatomo Shigenori and T. P. Kasulis. Albany: State University of New York Press, 1987.

FURTHER READING

Contemporary readers embarking on the study of Zen and looking for a handful of texts that could be considered "essential reading" are confronted now with a bewilderingly extensive body of literature. Fifty years ago, the number of English-language books in print that were related to Zen might have filled a small bookshelf. Today, there are thousands of such books in print, many of them available at any major bookstore and a vast many more online. This remarkable expansion of books in print has included everything from citation-laden academic works and transcriptions of talks given by contemporary Zen teachers to popular books applying "zen" ideas to everything from driving to playing guitar.

My aim here is not to select the "best" books on Zen. That judgment ultimately depends on the exact nature of one's interests. Instead, I want simply to offer some initial guidance in approaching the wealth of materials available on Zen. For convenience, these suggestions are grouped as follows: books suited to developing a historical understanding of the advent and evolution of Zen; a short list of academic works that offer readers with more scholarly interests a responsible introduction to the vast (and still growing) specialist literature on Zen; English translations of works by the Zen teachers who figured most prominently in this book; and, finally, a very small set of books by contemporary Zen teachers aimed primarily at those interested in Zen practice.

HISTORICAL BACKGROUND: BUDDHISM

For a very brief, but still comprehensive introduction to Buddhism, I would recommend the introduction, written by Donald S. Lopez Jr., to his edited volume, *Buddhism in Practice* (Princeton University Press, 1995). For a relatively short and user-friendly treatment of the full range of Buddhist traditions and their historical development, consider *The Buddhist Religion: A Historical Introduction*, edited by Richard H. Robinson and Willard L. Johnson (Wadsworth Publishing, 1997). *The Sociology of Early Buddhism* by Greg Bailey and Ian Mabbett (Cambridge, 2003) offers one of the few treatments of the larger socioeconomic and political conditions that shaped the beginnings of Buddhism and is useful in showing how Buddhism was from the outset "socially engaged." For an introduction to Mahāyāna Buddhism by both tradition and region, consider Paul Williams' *Mahayana Buddhism: The Doctrinal Foundations* (Routledge, 1989).

HISTORICAL BACKGROUND: ZEN

Perhaps the most accessible and reliable overall history of Chan and Zen is Heinrich Dumoulin's *Zen Buddhism: A History* (New York: Macmillan, 1994). The first volume of this two-part series focuses on India and China, while volume 2 focuses on Zen in Japan. Both volumes are replete with stories about major figures as well as considerable historical background informed by some of the newer scholarship being done in the 1980s.

Chinese Chan

For an accessible and brief introduction to Chinese Chan, see my own *Chan Buddhism* (University of Hawaii Press, 2005). Two fine scholarly works on aspects of Chan's development in China that would have major impacts on the complexion of Japanese Zen are Jinhua Jia's *The Hongzhou School of Chan Buddhism in Eighth- through Tenth-Century China* (SUNY Press, 2006) and Morten Schlütter's *How Zen Became Zen: The Dispute over Original Enlightenment and the Formation of Chan Buddhism in Song Dynasty China* (University of Hawaii Press, 2008). An insightful treatment of the socioeconomic and political contexts and the institutional dimensions of Chan during the Song dynasty—the period when serious Japanese interest in Chan/Zen first developed—see Albert Welter's *Monks, Rulers and Literati: The Political Ascendancy of Chan Buddhism* (Oxford, 2006). And, finally, for background on the changes that Chan underwent in the Ming dynasty—changes crucial to the development of Ōbaku Zen in Japan—see Jiang Wu's *Enlightenment in Dispute: The Reinvention of Chan Buddhism in 17th Century China* (Oxford, 2008).

Japanese Zen

Two now classic studies of the history of Zen in English are Martin Collcutt's *Five Mountains: The Rinzai Zen Monastic Institution in Medieval Japan* (Harvard, 1981) and William Bodiford's *Sōtō Zen in Medieval Japan* (University of Hawaii Press, 1993). For a work that carefully examines the power dynamics informing the development of Japanese Buddhism and Zen, see *The Gates of Power: Monks, Courtiers, and Warriors in Pre-Modern Japan* (University of Hawaii Press, 2000) by Mikael Adolphson. Duncan Williams' *The Other Side of Zen: A Social History of Sōtō Zen in Tokugawa Japan* (Princeton, 2006) is an excellent study of the public dimensions of late premodern Sōtō. The persecutions of Buddhism during the early phases of Japan's modernization and national strengthening had important impacts on Zen. A seminal study of this period is James Ketelaar's *Of Heretics and Martyrs in Meiji Japan: Buddhism and Its Persecution* (Princeton, 1990). And for a brief but effective introduction to the transformation of Zen during the early twentieth century and the eventual rise of so-called critical Buddhism, see James Mark Shields' *Critical Buddhism: Engaging with Modern Japanese Buddhist Thought* (Ashgate, 2011).

There are a number of academics who approach Zen from more philosophical and cultural perspectives. *Zen Action/Zen Person* (University of Hawaii Press, 1981) by Thomas P. Kasulis is a highly readable classic of comparative philosophy. Two quite sophisticated entry points to the scholarship on Chan and Zen are *Ch'an Insights and Oversights: An Epistemological Critique of the Ch'an Tradition* (Princeton, 1993) and *The Rhetoric of Immediacy: A Cultural Critique of Ch'an/Zen* (Princeton, 1991) by Bernard Faure. Steven Heine and Dale Wright have collaborated on a large number of edited volumes as well as individually penning thoughtful monographs on various aspects of Zen. Two of the more useful of their edited works are *The Kōan: Texts and Contexts in Zen Buddhism* (Oxford, 2000) and *Zen Ritual: Studies of Zen Buddhist Theory in Practice* (Oxford, 2007). I would also recommend Carl Bielefeldt's book, *Dōgen's Manuals of Zen Meditation* (University of California Press, 1988), as a textually and philosophically sophisticated introduction to Dōgen's early thought.

PRIMARY SOURCES IN TRANSLATION

A comprehensive sourcebook on Japanese philosophical and religious thought, with an excellent glossary and considerable attention given to Zen thinkers, is *Japanese Philosophy: A Sourcebook* (University of Hawaii Press, 2011), edited by James W. Heisig, Thomas P. Kasulis, and John C. Maraldo. A quite comprehensive, lightly annotated collection of Chinese Chan and Japanese Zen writings is Nelson Foster and Jack Shoemaker, *The Roaring Stream: A New Zen Reader* (HarperPerennial, 1997).

Translations of selected writings by Dōgen, Ikkyū, Hakuin, and Ryōkan are readily available, though with the exception of Dōgen, a great deal of their literary output remains available only in Japanese. For Dōgen, I would recommend two translations as points of departure: *Dōgen's Extensive Record* (Wisdom, 2010), translated by Taigen Dan Leighton and Shohaku Okumura, a monumental text of Dōgen's Dharma talks, poems, and letters with a substantial biographical and textual introduction; and Francis H. Cook's *Sounds of Valley Streams: Translations of Nine Essays from Shōbōgenzō* (SUNY Press, 1989), a collection of well-translated classics from Dōgen's most philosophically influential work.

Dōgen is far and away the most widely translated of all Zen writers. Translations of works by Ikkyū, Hakuin, and Ryōkan are much more limited but nevertheless offer useful insights into the character of their personifications of Zen. A well-introduced selection of Ikkyū's poetry is Sonja Arntzen's *Ikkyū and the Crazy Cloud Anthology* (University of Tokyo Press, 1986), which can be supplemented with freer translations of many of the same poems by John Stevens' collection, *Wild Ways: Zen Poems of Ikkyū* (White Pine Press, 2003). Stevens also includes selected translations in his biographical introduction, *Three Zen Masters: Ikkyū,*

Hakuin, Ryōkan (Kodansha International Press, 1993). A fine scholarly introduction to and translation of a collection of Hakuin's work is Philip Yampolsky's *Zen Master Hakuin: Selected Writings* (Columbia University, 1973). Norman Waddell has also produced a translation of selected works by Hakuin, including some of Hakuin's most colorfully critical works on the state of Zen during his lifetime: *The Essential Teachings of Zen Master Hakuin* (Shambhala, 2010). Ryūichi Abé and Peter Haskel have compiled a wide-ranging selection of Ryōkan's writings in *Great Fool: Zen Master Ryokan; Poems, Letters, and Other Writings* (University of Hawaii, 1996), while an affordable and compact introduction to Ryōkan's life and work is Kazuaki Tanahashi's *Sky Above, Great Wind: The Life and Poetry of Zen Master Ryokan* (Shambhala, 2012).

CONTEMPORARY WORKS ON ZEN PRACTICE

Perhaps the most enduring contemporary English-language book on Zen was written in the mid-1960s by one of the first Americans to be given transmission in a Japanese Zen lineage: Philip Kapleau Roshi's *The Three Pillars of Zen* (Beacon Press, 1967). One of the first books to effectively introduce English reading audiences to the teachings of a contemporary Japanese Zen teacher was *Zen Mind, Beginner's Mind* (Weatherhill, 1970)—a collection of wonderfully lucid talks given by Soto Zen master Shunryu Suzuki to his American students. Another book based on a teacher's talks to American students is Katagiri Roshi's *Returning to Silence: Zen Practice in Daily Life* (Shambhala, 1988). A more systematic contemporary discussion of Zen practice is *Opening the Hand of Thought: Foundations of Zen Buddhist Practice* (Wisdom, 2004) by Kosho Uchiyama Roshi, translated by Tom Wright, Jisho Warner, and Shohaku Okumura. John Daido Loori, one of the more prolific writers on Zen in English, presents a comprehensive Zen training program for American Zen students in *The Eight Gates of Zen: A Program of Zen Training* (Shambhala, 2002).

By no means are these the only contemporary teachers of Zen whose teachings are available in English. But they are readily available gateways for exploring living traditions of Zen. Readers may also want to explore websites like the Zensite (www.thezensite.com), which offers access to teachings, translations, book reviews, and reading lists, or the more comprehensive Zen Buddhism WWW Virtual Library (http://www.ciolek.com/WWWVL-Zen.html). Many Zen training centers also maintain websites that can provide even more finely grained views of Zen "from within."

INDEX

ABOUT THE AUTHOR

Peter Hershock is director of the Asian Studies Development Program at the East West Center in Honolulu. Alongside his work designing and implementing faculty development programs aimed at globalizing undergraduate higher education, his research has focused on using Buddhist philosophical perspectives to address such contemporary issues as technology, human rights, and the role of values in cultural and social change. His books include *Liberating Intimacy: Enlightenment and Social Virtuosity in Ch'an Buddhism* (1996); *Reinventing the Wheel: A Buddhist Response to the Information Age* (1999); *Technology and Cultural Values* (edited, 2003); *Chan Buddhism* (2005); *Buddhism in the Public Sphere: Reorienting Global Interdependence* (2006); and *Valuing Diversity: Buddhist Reflection on Realizing a More Equitable Global Future* (2012).